BULG...

Aegean Sea

Anzac Cove
Imbros

Lemnos

The Dardanelles

Gallipoli Peninsula

TURKEY

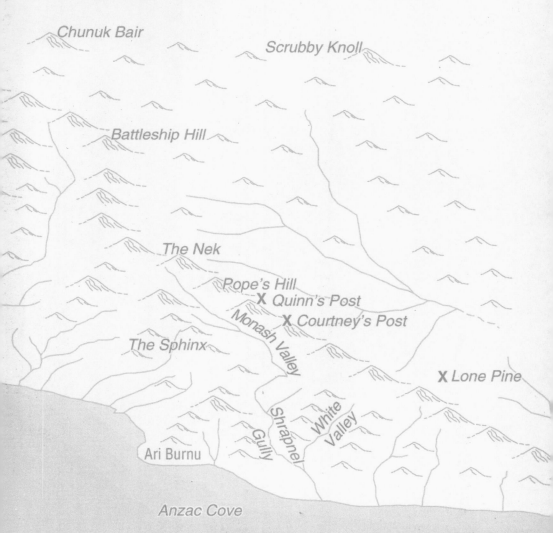

Chunuk Bair

Scrubby Knoll

Battleship Hill

The Nek

Pope's Hill
X Quinn's Post
X Courtney's Post

Monash Valley

The Sphinx

X Lone Pine

Gully

Shrapnel

White

Valley

Ari Burnu

Anzac Cove

GALLIPOLI:
OUR LAST MAN STANDING

GALLIPOLI:
OUR LAST MAN STANDING

The Extraordinary Life
of Alec Campbell

JONATHAN KING

John Wiley & Sons Australia, Ltd

First published 2003 by
John Wiley & Sons Australia, Ltd
33 Park Road, Milton, Qld 4064

Offices also in Sydney and Melbourne

Typeset in 11.5/15 pt Berkeley

© Jonathan King 2003

National Library of Australia
Cataloguing-in-Publication data

King, Jonathan, 1942– .
   Gallipoli : our last man standing : the extraordinary life of
   Alec Campbell

   ISBN 1 74031 066 7.

   1. Campbell, Alec, 1899–2002. 2. Veterans — Australia —
   Biography. 3. Centenarians — Australia — Biography.
   4. World War, 1914–1918 — Veterans — Australia.
   I. Smout, Arthur H. (Arthur Henry). II. Title.

940.40092

All rights reserved. No part of this publication
may be reproduced, stored in a retrieval system,
or transmitted in any form or by any means,
electronic, mechanical, photocopying, recording,
or otherwise, without the prior permission of
the publisher.

Printed in Australia by
Griffin Press Pty Ltd

10 9 8 7 6 5 4 3 2 1

To Jane, my life partner, best friend, co-author, reader and wife

CONTENTS

INTRODUCTION

MAN IN A MILLION

When fate picked out Alec Campbell to be the last man standing from the Gallipoli campaign, it could not have found a better representative of the 50,000 Australians who fought there. This is not to suggest his brief service as an Anzac soldier was typical, but rather that the extraordinary life he led encapsulated what it means to be Australian. In so many ways he demonstrated the attitudes, behaviour and characteristics, both good and bad, of the quintessential Australian. As a biographer, I could not have asked for a richer subject; at times, it seemed as though he had led his multi-faceted life in chapters in anticipation of this book.

From the moment I first met Alec in 1997 in his warm Hobart home, it struck me that he was a man apart, destined for a great historical role. This meeting and the first long interview that ensued were part of my project to capture on film a permanent record of the last ten Anzac veterans of the Gallipoli campaign. They were, after all, the last living link with a breed of Australians who were larger than life, judging by reports of the day. Of these ten, only Alec — the baby of the group — still lived at home. It seemed to me then that he was earmarked by history. During that first, intense meeting Alec shared so much of his remarkable and inspirational life that his character and story stayed with me long afterwards. Transcribing Alec's words in this book, I could still hear his voice, that singular, old-world tone at once gentle, reassuring and mellow

— especially once the malt whisky was brought out at the end of the session.

He was not at Gallipoli for long, just six weeks in fact, but he was at Anzac Cove long enough to get to know it well; he dodged his share of bullets, saw his mates shot, got sick as so many did, and served until the evacuation. He never went 'over the top' to attack the Nek or fought desperately hand-to-hand to dislodge the foe from Lone Pine, as his brave predecessors had. He did not endure the slaughter of that first terrible day, 25 April 1915, but he did land under enemy fire and earned his full credentials as an Anzac.

To get the feel of Alec's war I visited Gallipoli in 2002, walking the beach that Alec had walked, wandering through the remains of some of the trenches where he carried water to his mates; I even discovered Alec's dugout under Hill 971. I spent a night camped by a fire on the open beach at Anzac Cove under the overhanging cliff where Alec had landed. No matter how short a time he was there, it would still have been dangerous and frightening. Even today the atmosphere is spooky. Late that night I felt the need to move my swag away from the graves at nearby Shrapnel Gully and Ari Burnu. Alec's Hill 971 camp was very exposed, in clear line of sight from the high ground around the Nek and Chunuk Bair held by the Turks. I had no doubts that the kid soldier did well to survive in this exposed terrain, especially once winter set in.

But Alec Campbell was far from just a Gallipoli veteran. As my research evolved, I discovered that there were many Alec Campbells, and this story introduces each one as he comes out onto the field, before passing on the baton to the next runner in the Alec Campbell relay race of life. The book started out to tell the story of a Gallipoli veteran; it became the tale of a 'little Aussie battler' who overcame all obstacles to live an amazing life, a man who also happened to serve at Gallipoli. Even without his war experience, his life was a story worth telling, full of adventure and idealism, struggle and determination.

Alec's is also the story of the first hundred years of the Commonwealth of Australia. Born two years before federation, he lived across three centuries. His story, then, also chronicles the growth of a nation, from horse and buggy to tense global village, from the Boer War in distant South Africa to the global war against terrorism. He survived some of the worst ravages of the twentieth century, including the Great War, the postwar influenza pandemic, the Depression and the Second World War, all the social and political upheavals that shaped the century. Born before motorcars, manned flight or the widespread use of electricity in the home, he could look back on a century that brought greater change than any previous period in human history. Alec adapted exuberantly to change. A fighter from boyhood, he rolled with life's punches, always bouncing back to fight another day.

Over his long life, Alec, the great all-rounder, had many identities. But it is the themes that run consistently through this varied life that are most impressive. As a young man he set himself the challenge of lifelong self-improvement, and his story bears testimony to his success. Brought up a Christian, his life embodied a strong moral code, putting the greater good ahead of personal gain and helping those in need. Confronted by challenges, he sought to understand them and to learn from them — to grow from the experience. He never complained about the facial disfigurement he suffered as the result of an injury sustained at Gallipoli; rather, he turned it to his advantage, using the setback to spur him on. Inspired by his school headmaster's encomium to persistence, Alec was resolute and tenacious in everything he did, never letting go until he had achieved his goal. Of course, for every positive trait there exists a negative. The determined achiever could be a selfish opportunist, and Alec had his share of faults (for willpower, read self-centred bloody-mindedness). Like all of us, he had a shadow side. His first wife Kathleen, an extraordinary woman in her own right, contributed greatly to his success, bearing more than her share of the burden of providing for the family through the lean times, yet when life became easier he chose to share his life with a younger woman. Nobody wants their heroes to have feet of clay, and biographers are often tempted to build their subjects up; in the end, Alec Campbell was just 'an ordinary bloke', as he said himself, who did extraordinary things.

His political transformation is another interesting theme in his life story. Despite conservative, middle-class origins, after his war experience this poorly educated Gallipoli veteran turned his back on conventional notions of serving his country to become a dedicated opponent of war and the monarchy, a passionate trade unionist who advocated government ownership and the redistribution of wealth. An admirer of John Curtin and Ben Chifley, Alec embraced their political philosophy of compassionate socialism. The experience of this transformation, in fact, was shared by many who lived through those calamitous times. But Alec was no armchair socialist; as with all his enthusiasms, he threw himself into the political struggle, determined to make a difference. And as a union leader and workers' advocate, he did.

His personal and professional evolution demonstrated his tireless zest for life. 'After his brush with death he decided to live life to the full,' says his daughter Mary. 'He put all he could into life and tried everything. If he thought of something new, or saw someone else doing something he had not done, then bingo, he gave it a try!' An experimenter and risk-taker to the last, there was nothing he did not think he could take on, and he never entertained the thought that advancing years should slow him down. Alec Campbell was the living expression of *carpe diem*.

He realised his personal and professional achievements through a remarkably diverse range of activities. Alec set so many examples by the way he led his life that his story offers inspiration for anyone tempted to 'have a go'. He was the classic self-made man: a bush-savvy country boy and all-round sportsman who carried boyhood accomplishments into manhood; a loving family man who provided for his children through modern history's worst economic slump; a burning idealist who fought for justice for his fellows; a man of compassion who sought to help the disadvantaged; a lifelong student; an evergreen adventurer. He was also a man of great integrity and steadfastness, with a still calm centre of self-knowledge. Content with himself, he was able to meet the world with the broadest and most inquiring of minds.

Alec was one of 50,000 volunteer soldiers in the Australian Imperial Force who served during the nine-month campaign on the Gallipoli Peninsula in 1915, one of an estimated million combatants who participated on all sides in this conflict. The Anzacs formed part of the British-led Mediterranean Expeditionary Force sent out to seize the peninsula from the Turks. The initial plan had been for a combined British–French naval force to open sea communications with Russia and force Turkey out of the war, raising the possibility of a new front behind the Central Powers. Partly hatched by Britain's First Sea Lord, Winston Churchill, the plan unravelled when the joint naval force was forced to withdraw after heavy losses from mines and the entrenched Turkish gun emplacements in the Dardanelles. With this naval failure in March, the War Council decided to send in a land force to capture the Turkish guns. As Charles Bean, Australia's official First World War historian (who also founded the Australian War Memorial), observed, 'Through Churchill's excess of imagination, a layman's ignorance of artillery and the fatal power of a young enthusiast like Churchill to convince older and more cautious brains, the tragedy of Gallipoli was born.'

A number of simultaneous landings were to be made on the peninsula and the Asian shore of the straits with the goal of overwhelming the relatively light Turkish defences, seizing the Turkish forts from behind and marching on Constantinople. On paper it was an attractive plan; in reality the rugged terrain of the peninsula made it an impossible task. Allied intelligence of the terrain was entirely inadequate; the Turks, perched on cliff tops overlooking the beaches chosen for the landings, had the advantage of knowing their ground and were ably led by experienced German officers. To make matters worse, the Anzacs were landed on the wrong beach, where the cliffs made any advance impracticable. It would be nine months before Kitchener and the War Council in London would accept what was obvious to many on the ground and abandon the ill-conceived campaign. By that time it would have cost nearly 50,000 Allied lives, and approaching twice that many Turks.

Just 16 when he enlisted in June that year, Alec was fortunate to miss the bloody landings in April, arriving on the peninsula only in November, when most of the fighting was over. It was from that first terrible day that the Anzac myth was born. Contemporary newspaper correspondents and observers would portray the event in such colourful terms as to create the foundation of our national legend. Ellis Ashmead-Bartlett wrote in the London *Times*, 'In the face of murderous enemy fire this bold race of athletes continued to scale the highest cliffs'. April 25 became a defining moment in the nation's history. Through the harrowing events of the ensuing months, stories of sacrifice and dignity would help to nurture the Anzac legend. The English poet John Masefield waxed especially lyrical: The Anzacs, he suggested, 'were the finest body of young men ever brought together in modern times. For physical beauty and nobility of bearing they surpassed any man I have ever seen; they walked and looked like the kings in old poems, and reminded me of the Shakespearean line "Baited like eagles having lately bathed".' The Anzacs' normally restrained British commanding officer sang their praises in his official reports. Lieutenant-General Sir William Birdwood wrote after the campaign, 'No words of mine could ever convey to readers at their firesides in Australia, New Zealand and the Old Country one half of what all their boys have been through, nor is my poor pen capable of telling them of the never-failing courage, determination and cheerfulness of those who have so willingly fought and given their lives for King and country's sake.' Charles Bean had the last word: 'ANZAC stood, and still stands, for reckless valour in a good cause, for enterprise, resourcefulness, fidelity, comradeship and endurance that will never admit defeat.'

There were of course much bigger and more important battles in Flanders and France, especially on the Somme in 1917 and 1918, where so many Anzacs fought and died. Gallipoli was different, though. Here the young Australian nation was truly blooded. Stories and images from the campaign captured the imagination and created a national legend that has never been dislodged from the popular psyche, where it seems to grow in stature year by year. By the turn of the millennium so many Australians were turning up for the annual dawn service that the little Ari Burnu cemetery beside the beach where the first casualties of the tragedy fell could no longer contain them. The Anzac Day commemoration has since been transferred to a nearby site at North Beach that anticipates the 25,000 visitors expected for the 2015 centenary. In a joint venture involving the Australian, New Zealand and Turkish governments, a new memorial at North Beach has become the showpiece of the Gallipoli Peninsula Peace Park, created to preserve the military, cultural and archaeological heritage of this international sacred site. A memorial commemorative stone wall features a series of panels depicting different stages of the Gallipoli story. From a line of flagpoles fly the flags of the Allied nations beside the Turkish flag.

Alec's death on 17 May 2002, as the last man standing out of one million who fought there, was reported in newspapers in Britain, Europe and North America, as well as Turkey, India, China and Japan. Features and obituaries appeared in *The Times* of London and the *New York Times*. Perhaps no other private soldier has received such attention on his death.

With his passing a door has closed to which no one still has the key. Australia has lost the last direct link with one of the most significant events in the nation's first century. No one can ever again explain what it was really like, which makes this memorial to him all the more important. For Alec Campbell was not only our last Gallipoli witness but also the last representative of an age now gone forever, an age when young men believed in Empire so strongly they eagerly volunteered to fight for 'king and country', happy to risk their lives for a cause they little understood. And even if capturing Constantinople was an ill-conceived, even hopeless adventure, they gave it their best shot with good cheer. The young men who volunteered to fight at Gallipoli were a special breed, and Australia will never see their like again.

Ironically, perhaps the most poignant memorial to the Anzacs comes from one of their most implacable enemies. In 1935, to commemorate the twentieth anniversary of the campaign, Turkish president and poet Kemal Atatürk, his country's most brilliant commander in 1915, erected a monument at Anzac Cove on which was inscribed his own poem to the fallen:

Those heroes that shed their blood
and lost their lives . . .
You are now lying in the soil of a friendly country
Therefore rest in peace
There is no difference between the Johnnies
and the Mehmets to us where they lie side by side
here in this country of ours . . .
You the mothers
who sent their sons from faraway countries
Wipe away your tears
Your sons are now lying in our bosom
and are in peace
After having lost their lives on this land they have
become our sons as well

It is against this background that the story of Alec Campbell unfolds.

One night off Anzac Cove ...

The night was black as pitch and the boat was being tossed about like a cork on the tumbling sea. It was about one o'clock on the morning of 2 November 1915.

He couldn't see a thing, but surely they weren't far from the beach now. All his mates were silent, running through their last instructions over and over: *As soon as you're out of the boat, bolt for the first line of cover you see.* The kid soldier's nerves were on edge. His heart beat against his rib cage as he clutched his .303 rifle tightly to his chest. He couldn't wait to feel the sand under his feet, to run for cover. The journey seemed to be taking forever. The fierce wind kicked up the sea about them. He knew one fellow had been killed on the ship the night before, taking a stray bullet in the head while sleeping on deck. And just now he had heard a muffled cry up forward as a soldier crumpled to the bottom of the boat. They must be within rifle range now. The kid soldier could be next.

Of course he had heard about the Anzacs' first landings, just a few months earlier, when more than two thousand of his countrymen had been slaughtered in the first twenty-four hours — an unthinkable death toll that had shocked all Australians to the core. Thousands more had been killed since as the Turks, perched high on the ridges, rained fire down on the beach. He'd heard rumours that many of the Anzacs had not even been buried. It was too dangerous to duck out into no-man's-land to bring back their bodies. He'd also heard that the Turkish forces had since been reinforced and now heavily outnumbered the Anzacs, who had been clinging to their precarious beachhead ever since the April landings.

The kid's skinny, five-foot-five frame shuddered as he hunched in his seat, squeezed between the rows of grown men. Squinting against the gun flashes from the dimly outlined heights ahead, and inwardly recoiling as another shower of metal spattered the sea nearby, he searched anxiously for signs of the promised landing. Yet with every desperate stroke the tumbling tide seemed to pull their little craft back to sea. He was reminded momentarily of the sitting ducks he used to shoot as a child on the still waters of the river Tamar back in Launceston, in a world that suddenly seemed so far away.

But wait a minute. Was this some kind of mistake? What on earth was a scrawny 16-year-old boy doing here, among these veterans of the battle-scarred 15th Battalion, which had been at Gallipoli since the landings and had suffered the highest mortality rate of any Australian unit? Who was this kid anyway? How did he get past the recruitment authorities? And how did he come to be sitting in the dead of night in a flimsy boat off Anzac Cove, about to gamble with his life by leaping ashore on an alien scrap of land on the edge of Europe that had already claimed so many Australian lives? If he had been shot then and there, some of the men in the boat might have recalled him as Private Campbell, nicknamed 'the kid soldier'. Any well-versed Scot on board might have linked the name to that of the highlands' most martial clan, whose famous war cry — 'Cruachan!' — had for centuries sent shivers down the spines of their enemies in battle. But this squeaky-voiced Campbell had not even started shaving.

To understand the path that had brought the kid to this pass, we have to go back to the beginning — the roots of the Clan Campbell.

CRUACHAN!

ANZAC stood, and still stands, for reckless valour in a good cause, for enterprise, resourcefulness, fidelity, comradeship and endurance that will never admit defeat.

C.E.W. Bean, Australia's official Gallipoli historian

CHAPTER 1
THE ROOTS OF THE TREE

'My grandfather Donald Campbell arrived on the sailing ship Storm Cloud from Scotland in 1855. He always said he was an Argyll Campbell. He probably lived at Inverlochy, not far from Fort William. He married a fellow passenger on the Storm Cloud, a young Lady named Sarah Ryley. They were married in St. Andrews Church, Launceston.'

Soon after the outbreak of the First World War Alec Campbell made up his mind to join up if he could. He would become one of the youngest serving soldiers in Australian history. This did not happen by chance. Alec was in essence a Campbell, and an Argyll Campbell at that. His grandfather had told him stories of his Scottish heritage from an early age. It was in his blood — even at 16, and even in Launceston, Tasmania, at the opposite end of the world from Argyllshire. Alec had also grown up in the bush with a gun in his hands and a natural love of shooting. He was a good shot, and he could ride and box. So when the call came he could not have done other than enlist. His destiny had been predetermined — not least by 500 years of Scottish history, for the Campbells of Argyll were the greatest warrior clan of a famously combative tribe. The fearsome reputation of the Scottish fighter, built up over centuries, was sustained during the Great War. According to Ted Matthews, the last survivor of the Anzacs who landed at Gallipoli on that first savage day in April 1915, 'The Germans only feared two types of soldiers — Australians and Scots. With their kilts flying as they charged we used to call the Scots "the wild women from hell".'

For centuries the Scottish highlands had echoed to the clamour of war, but one sound in particular never failed to provoke terror even among other warriors, let alone ordinary folk — that was the war cry of the dreaded Campbell clan, *'Cruachan!'* Raised on these traditions, as passed down by his grandfather and father, young Alec would have been well aware of Campbell legend. Theirs, of course, was one of the commonest Scottish surnames, and when Campbells emigrated in their thousands they transplanted the name to Britain's colonies, where they exerted an enduring influence. Until the sixteenth century the name was spelt *Cambel*. According to clan legend, it derived from two Celtic words meaning 'curved' or 'crooked' and 'mouth', and alluded to the aspect of these warriors when howling their war cry as they entered battle. In a strange quirk of fate, Alec Campbell himself came to be afflicted by a crooked mouth and face, permanently disfigured by the palsy he contracted under the harsh conditions at Gallipoli.

The Campbell clan had always been dominant players in Scotland. The name is linked to such legendary fighters as William Wallace, Robert Bruce and Rob Roy. It is also associated with some of the bloodiest battles — from Bannockburn to Flodden Field to the infamous massacre of the MacDonalds at Glencoe. Thus the name appears and reappears on page after page of Scotland's bloody history. Growing up, Alec heard how the Campbells made their name by supporting the independence fighter Robert Bruce. According to legend, Bruce once watched a spider attempt to cross a ceiling by swinging from beam to beam; it succeeded on the seventh attempt — incidentally imbuing Bruce with his characteristic qualities of determination and persistence. Having failed to better the English on six occasions, Bruce famously mounted a seventh battle, which he won with the support of his Campbell allies. Bruce's most important supporter was the pre-eminent warrior and statesman Sir Neil Campbell, after whom Alec would name his ninth child.

Over many generations the clan steadily built up its power base in the western highlands, where the house of Argyll dominated. Even in 1800 a man could ride a hundred miles in any direction in Argyllshire and still be on Campbell land, and the dukes of Argyll were based at the heart of this dominion — Inverary Castle. From their origins as an obscure highland tribe in the early thirteenth century, the Campbells had become legendary regional magnates and won a place as one of the principal noble houses of Scotland. As historian David Campbell put it, 'What the Campbells did not achieve by conquest they achieved by marriage. They always managed to choose the right side in battle or marriage, which is why they were so disliked by so many other clans. They were such persistent and ruthless winners.' As time passed, the heirs to the title came to serve not in battle but as politicians in the English Parliament, usually for the Tory Party, initially under the leadership of such figures as Lord Aberdeen, Palmerston and Gladstone. Other Campbells developed agricultural interests or went into business. Still others sought opportunity beyond the land of their birth. After the industrial revolution, with the growth of towns and increasing rural poverty, the Campbell power base began to weaken as land was divided among growing numbers of kinsmen, and traditional loyalties and values gave way before modern practicalities. By the mid nineteenth century the Campbells' glory days were over, and many younger clan members looked to the new world for fresh opportunities. Men who would once have turned to the traditional expedient of clan warfare now chose migration — to North America or to the colonies of Canada, Australia or New Zealand.

So it was that Alec Campbell's great-grandfather John, along with his children, set sail for Tasmania in 1855. Given the clan's powerful position in the community and the strength of the family culture, John's decision to turn his back on centuries of tradition to sail off into the unknown would have demanded enormous resolution and courage. Intrepid though these trailblazers undoubtedly were, however, they could not have predicted how many migrant ships would be lost before reaching their destination, or the hardships involved in transplanting the roots of this ancient Scottish tree to an untamed colony like Van Diemen's Land, notorious for convicts, hostile Aboriginals and bushrangers. Nor, most importantly for a clan with such a strong family tradition, could John have foreseen how this dramatic upheaval would sunder the family, as fortune drove its disparate members apart.

Nineteenth-century Tasmania was steeped in the cultural heritage of its Scottish immigrants, who attached ancestral names to their settlements, streets, houses and ships to maintain visible, tangible links to the past. Many settlers perpetuated Scottish names through their offspring too, and in time Alec would continue this tradition through his own children. The Launceston region, where Alec was born, had more than its share of these reminders, including several Argyll names. This sense of identity with Argyll was passed down through Alec's great-grandfather John Campbell and his eldest son, Donald, to Donald's son Sam and, in turn, to Alec. Donald had even carried his kilt, sporran and dirk on board ship along with a Gaelic bible inscribed with the Gaelic version of his name, 'Domhuil Caimbealaich'. To understand the cultural context into which Alec would be born, we need to begin with that original transplanting.

John Campbell, aged 54, with his eldest son, Donald, 21, and Donald's younger siblings, sailed for the new world determined to make a fresh start and to found a new branch of the Campbell clan. Ambitious though this goal might have sounded, within two decades the family had accrued sufficient land and commercial interests in Tasmania to achieve it. By Alec Campbell's death the Tasmanian branch of the clan would number more than one hundred members, rivalling the growth of any branch of the Argyllshire clan. It was nevertheless characteristic of the clan's migration patterns — by the end of Alec's life three million Campbells lived outside of Scotland.

John's wife, Catherine, had died before they left home. Donald, who gave his father indispensable support on the passage out and on their arrival, met a girl on the ship whom he married soon after they were settled. Within a year John Campbell had mysteriously disappeared from the records, and the Tasmanian clan came to regard Donald as its true founder. Yet it was John who had first led the family to Van Diemen's Land.

From Corran of Ardgour, John had married Catherine (née McLachlan) in 1833 in the parish of Ballachulish. Before her early death they had raised their family in several parishes in the Loche Linnhe region, at Buachille, Kilmallie, Kilmonivaig and Inverlochy, where John had worked as a rural labourer and shepherd. The family was recruited by the St Andrews Immigration Society, established in 1841 to populate Van Diemen's Land. The young island colony's settler population of 60,000 had declined rapidly when able-bodied men began deserting the island to join the gold rush set off by prospector Edward Hargraves, who had discovered gold near Bathurst in New South Wales in 1851. Understanding the urgent need to replace this labour force, the 82-member society raised £3,450 to cover the fares of 110 families and 305 single migrants. Joseph Bonney was sent to Argyll to recruit highlanders to work as shepherds for the growing wool industry in the colony. Bonney needed to ensure only that his recruits were 'of sound mental and bodily health and of good character' and under 40 years of age. He would certainly have eulogised the virtues of life in the colonies, but to persuade shepherds like John to take the plunge Bonney also guaranteed immediate work on arrival — on condition that the migrants signed an agreement to remain in the colony for four years. By 1855 such immigration societies had recruited 5,472 migrants. To qualify, John had to drop his age (by 14 years), just as his great-grandson would raise his 60 years later.

In June 1855 the family packed their bags, caught a carriage to Glasgow and boarded the new 906-ton Glaswegian iron clipper *Storm Cloud*. Described in the local newspaper *The Artizan* as 'the pride of the Scottish fleet', it was generally believed that 'its daring build and configuration were so far out of the usual run of clipper ships that the "Storm Cloud" would prove one of the fastest, if not the quickest, that ever left the Clyde'. The ship was 'neatly rigged and sailed like a witch', and the Glasgow shipping industry expected great things of her. The ship carried a cargo of farm equipment, coal and 314 immigrants, including a number of Argyll Campbells. Along with Donald came siblings Robert, 19, Ann, 17, Lachlan, 15, Catherine, 13, Christina, 10, Alexander, 7, and Allan, 4. The family travelled as assisted migrants on bounty ticket number 438. Twenty-three Campbells were listed on the ship's register, including the master. Captain James Campbell, a sailor in the traditional mould described as 'decidedly smart and gentlemanly', had already spread the clan's name across the oceans of the world.

During the long voyage the passengers whiled away the evenings dancing and singing to the pipes, and Donald fell in love with one of the prettiest singers, Sarah Ryley, also bound for Launceston. The 20-year-old Presbyterian housemaid, who could read and write, had made the voyage for health reasons. The immigration authorities in Launceston nevertheless described her as 'free from any organic disease' and 'a healthy, stout and good looking girl'. She seemed a good catch to young Donald.

The island's first convict settlement had been founded in the north in July 1804. Governor Philip Gidley King had advanced the settlement to forestall French claims to the island. The settlement was named Launceston after King's home town and was situated on the Tamar, after the river running through that town in England's west country. The first settlers were led by Colonel William Paterson, whose military guard included Sergeant James Brumby. A descendant of Brumby's, Elizabeth, would become Donald Campbell's second wife. (The *Australian Dictionary of Biography* contains an article on Brumby's achievements, written by Alec Campbell.) After a record voyage of just 71 days, *Storm Cloud* steamed past Low Head (where Alec would spend several childhood holidays), entered the Tamar Heads and dropped anchor off George Town, north of Launceston. John Campbell must have found the setting at once picturesque and strangely familiar, since like his native Fort William, on Loch Linnhe, Launceston sat at the end of a long, thin tidal estuary.

They got off to a bad start. Having reason to fear that his crew would try to jump ship and head for the goldfields, Captain Campbell decided against taking the ship upriver to Launceston and directed that the passengers remain on board. From their anchorage off George Town, John and his family were eventually disembarked in the ship's only boat and sailed up to Launceston. The captain had hoped that by this expedient he would contain his restive crew, but sailors are known for their resourcefulness, and it was not long before the men had made off on a hastily contrived raft constructed of chests and spars secured by hammock lashings. Despite a bounty of £11 for each man returned, and the cooperation of the local authorities, only three sailors were apprehended. The unfortunate trio were punished with eight weeks' hard labour and loss of wages for the voyage from Glasgow, and a replacement crew was eventually delivered from Victoria. Whether or not the deserters found gold on the mainland, they were probably the lucky ones, for on a subsequent voyage *Storm Cloud* was wrecked off the coast of Sittwe Akyab, Burma.

On shore at last, John and his young family were shocked to see chained work parties of convicts being marched through the streets. Although convict transportation to Van Diemen's Land had been abolished in 1848, there remained thousands of convicts in the colony, as on the mainland. Indeed, convict transportation to Western Australia persisted until 1868. By the time the practice ceased, at least 166,000 convicts had been offloaded in the colonies. It was hardly surprising, then, that convicts were much in evidence that day. To compound their rude introduction to the penal colony, however, the Campbells were then informed that the only accommodation available to them, at least until they started work, was in the local prison barracks. With their expectations dampened, they could have been forgiven for questioning the rosy picture painted by the St Andrews Society for Immigration.

John's last appearance in the historical records occurred about a year after their establishment in Launceston, when he gave away his eldest daughter, Ann, to a local man. Donald, however, remained in Launceston all his life. His granddaughter Estelle, Alec's sister, who became a journalist and the family's chronicler through her book *Donald Started It All*, firmly established him as the clan founder. Several of his siblings also vanished. Robert fell out with his father and left Van Diemen's Land soon after they arrived. Lachlan migrated to New Zealand (where he married an Australian woman and founded another large Campbell clan). Catherine disappeared from the record, perhaps marrying and taking her husband's name, or leaving the struggling colony for work in the goldfields. Christina died of tuberculosis. Alexander later moved to Victoria, and the fate of Allan is unknown.

Eighteen fifty-five was a good time for fresh beginnings. In January the following year the colony dropped its old name (bestowed upon it in honour of his patron by the seventeenth-century Dutch navigator Abel Tasman) and became simply Tasmania. It also achieved self-government, on a responsible democratic Westminster model, and established its own constitution. The first elections were held in October and the fledgling democracy opened its first Parliament in December. The colony would offer a much more egalitarian model than its Scottish migrants had known, with many opportunities for advancement. It was the perfect environment in which hard-working, entrepreneurial migrants like the Campbells could rise.

With typical adaptability, Donald immediately found work as a storekeeper's assistant. He married Sarah Ryley on 25 July 1856 in Launceston according to the rites of the Church of Scotland. Despite her poor constitution, Sarah had four children in quick succession, three (William, Donald and Lachlan) while they lived at Distillery Creek and a fourth (Allan) after they moved to Cressy. Donald and Sarah had chosen a good place to bring up a family: in 1858 Launceston was incorporated, and just two years later it opened one of the first local government libraries. In 1861 Donald was appointed assistant manager of retailer H. B. Nickolls, based in Cressy, where he became manager in 1863. Sarah, however, never fully recovered from the ill-health that had inspired her to leave the cold winters of Scotland, and on 15 November 1865 she died, aged just 31 years. When she received the news, Sarah's sister in North America offered to take in their four young children, but Donald decided to battle on, and three years later he remarried. He and Elizabeth Brumby were married in 1868 at her brother Samuel's house in Glenburnie. Elizabeth's grandfather Sergeant James Brumby, of Richmond Hill, one of the founding fathers of the colony, had served in Port Jackson, Sydney, with the New South Wales Corps in the 1790s before pioneering the settlements of George Town and York Town, near Launceston, in 1804. Elizabeth bore Donald three more sons — James (in 1868), who moved to Melbourne; Samuel (in 1870), the only one of them to stay in Launceston; and Colin (in 1872), who also moved to Melbourne, where he would later be one of the stars of the Essendon football team's 1897 premiership side. Colin died of pneumonia in England in 1907 after completing his medical degree.

Now a successful businessman, Donald could provide for his second family in some comfort. Elizabeth had herself brought money to the marriage, and Donald was going from strength to strength professionally — 'everything he touched turning to gold', according to the local newspaper. After saving his wages, and having learned the business while working for the H. B. Nickolls company, in April 1874 he bought a store of his own in Cressy. It was a good time for business growth, for with the Launceston–Hobart railway opening in 1876 he could obtain fresh supplies much faster and cheaper than was previously possible. The *Cyclopedia of Tasmania* records that, from a modest start, Donald Campbell, 'by dint of energy and perseverance' built up 'a very extensive business' under his own name. His stores were 'very commodious and contained a most complete and superior stock' that was 'delivered to customers by his own delivery carts for twenty miles around'. The buildings, with stabling, covered about an acre of ground. He had 'four wagons and teams always on the road', which were further described as 'splendid specimens of what such teams should be'. Donald employed ten staff and appointed his eldest son, William, as manager.

As he got older, Donald turned increasingly to community work, sponsoring a church, serving as a justice of the peace and managing Richmond Hill Estate, which had been bequeathed by James Denton Toosey in trust to the Bishop of Tasmania as an educational college. The prosperous businessman apparently had everything, but his health began to decline after he was injured in a buggy accident near Cressy in early 1906. The final blow to his spirits, however, was the news of Colin's death in England in April 1907, aged 35. Broken-hearted, Donald died three months later, on 30 July 1907. In the *Weekly Courier* obituary, he was described as 'a good-hearted man who had done many great things for the community'.

Fortunately for the Campbells, Donald's second son, Samuel, stayed in the region and continued to foster the clan, building on his father's commercial assets and reputation. Sparing nothing in the education of his sons, Donald had sent Sam to the prestigious Horton College boarding school for boys near Ross, founded in 1855. Sam did well in school, winning prizes in arithmetic, English and Greek, but a chance swimming accident (he struck an unseen stake while swimming in the river at Ross) left him with a limp for the rest of his life. With a better diagnosis and adequate treatment he might have made a full recovery, but the main remedy prescribed by local doctors was regular doses of champagne — not all of which got past the vigilant Horton College masters.

Through his academic success and his father's commercial influence in the town, Sam landed a job with Launceston retailer W. Hart & Sons soon after leaving school. After serving his apprenticeship with Harts he was recruited by Lindsay Tulloch and Co. as their principal commercial traveller, eventually taking responsibility for the whole state. When Tulloch's closed down, he had no trouble graduating to the stronger firm of A. C. Ferrall & Co., with whom he would work until retirement in his seventies.

In the last years of the century the growing colony of Tasmania was abuzz with talk of union with the mainland and joining the modern nation to be called the Commonwealth of Australia. In 1898 Tasmanians were given the opportunity to vote on the proposal in a referendum in which a clear majority supported the union. Change was in the air, as it was in Sam Campbell's personal life. With a steady, reliable job, 'the short but good-looking and broad-shouldered' young man wasted no time in proposing to one of the town's most sought-after beauties, Marian Thrower, who would be described by Estelle as a 'tall slim brunette, with big brown eyes, a lovely straight classical nose and a flawless skin'. Frequently referred to simply as 'the beautiful Miss Thrower', Marian was the daughter of William Thrower of Launceston, and his wife, also Marian. Mrs Thrower, an extensively published, well-travelled author and journalist who used the nom-de-plume 'Gitana', was descended from two pioneer families, both of which had interesting backgrounds. On the maternal side were Irish Catholics originally called Keane, O'Keene or O'Cahan, from Dungiven in County Derry, who had arrived in Van Diemen's Land on the *Eliza* in 1833. Hugh Keane went on to design and build several notable landmarks, including Campbell Town's Foxhunter's Return Hotel. The paternal side of the family could be traced to Robert Thrower, convicted at the Norfolk Assizes for sheep stealing and sentenced to transportation in 1836. After serving out his sentence of seven years' hard labour he evidently reformed dramatically, working as a police constable before contributing to the wealth of the combined families through property development.

Along with her fine looks, Marian, like her mother, 'had brains too and a great sense of fun'. After studying painting under Launceston artist Joshua Higgs and 'prominent artists at a leading art school in Melbourne', she was described as 'a courageous woman and an accomplished pianist with a good singing voice and also a fine artist, working in oils'. A few years later, when he overheard the local doctor asking his father, 'Whatever happened to those beautiful Thrower girls?', Sam spun round and announced proudly, 'I married the most beautiful one!'

The wedding took place on 22 February 1898. Following family tradition the event was held at home, at the Throwers' residence at 39 Elphin Road, officiated by the Rector of St. John's Church. The couple rented a series of houses, occupying at least a dozen different homes in the Launceston region, before finally settling down in a rambling old colonial bungalow with a deep verandah in large grounds at 20 Claremont Street. In later years Estelle would buy the house, naming it 'Younah' after the title of a book written by her grandmother about life among the Aborigines in colonial Van Diemen's Land. Sam and Marian had five children — Alec, born in 1899, Malcolm (aka Mac) in 1901, Hector (aka Angus) in 1903, Estelle in 1905 and Colin in 1910. Mac, too, became a successful retailer, running a store in Rossarden in the north-east. Angus, an amateur boxer and racehorse owner as a young man, became a commercial traveller like his father. Estelle became a journalist. Colin drove cabs before serving in the Second World War, and subsequently became a public servant. All but Estelle raised families of their own.

Sam and Marian's home was a happy one, although Marian had to shoulder much of the burden of bringing up the children since Sam was so often on the road. As he travelled about the island mainly by train, and never owned or drove a car, Sam got to know many Tasmanians during his long working life and became one of the most popular commercial travellers of the time. An old-fashioned man, with his father's impeccable manners, he was renowned for raising his hat politely after speaking with someone in the street, and was reputed to have done so even at the end of a telephone conversation — at least in the early days of that new-fangled contraption. Since he also used to hand out threepenny coins to young children wherever he went, he was also famous for his generosity. Watching their family grow in the quiet little town of Launceston, Sam and Marian Campbell must have imagined their children would know nothing but the peace and tranquillity they had enjoyed. They could not have guessed that two of their sons would leave home to fight in bloody wars overseas.

Sam Campbell, *c.* 1898   Marian Campbell, *née* Thrower, *c.* 1898

Family patriarch Donald Campbell, Elizabeth, *née* Brumby, and Alec, *c.* 1900

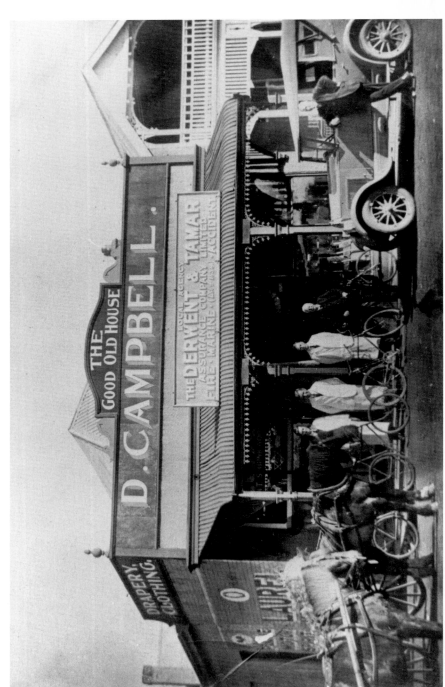

Donald Campbell's store at Cressy, managed by his son Donald (Dan) (centre, in dark suit)

Alec and his mother Marian, 1902

Alec (third row, centre) and the Invermay State School fife band, *c.* 1905

Scotch College, *c.* 1910   (Scotch College Collection)

Scotch College principal
Andrew Raeburn, *c.* 1912
(Scotch College Collection)

CHAPTER 2
FAR FROM THE DRUMS OF WAR

'My father would often drive to Cressy from Launceston in a vehicle we called the Phaeton drawn by a big brown mare named Posy. It took a little over two hours.'

Alec was born in Launceston on 26 February 1899, a year after his parents were married, eight months before the Boer War broke out, and two years before the proclamation of the Commonwealth of Australia at a spectacular ceremony in Centennial Park, Sydney. The population of Australia stood at 3,715,988, of whom 172,362 lived in the colony of Tasmania. Launceston was growing hand over fist as mining and agriculture boomed and new industries and factories were established in the town. These were the days of horse-drawn vehicles, steam or electric trains, electric trams and steamships. There were few cars on the roads, few electrical appliances or telephones in ordinary people's homes; radios were still 25 years off; televisions, 55.

Despite the Campbell clan's warrior heritage, when the Boer War broke out on 11 October 1899 Sam, the courtly commercial traveller, felt no call to volunteer. The news from South Africa nevertheless inspired the first rush of enthusiastic Tasmanian volunteers to enlist in one of the Empire's foreign wars. The *Medic* troop carrier left Hobart with a full complement on 28 October. For the Campbells there was no shortage of action on the home front.

Delivered by a visiting nurse, Alec was born at home at French Street, a colonial bungalow with a traditional wrap-around verandah and backyard. A few months later Sam found himself in the firing line when a 'lunatic' absconded from the detention centre beside the nearby Launceston General Hospital, just behind their house. The first he knew of it, their local doctor, George Clemens, bowled into the house and breathlessly recounted the story: 'Quick, Sam, get your gun. He's heading this way. He's got an axe, and he's threatening to kill anyone who comes near him.' Leaving Marian clutching baby Alec, Sam grabbed one of his sporting guns and rushed out with the doctor. Clemens warned, 'He's dangerous, Sam, so if he comes too close don't hesitate to shoot.' Within minutes Sam was confronting the man, who still carried the axe. Calmly levelling his rifle, Sam demanded, 'Put the axe down immediately or I'll shoot you dead.' To the satisfaction of the assembled crowd the man quickly did so, allowing hospital attendants to hustle him away. Sam and Marian had grown used to hearing the inmates 'calling out and screaming at night', but this little adventure had been too close for comfort. They decided to move to a more respectable area of town, taking up residence in a house called 'Shanikell' at 229 Invermay Road, where within two years Mac was born.

The Commonwealth of Australia was also born in 1901, on 1 January in Sydney's Centennial Park, before an enormous crowd gathered around a rotunda packed with distinguished guests including the governor-general, Lord Hopetoun; the interim prime minister, Edmund Barton, and his cabinet; and governors and premiers from all the newly created states, including Tasmania. Most Tasmanians had supported federation from the time it was first mooted in the 1850s. Alec's well-connected father would have been invited to the public celebrations in Launceston's Royal Park. Here Sam, Marian (then expecting Mac) and toddler Alec would have watched the flag-raising, listened to the patriotic speeches and the municipal band, and generally enjoyed the festivities. It was a great day for the struggling little state of Tasmania, which would always rely on financial support from the mainland. Later that month, however, the death of Queen Victoria would cast a brief pall over the little town. The passing of this legendary figure had a huge impact around the British world, even in Tasmania. She had, after all, already ruled the Empire for nearly twenty years when Sam's paternal grandfather set out from Argyllshire for the new world. Her passing truly marked the end of an era.

Looking back on the federation celebrations years later, Alec could recall little of the event. He had 'some idea that something big was going on. And I can remember Uncle Harry Pybus pulling a flag up the mast, and little things like that.' His father voted in the first national elections in May that year (it would be two more years before women's suffrage was achieved across Australia). The federal parliament was temporarily located in the Victorian Parliament House, Melbourne, until a site was selected for the planned federal capital. (Many years later Alec would help to build the first permanent parliament building in the new capital of Canberra.)

In 1902 Sam and Marian took three-year-old Alec and his younger brother to Hobart for a few months while their father worked out of the state capital. For the Campbells, the two big events that year were Marian's new pregnancy and the end of the Boer War. They read in the Hobart *Mercury* of the final victory that brought hostilities to a close on 31 May. For many Australians at home, the war in South Africa seemed to offer an optimistic precedent for the next imperial adventure into which they would be drawn, just 12 years later. As the returning troops paraded through the streets of Hobart, Alec's patriotic parents took the toddler to watch the colourful parade. But now his second brother's impending birth sent his parents hurrying back to Launceston. Sam took a job at Harts and they rented a house in Abbott Street, just in time for Angus's arrival in 1903.

Always proud of their first-born, Alec's parents had him photographed professionally in 1902 at a studio in Launceston dressed up like a little girl in an ostentatious dress and elaborate hat, after the fashion of the time. Alec's earliest memory was of pulling his hand free of his mother's and lagging behind her as they strolled across the bridge over the river Tamar on the way home from the studio, before defiantly tearing off the ridiculous hat, throwing it into the river and watching it drift downstream. Perhaps vying for his father's attention after his two younger brothers had seized the limelight, the precocious Alec, aged four, left home without permission one afternoon in 1903, planning to meet his father returning from work. Distracted by workers operating a traction engine, the young adventurer failed to make the rendezvous. When his father got home, the police were called and the neighbourhood scoured before the wandering toddler was returned to the fold. Not long after this adventure Alec made amends by loosing his dog Ruffy in the nearby bush to catch a rabbit, which it promptly did, providing a welcome supplement to the food on the table. Never one to miss an opportunity to show off, the five-year-old huntsman, clutching the dead rabbit, and pursued by his excited dog, set off to announce the kill to the whole neighbourhood.

The following year the family moved to Mulgrave Street, where Estelle was born in 1905. As she grew up, Estelle introduced a musical note into the house, and they took to holding singsongs that graduated into elaborate musical productions 'including many Gilbert and Sullivan operas around a beautiful upright grand Collard and Collard piano'. To house this fine piano and other furniture inherited from their respective parents, the Campbells finally bought the spacious 'Chesney', at 81 Mayne Street, a traditional weatherboard house with generous verandahs behind a white picket fence on a large block. Here they settled for some years. It was at Chesney that their fifth and last child, Colin, was born, and it was from this happy family home that Alec would set off for Gallipoli just five years later.

Alec's first significant memories of childhood, and those that really shaped the young boy, were of the adventures he enjoyed at the country home of his grandfather Donald — what he called his

'Cressy days'. Donald and Elizabeth's home in the remote town of Cressy, 20 miles south of Launceston, was perhaps a colonial counterpart to the Scottish farm on which he had worked as a shepherd in his youth. With his father absent for much of the time, Alec evidently appreciated the stability of this country world. Holidays at Cressy began just after the turn of the century and continued for ten years, until both grandparents had died. These times were not just fun, either. It was at Cressy that he learned about his Scottish origins and developed the country skills that would prove so essential in later life. The things he learned during these interludes would equip him for a life of great challenges.

Alec and his siblings were taken to Cressy every possible weekend, for Sunday lunches, and for special holidays such as Easter and Christmas. Cressy represented 'long happy holidays with their doting grandparents, tolerant uncles and fun-loving cousins, with ponies to ride, a big store full of exciting things, a large garden and a rambling old house to explore'. Banjo Paterson, the new nation's favourite poet, whose ballads the Campbell family learned by heart, had said he pitied any young child who did not grow up in the bush or go to school in a country town, because that was what shaped 'a fair dinkum Australian'. Alec enjoyed the idyllic and secure bush childhood prescribed by Paterson. It was this solid foundation that would help him survive across three centuries, from the age of the horse-drawn buggy and the parish pump to one characterised by computerised high technology and the global community.

They normally travelled to Cressy by horse and buggy or the phaeton, although occasionally they went by train. The buggy, owned by Alec's grandfather, was a four-wheel affair with two bench seats, one behind the other, which carried six people comfortably. It was drawn by two horses, a mare called Maud and Posy, 'a beautiful, high spirited and high stepping carriage mare with a tendency to skittishness and to shy at the least excuse'. But Sam 'was a superb horseman who would not take any nonsense from her and would give her a flip across the rump with a long handled whip'. If they took the phaeton, Sam harnessed Posy. The phaeton was 'more elegant than the buggy and lower slung'; it had two seats facing each other and a small 'dickie' seat at the back for Alec and his brothers, and 'needless to say the boys did not like this seat as they could not see where they were going, only where they had been'. Estelle remembered the journey to Cressy as 'an exhilarating trip, especially on a spring or summer morning, with hawthorne blossom out along the hedges and the lambs chasing each other in the paddocks, and the magpies warbling melodiously with the joy of being alive on such a morning'. If the horse performed well, they normally made the 20-mile journey in two hours. Setting off early, with one stop at the Travellers' Rest Hotel en route to give Posy a drink from the horse trough, they would arrive well before lunch, although Alec and his brothers would always claim to be 'hungry as hunters'. The train journey was equally diverting: 'The steam engine puffed and whistled its way along and once the family and the luggage tumbled out there was always someone to meet them — usually Wattie Wall the groom with the buggy and pony.' Among the thoroughbreds, work horses, wagon horses and plough teams at Cressy, Alec had a favourite, 'my special chestnut mare'. After one of his grandfather's best-loved horses was killed by a snake, Alec always checked on arrival that his chestnut mare was alive and well.

Alec drew up a plan of his grandparents' Cressy home in which he carefully recorded the layout of the complicated arrangement of buildings and gardens that for a decade formed his special world. The plan included the stables, coach house, barns, summerhouse, dovecote and of course the main house itself. The homestead was built above and around the store and was dominated by a wide verandah beneath five dormer windows, behind which, over the store itself, were the upstairs bedrooms used by Alec and his siblings. These bedrooms opened into one another and were reached by a staircase leading up from a large parlour below. In the end attic bedroom, Alec's paternal uncle William slept next to a large storeroom, from which another very steep flight of stairs descended to the shop itself. The plan included sketches of the immense dining room with its long table that seated gatherings of 20 people in front of a roaring fireplace during family celebrations. The meals, covered with big silver dish covers, were wheeled along the verandah from the kitchen. There were no mod cons at Cressy, of course, as Alec's plan confirmed. 'The little house was a long way from the main house and contained a three seater, one long seat with three holes side by side, a big hole, middle sized hole and small hole for different family members. Instead of pulling a chain the user threw a bucket of cinders down after their deposit to keep the smells down and minimize the flies.'

Alec was always first up in the mornings at Cressy, leading his little brothers noisily out into the yard amid protests from his elders — 'Go back to sleep, you little devils!' The big yard was 'full of never to be forgotten sights and sounds where there was always something exciting happening as wagon horses were being fed and harnessed, workmen were shouting, dogs barking, impatient horses stamping and snorting and loads of goods arriving with exquisite nose-tingling perfumes'. The yard was 'surrounded by stables, lofts full of hay, harness rooms with their own pungent odours, a coach house and endless outbuildings'. At night the irrepressible Alec would sneak out to watch Jimmy, the head man, 'doing his rounds of the horses with a hurricane lamp bobbing about in the dark as he checked and fed them'. Alec and his brothers added a little chaos of their own to the proceedings whenever they decided to hold a cricket or football match in the yard.

'The boys got up to all sorts of mischief,' Estelle recalled in her family memoir, 'and Alec was always the ringleader.' Having learned to swim in nearby Brumby Creek, Alec gave his father 'many a near heart attack by his rashness in swimming across the strong flowing river when it was in flood'. It was here that he learned to fish. Alec loved to take risks and cause mayhem. One day, playing Red Indians with his brothers, he 'ordered them to take their clothes off, poured red ink all over them, stuck a couple of rooster feathers in their hair, and calling out blood-curdling "Whoopees" started chasing unsuspecting maids and station hands around the property'. Another time, to avoid being dragged off to yet another boring church service, he ran off down the paddock in his Sunday best, and had to be hunted down on horseback, scooped up by the stockman, and delivered to the local church, direct from the saddle and brimming with indignation. To compound his offence, during the service, when his grandfather gave him a half-crown to deposit in the collection plate, Alec decided this was too much for a humble village church so calmly took out one shilling as change before depositing the half-crown.

When in trouble he would sometimes escape to the Cressy butcher's shop, where a sympathetic relative would hide him in the back room with the carcasses. By age five Alec's precocious language skills could cause his parents public embarrassment. Once, asked to recite a poem for visiting guests, he declaimed, 'There once was a blooming sparrow / Got in a blooming spout / Then came a blooming thunderstorm / And flushed that sparrow out.' Asked by his mother some time later why he was sitting watching a ploughman eating his lunch, he replied that since she had criticised his table manners, claiming he ate like a ploughman, he had decided to see what that looked like. As he got older, Alec became more useful, especially on neighbouring Glen Roy farm (owned by another relative) during harvest time, when he stayed in the caboose with the seasonal workers and did odd jobs.

Alec was fascinated by a 'fearsome looking bayonet', probably a memento from the Boer War, owned by one of his grandfather's storemen. The man used it to dig out dried fruits from their bulk supply tubs; with great relish he would plunge the bayonet deep into the barrel. Alec remembered this first bayonet as 'triple edged and deadly'. Probably not coincidentally, in his first childhood nightmare, at Cressy, he dreamed he was being chased 'by a huge ugly giant with a bayonet in the large scary store room as he ran around in between the boxes of stock, before eventually escaping down the narrow stairs and waking up'. Not that this was the only weapon he became accustomed to. While still very young Alec learned to use a gun and was allowed to join his elders on game-shooting expeditions, during which they would bag hares, rabbits, deer, wattle birds, pigeons and quail. He was most excited one day when they came home with 'a magnificent stag with spectacular antlers'.

The idyll of early childhood at Cressy could not last forever. Back home after another rural holiday, his parents one day advised him that he would have to spend more time in Launceston and prepare to face the real world. It might even mean being sent away to boarding school. Alec, who hated the prospect, embarked on a campaign to dissuade his parents from such a draconian move. His schooling began at a small school in Mulgrave Crescent near home, which was convenient for his busy mother, given Sam's frequent absence. When he turned six in 1905, Alec was enrolled at Invermay State School, where he attended his first serious classes and played in the school's fife band, with younger brother Mac tagging along. Fife bands were popular in state schools then, and it was considered an honour for young lads to represent their school in this way. But when he complained to his parents that one of the teachers mistreated him, he was withdrawn from both band and school and sent to a private establishment run by a Frenchman named Monsieur Henri, not far from Mayne Street. According to Estelle, however, the 'wild and restless' boy, who just wanted to be out in the bush with his gun, 'did not learn a great deal' at either institution. Of Henri's School all he later could recall was being taught by the Frenchman's wife, who 'always smelt of stale eucalyptus'. Eventually Alec's parents recognised that his teachers could not discipline the unruly young country boy or even interest him in indoor activities. Something had to be done.

Sam and Marian had wanted to send their eldest son to boarding school, but Horton College had closed down and the alternatives were too expensive, especially with five children to educate. The death of Alec's beloved grandfather in 1907 severed the last living link with their Argyllshire roots. When Elizabeth, who never fully recovered from Donald's death, died three years later, she left an inheritance sufficient to send Alec to a private school, if they could find one. Alec — who at eight years old already knew how to milk a cow, skin a rabbit, ride, swim, fish and hunt for the table — doubted there was much useful a school could teach him, especially a boarding school. His parents disagreed, and so began the search for a school that could tame the barefoot kid from Launceston, hold the restless interest of this intelligent but incorrigible child, and perhaps even teach him a thing or two.

CHAPTER 3
SCHOOL DAYS

'I was a student at the Launceston Scotch College when the war broke out in August 1914.'

S am and Marian decided against sending Alec off to boarding school in Hobart (the closest option), enrolling him instead at Launceston's most prestigious private school, Scotch College. The fees were 12 guineas for the full year of four equal terms, with the option of paying 3 guineas term by term. This was still a lot of money when a family cottage in Launceston could be bought for just 300 guineas, but his grandparents' legacy meant they could just afford it.

Scotch College, based on Launceston's City School, was opened in 1901, with Andrew Raeburn taking up the post of inaugural headmaster. Raeburn, a Scotsman dedicated to passing down the values of the old country, applied the same high educational standards he had inculcated at Melbourne's prestigious Scotch College. He insisted on hard work and long school days. The school was housed in an old building behind a white picket fence in York Street before it moved to Penquite Road. In Alec's day there were at best one hundred pupils, most the sons of doctors, lawyers, engineers and assorted professionals along with small businessmen and other members of the commercial class.

Andrew Raeburn proved to be the most influential figure, after his grandfather, in Alec's childhood. Apart from their shared Scottish heritage and religious background, he believed in developing boys' 'all around qualities' rather than simply the three 'Rs'. Alec, at first, was not interested in 'book learning', and fortunately the school was small enough to permit personal attention. A man named Harris was employed to teach religion and scripture, implanting in them the sense of a moral duty to contribute to their community. Raeburn, a devout and clean-living Presbyterian, was an unusually sensitive and caring man for his time. He believed that 'a schoolmaster must consider not only the boy's mental and physical nature but also his personal and individual temperament'. He held that it was 'wrong to merely cram a boy's head with facts to pass examinations, as every aspect of the boy's development had to be considered'. He also believed that every child had a special talent that would emerge in the right nurturing environment, and that 'each boy has varying natural abilities and we must be aware of the psychological reasons why some boys are under-achievers at school work'.

Accustomed to a more informal environment, Alec would recall the headmaster as 'an authoritarian figure who always stood tall and dressed very well in a dark suit...we were all attired in dark suits and polished boots. I studied several languages including Latin and German. I enjoyed them greatly as well as English and Maths. We were all very well behaved, as I remember, but if we misbehaved punishment was strict. The lessons were all very regimented and Mr Raeburn was always very much in control — very authoritarian indeed. I remember him as a large, stern man.' Yet Alec could not have received greater support and encouragement in building the self-confidence he would need to lead his life in the individualistic way he chose. Raeburn never caned the boys, utterly rejecting the enduring nineteenth-century Victorian theories on disciplining children. He once said, 'I would rather spend the time talking to the boy who misbehaved to find his unique interest so I can cultivate this.' Luckily for Alec, the headmaster's special focus was those boys who were lagging behind in class. All this must have been music to the ears of his parents for, given his preoccupation with outdoor activities, Alec did not perform well in class.

One of the best features of Scotch College for Alec was the sport — especially Australian Rules football, which he played well; he had, after all, the example of his uncle Colin to look to. After school he liked to take a gun 'with the dogs out in the stubble paddocks bagging quail'. He loved to ride to school too, until the day Mac's borrowed grey mare, Heart's Desire, broke free onto the school lawn, which it cropped rather overenthusiastically. Alec was severely reprimanded and warned never again to bring horses onto the school grounds.

Raeburn's greatest influence on Alec may have been exerted through the Cadet Corps, which he founded shortly before Alec arrived and which he himself led. Here he instilled in the boys the value of duty and of serving 'King and country'. Alec joined the corps at the age of 12, at the start of his second year at Scotch. The cadets were very active at the time. Australia was on the move: it had just established its own navy, and the government was talking about starting a flying corps. As a good shot, and the proud owner of a range of hunting guns, Alec relished his time in the Cadet Corps and, despite his youth, had plenty to contribute. Raeburn employed a Boer War veteran, Sergeant-Major William Welsh, who inspired the boys with his war stories, drumming into them the importance of fighting for one's country if called upon, as he had during the South African war — which he liked to tell the boys he played no small part in winning. Welsh issued uniforms, taught them how to present themselves to a military standard, showed them how to handle the heavy .303 rifle, fit and use a bayonet, pitch tents in the bush, march and advance into battle. The young corps, with Alec a proud member, did so well that in 1913 they were asked to parade through the streets of Launceston, with 'a large crowd lining the streets as the boys passed'. The local reporter for the *Examiner* wrote up the story: 'With their equipment specially polished for the occasion, the young guard presented an impressive spectacle, as, headed by the Military Band, they marched through the main streets of the city.' He congratulated the cadets on 'attaining an all-round proficiency, not only in drill and rifle exercises, but also in discipline, good conduct and other qualities that go so far towards the making of an ideal soldier. It was a good thing,' the reporter concluded, 'that the Cadet Corps was arousing such an enthusiasm among the lads and that compulsory military training has come to stay because it was this training more than anything else that led to success in war.'

The school expected boys to serve their country. When war broke out, Scotch College would actively encourage old boys to enlist and would criticise any 'shirkers' who did not do their duty to 'God, King and Country'. Unsurprisingly, Scotch boys would volunteer for the war in large numbers. Twenty old boys from this relatively small school would sign up in the first patriotic rush before the end of 1914, with many more answering the call in the succeeding years, so that by the end of the war nearly 50 per cent of the school's enrolment register had enlisted. Twenty-two boys from this tiny Launceston school alone would not return from the war.

Despite the school's best efforts, Alec continued to learn most about life outside of school in the paddocks and bush around Chesney. Here he and his brothers got on with the real business of living. Alec would remember Launceston as 'just a nice little country town. It was so compact, and we used to swim in the Tamar or walk in the bushy hills beyond Trevallyn.' Chesney had the advantage of a very large yard for the horse and carriage and even larger paddocks around the house, with orchards, vegetable gardens, chooks, dogs, cats, pigs, a pony called Nigger and grazing cows like the black and white Beauty, whom Alec milked for the table as soon as he was old enough to become a 'junior yard boy'. There was always plenty to learn from the tradesmen who announced their arrival by calling out 'Butcher!', 'Grocer!' or Rabbito!'. Since he slept on the side verandah outside the dining-room windows, Alec was in a good position to study their wares. He was also well placed for late-night excursions, and would often sneak off with Mac after dark. Sometimes, rather than being cooped up indoors, they would pitch a tent in the garden.

Most of all Alec loved the shooting expeditions, during which he might bag a brace of rabbits for the table, which he would then skin, gut, cook and eat. As a result of these hunting trips, he became one of the better marksmen in the Scotch College Cadet Corps. He brought home birds' nests complete with eggs, fruit from the trees in the surrounding orchards and vegetables from the nearby 'Chinaman's' vegetable patch. Nothing, it seemed, was out of reach of the resourceful Alec and his brothers. He built elaborate kites, which they flew in the paddock. He made bowling hoops and spinning tops, which they lashed to great speeds using homemade whips. He taught his brothers how to 'swing right up to the sky' on a tree swing in an old mulberry tree that in season carried fruit for the picking. He would also frighten them all, Estelle recalled, by letting off fire crackers, rockets, jumping jacks and bungers, 'which were the most dangerous if you stood too close'. And he loved to light the huge bonfires they built for special occasions — especially 24 May, Empire Night.

His pungent language was a problem the school did not seem to be resolving, so his mother gave him private lessons at the kitchen table to discourage him from imitating the rougher boys at Invermay State School. She also insisted that the reluctant country kid take dancing lessons. Every Saturday morning, after forcing his toughened bare feet into shining black shoes and dressing him in smart slacks, white shirt, jacket and tie, she packed him off to the home of local dancing teacher Miss Amy Barnard in Invermay, where the unenthusiastic dandy mastered the basic steps of the barn dance, the veleta and the two-step. Estelle remembered 'many happy hours spent at Chesney with the whole family gathered around the breakfast table, and in the evenings school books scattered on the table, or playing indoor games, reading or roasting chestnuts from the garden on the fire grate'. It was around the same table that the children would sit a few short years later to 'painstakingly write letters to Alec at war'.

After the death of Alec's grandparents, they holidayed at a beach resort north of Launceston called Low Head, overlooking the mouth of the Tamar, where his great-grandfather had first arrived in the new world with his family. It was in the safety of these sheltered waters that Alec learned to sail. Now the family caught the ferry to nearby George Town, where they rented an old two-storey house, Tara Hall, which was rumoured to be haunted. To reassure his worried siblings, Alec had promised to bring his trusty gun and shoot any ghost that dared to make an appearance. Alec was always ready to help his younger siblings. One day during a swimming outing, Estelle recalled, some local bullies threw his baby brother Angus (who could not swim) into the Tamar. In a flash Alec had dived in, fished out the startled Angus and set him on course for home before alone chasing off the three young ruffians.

In 1913, at age 14, Alec surprised his family with an unexpected eighth birthday present for his kid sister, whom he presented with a revolver and enough bullets to learn to shoot straight. 'Needless to say I did not own it for long after Mother saw it,' Estelle wrote, 'but I had it long enough to shoot a few bullets into the huge old oak tree at the bottom of the back garden.' Alec was 'very gun and explosives minded in those days, and I think the old oak tree must have been riddled with bullets from his various firearms'. Estelle was accustomed to her brother's preoccupation, but she vividly remembered how, when one of her friends 'first saw Alec nonchalantly cleaning one of his guns, she burst into tears, to my amazement and Alec's'.

The young gunman's competence proved useful to the family on more than one occasion. One night when Sam and Marian were out, leaving their eldest son in charge, Alec, who was in the breakfast room with his brothers, heard the side door open. He knew instantly it was not his parents, who always used the front door. 'So Alec got his gun and ammunition and rushed through the house towards the door, surprising the intruder, who ran across the garden.' Alec shouted, 'Stand or I will fire!' He later commented laconically, 'He didn't stop so I put a shot over his head.' The young sentry then stood guard under a streetlight outside the house until the return of his parents, to whom the 15-year-old explained calmly, 'We had a burglar and I had to deal with him.'

Being a good marksman, Alec was sometimes called on as a hired gun by neighbours, such as Fred Lamb, who on one occasion shook Alec awake at midnight. 'Alec, bring your gun quick!' Assuming another intruder was causing problems, and nothing loath, Alec grabbed his gun and, still in pyjamas and bare feet, rushed after his distracted neighbour, who suddenly froze in the yard and hissed, 'There he is, Alec! There he is — shoot him!' Alec looked up to see an old owl blinking back at him. 'He ate my pet seagull,' his neighbour complained. 'Shoot him!' The young marksman did as he was asked.

Alec never got into trouble with the police over his guns, since they knew the family understood firearms. The Campbells had always had guns in the house. 'Alec and his brothers were such good shots, and huntsmen thanks to their gun dogs, retrievers and setters.' Sam was 'very strict about the handling of firearms and all the boys were taught how to always break a gun and unload it before getting through or over a fence and never to point a firearm at anyone, even when they were certain it was not loaded. Alec as the oldest was also taught how to clean a gun immediately on returning home after a shooting expedition and everything else to do with the correct use and care of guns.' Gunpowder was also a 'familiar thing in our house', Estelle wrote. 'At least Alec always seemed to have plenty of gunpowder on hand, especially if a tree stump needed to be blown up, and he got rid of many a stump in that way. One day Alec called out to Mother, who was on her way to the clothes line, "Go back, go back!" and seconds later there was an almighty explosion and a tree stump went flying through the air.'

From the day news reached them of the outbreak of war in Europe in August 1914, all the young men in Launceston, as around Australia and throughout the British Empire, talked of little else. Even in Launceston the assassination of the exotic-sounding Archduke Franz Ferdinand at the end of June had been reported in the *Examiner*. Apparently this incident had helped bring about the war. Would they soon be fighting for king and country? The build-up to war was widely reported in Tasmania, and even at 15 Alec knew something of what was happening. 'I heard about it fairly soon after it started, because there were rumours of war coming, and then we heard immediately when war was declared — and that Australia was in it too, because England was in it.'

Overnight the mood in the country changed, and soon the papers were carrying stories of Germany's invasion of Belgium, Luxembourg and France and of atrocities against women and children. In the following months the *Examiner* would report the unprecedented slaughter in the battles of Marne, Ypres and the other killing fields of Europe. Boys like Alec talked of their school chums from Scotch College and other local schools who had enlisted and sailed out within weeks of the outbreak of war and were already setting up a base camp for Australian and New Zealand forces beneath the pyramids of Egypt. To young Australians, especially lads like Alec who knew how to handle a gun, the news was all very exciting.

Alec's school days were in any case drawing to a close. The 15-year-old needed only to sit his end-of-year exams before leaving school and finding a job. Given all that was happening in Europe, and the charged atmosphere at home in Australia, his final day at school in December would have had a big impact on him. The headmaster, Mr Tovell, who had replaced Andrew Raeburn, addressed the school leavers fervently on the theme of 'Persistence'. 'Delivering a passionate plea,' the *Examiner* reported, 'the head-master urged upon the lads the importance of recognising that of all personal characteristics they should recognise the necessity of perseverance as the most essential quality for success in life.' Campbell family lore already included the exemplary story of the thirteenth-century Scottish patriot Robert Bruce and the persistent spider; listening to the principal's speech that day in December 1914, Alec would certainly have made the connection. The headmaster threw the school's support enthusiastically behind the war. 'At the present moment,' he announced proudly, 'there is a list posted on the school's noticeboard of some twenty names of old Scotch Collegians who are on active service for the King and country, both at sea and on land, and we are frequently learning of others.'

School was over for Alec, and within days he had his first job, helping with the pre-Christmas rush at D. & W. Murray's warehouse in Paterson Street. Estelle recalled how he 'hated his first job so much that he soon left because it did not suit his adventurous spirit'. Nevertheless, he had received his first-ever pay packet, and he could do what he liked with his money. In the event, he rode his bicycle straight to town and bought Estelle 'the prettiest doll I ever saw with big brown eyes and black hair'. By early in the new year Alec had already gone up in the world, having secured a position as junior clerk with the Colonial Mutual Fire Insurance Company. Admittedly it was at the bottom of the ladder, but it gave him prospects, with a potential career in the insurance industry. He soon became bored, though, and once he turned 16, on 26 February 1915, Alec began to think more seriously about putting his skills to use in the war that was already more than six months old. In the months to come the idea would grow, finally forcing a decision that would change his life forever.

CHAPTER 4

A 16-YEAR-OLD ANSWERS THE CALL

'I had read stories about the South African war and of British troops in India. I made up my mind then to go to the war if I could.'

As 1915 unfolded the war seemed to turn against Britain. Working as an insurance clerk in Launceston, Alec would have heard about the German submarine attacks on British merchant ships, the sinking of the Cunard passenger liner *Lusitania* off Ireland, and the giant Zeppelins dropping bombs on London. Now Turkey had thrown its support behind Germany. These were troubling days for the mother country, to which many people in Launceston felt strong ties.

In early May the newspapers reported on the Allied attack against Turkey in the Dardanelles, and spoke for the first time of a peninsula with the unlikely and initially unpronounceable name of Gallipoli. Soon the papers were full of this dramatic news. Some correspondents reported that hundreds of young Australians, including Tasmanians, had been killed on the very first day. Later reports put the death toll in the thousands. It was enough to inspire some young men, even in quiet, isolated Launceston, to enlist — especially after they heard about that Melbourne bloke, Albert Jacka, who single-handedly killed five Turks and captured three more in one trench, earning himself a Victoria Cross. Some of the local fellows, emboldened by a few beers, might have suggested that Jacka needed a hand over there.

The *Examiner* explained that the Allies had attacked Turkey to gain control of the strategic Dardanelles sea lanes. The idea, advanced by Britain's First Sea Lord, Winston Churchill, was to knock Turkey out of the war and open sea communications with Russia. In March Allied warships had failed in their bid to push through to Constantinople, sustaining heavy losses from Turkish mines and from artillery in entrenched positions overlooking the straits. A land invasion was therefore deemed essential to knock out the Turkish defences on the Gallipoli Peninsula. The Gallipoli landings would soon dominate newspaper reports of the war. Heavy losses inspired the government to call for more recruits, an appeal enthusiastically supported by the jingoistic press. Cartoonist Norman Lindsay, of the *Bulletin*, who the previous year had drawn blood-curdling images of Germans spitting Belgian babies on bayonets, now depicted an empty trench at Gallipoli with a lone Australian volunteer calling out 'Coo-ee' and beckoning. Around the country, women nailed white feathers to the doors of young 'shirkers' who refused to volunteer. Patriotic leaders like federal Labor Party leader Billy Hughes began calling for conscription.

Even so, it would have taken a brave man to enlist. After months of news stories about the Allied losses in France, anyone who volunteered to join up would have been public spirited. But the event that lit the fire in many young men's bellies was Gallipoli. The daring landings on 25 April seemed easier to understand. To capture the Turkish positions now, surely they just needed more men. It was an irresistible call to arms for many, including one bright young office clerk in Launceston, a country boy used to shooting rabbits and birds and chasing off the odd human intruder. Believing he could be more use over there than in his boring office job, this young man of action itched to pick up the gun that had already served him well. He would probably have identified more with the young soldiers he was hearing about than with his fellow office clerks. Many young Launceston people were concerned about the war. Kathleen Connolly, Alec's future wife, wrote to the local paper: 'I am thirteen years and eight months old and am in the sixth class. There was a send off for some more boys last week; about six of them went away. A number of boys have gone from here to fight in this dreadful war, which is causing so much trouble and loss of life; but we all hope it will soon come to an end and we hope that peace will be proclaimed before next Empire Day. We pray for it every day in school. I trust our prayers may be heard by almighty God and bring this terrible war to an end.'

Prime Minister Andrew Fisher had promised to support Britain 'to the last man and the last shilling'. Some of those who stepped forward had returned from the Boer War just twelve years earlier; others, who recalled the triumphant return of the veterans of this imperial adventure, saw themselves following in these soldiers' footsteps. Nobody knew what a slaughterhouse this new war would be. In the event, Australia was the only country to field an all-volunteer army throughout the war. Before it was over 324,000 Australians (out of a population of five million) would go to war, of whom 61,000 were killed. Of those who saw active service, 12,907 were from Tasmania, where enlistment reached its peak in August 1915; and of these, 2,500 local boys would be killed, with the death toll worsening each year up to 1917 (16 per cent in 1915, 27 per cent in 1916, 33 per cent in 1917), before falling back to 24 per cent in 1918. (The Tasmanians were led by John Gellibrand, who commanded the 12th Battalion during the battles of Bullecourt in France in 1917.) When enlistments dropped off, the government conducted two referendums, in 1916 and 1917, to force through conscription; both were narrowly defeated. By the time young Alec made his fateful decision, having convinced himself that he had thought and talked about it enough, and that it was time to act, there was already a well-worn path to follow. Posters directing young men to recruiting stations were pasted up on walls every-where.

The big day came. 'I just suddenly decided,' Alec would recall later, 'so walked up to the building, went into their recruiting office and put myself in as a recruit. They were after young men. I was young. I was not very big, but I was strong, and that was all right. Oh yes. I think I said I was 18.' Alec's war records, now held in the National Archives of Australia, confirm that he enlisted in the Australian Imperial Force on 2 July 1915 and was placed in the 15th Battalion, made up of Tasmanians and Queenslanders.

The 15th Battalion formed part of the 4th Brigade under the command of the up-and-coming Melbourne engineer John Monash, who had been at Gallipoli since the landing. (In 1918 Monash would take command of Australia's first army on the western front when all five Australian divisions were united. He would be knighted on the battlefield by George V in August 1918 for his part in actions in France that turned the tide of the war; the first soldier to be knighted in battle for 200 years, he was also the last). By July 1915 the battalion had built up an impressive track record. They had landed at Gallipoli on day one and had fought in almost every significant action involving the Anzacs since. When Alec finally reached the last port of call before Anzac Cove, the Greek island of Lemnos, he would hear stories from these veterans that would raise the hair on the back of his neck.

Alec's official enlistment form states that he was working as a clerk, that he had served three years in the school cadets and that his religion was Church of England. It also 'confirmed' that he was 18 years old. Since the form did not require his date of birth, asking only for the volunteer's age, Alec simply added a couple of years. The attesting officer added his signature once Alec had signed the oath, which included the words, 'I swear that I will well and truly serve our Sovereign Lord the King in the Australian Imperial Forces until the end of the War' and that 'I will resist His Majesty's enemies and cause His Majesty's peace to be kept and maintained'.

At five feet five inches (162 cm), and weighing 135 lbs (61 kg), Alec just made the grade. Although smaller and lighter than most recruits, he would certainly have told the officers how well he could shoot and ride. One blemish in his past — he admitted to having been caught 'riding without a light' — evidently did not dissuade the Army from trying to make a soldier of him, so with the initial processing over he was referred to the medical authorities. He duly passed his medical with flying colours, the MO confirming that Alec 'did not present any of the following conditions: syphilis, scrofula, abnormal curvature of the spine, impaired constitution, defective intelligence, defects of vision, voice or hearing; haemorrhoids, varicose veins beyond a limited extent, traces of corporal punishment, nor marked varicocele with unusually pendant testicles nor any other physical defect calculated to unfit him for the duties of a soldier'. Most important (as he had learned many times in the past), he had the good eyesight ('could see the required distance with either eye') and steady hand of all good marksmen.

Like all recruits under the age of 21, Alec needed his parents' consent. Although this could have proved an unassailable obstacle, in his case it did not, partly because he was honest with them from the start. Nonetheless, his success was due to a series of misconceptions. 'Dad, never thinking they would take him, made Alec promise he would tell the recruiting office his correct age. Alec claimed he did this, and when they told him to go home and come back in two years, he replied: "Well, just stick me down as 18".' They did. When Sam heard this, he decided to let him go. 'Like most other people, he thought the war would be over in a few months, well before Alec got to the front. How mistaken he was. It continued for three more years after Alec enlisted, although he was returned home before it ended.' A commercial traveller with no experience and little understanding of war, Alec's father signed the enlistment papers as his first-born (just 16 years and four months old) hovered expectantly at his shoulder. Sam had been the most loving father imaginable, filling his children's lives with fun and games. Now he typed up the letter (dated 30 June 1915) that in a few words passed his son's fate into the hands of the Army.

30th. June .1915

Chessney.

8I.Mayne.Street.

Invermay.

To the Military Aurthourities.

Dear.Sirs.

I beg to advise you that my son Alec
has my full consent to his inlistment for the front.

I remain Yours truly

Samuel A. Campbell

Marian F. Campbell

At the time Marian felt she could do little but go along with her husband's wishes. Later she would express her anguish by changing her religious faith. 'She did not approve,' Alec's second wife, Kate, believed, 'but she did not stand in his way. I don't know what his father felt, but his parents were of different religions: she was a Catholic, he was a Presbyterian and a true Scot. When they married, they split the difference and were married in the Church of England. But when Alec came back his father said, "Well, you and I now are the only black Scots" (they were known as black Presybterians), because Marian had gone back to the Catholic Church. Because of the shocking slaughter happening on Gallipoli she was making her peace with her God and praying Alec would get back. She felt very bad about what was happening in Gallipoli and very afraid.'

Alec had read and heard about the Boer War and British troops in India, but he would also have been inspired by the Scotch College boys who joined up with the school's full support. As a kid who had grown up with guns and explosives, hunting animals for the table and blowing up tree stumps to clear the land, he felt he was qualified. Later he would simply say that 'everyone was doing it', and that he 'did not have much sense, and most of my mates were joining up for a bit of fun'. He also recalled, 'I suppose we had some sort of idea that it was to protect Australia, and in a way England, because we used to think a lot more of England in those days than we do now!' Towards the end of his life he would add, 'I did not look for a reason. I just did it. Most young fellows were going, and I was only 16 so not very mature to make decisions of any sort. And my parents did not realise what the war was, until afterwards.'

Alec was not the youngest Australian to enlist. James Martin, a tall, strapping country boy from Tocumwall near the Victoria and New South Wales border, was 14 when he enlisted. How he got past the authorities no one knows, but unlike Alec he did not come back. James Martin died at Gallipoli just before his fifteenth birthday — a sad footnote to a desperate and irresponsible government recruiting policy.

With the paperwork behind him, Alec William Campbell left home as Private Campbell, service number 2731, AIF. The 8th Reinforcements became his new home, where his comrades nick-named him 'the kid soldier' or just 'the kid'. After a short period of preliminary training in Launceston, and an even briefer final leave, Alec was sent south to train at an army reinforcements camp outside Claremont, near Hobart. In his first letter home he told his mother, 'We have nearly 900 men in Camp now' and 'about half the camp have got Influenza. I had a touch of it myself but am alright now.' To begin with it seemed to Alec just like the school cadets: 'We did rifle shooting and we did marching. Not much training really — it got you in decent physical nick because we did running in the morning, doing exercises. But there was nothing over-strenuous.'

Alec's letters before leaving Tasmania were written on letter-head supplied by the YMCA that carried the grand header 'With his Majesty's Commonwealth Forces on Active Service' and 'For God, for King, and for Country' beside a depiction of a handsome British officer resplendent in full dress uniform and a flamboyant handlebar moustache. It was, of course, Britain's celebrated Minister for War,

Lord Kitchener, whom Alec himself would meet on a crowded beach at Gallipoli before the end of the year. Writing to his father between tiring stints on guard duty, Alec noted, 'We don't know when we are going for a certainty,' but 'from what I hear we will go to Sydney for about a week (so I might be able to see Uncle Jim) and then we go straight to Egypt and finish our training there.' In the meantime he would not be short of money as 'they bank one shilling a day for us and pay us the rest, and when we get away I will get two shillings a day and the rest you draw and keep till I get back'. He had a series of photos taken by a photographer at Claremont Camp, Estelle recorded, 'with a bayonet nearly as big as himself, looking for all the world like a child in fancy dress'. Alec wrote, 'I got my photos and liked them well, the one sitting down is the best I think. I will send that one to Olga' (an early girlfriend, according to family legend). Meanwhile Marian could not bear the thought of her son preparing for war, and 'tears never failed to come to her eyes whenever she looked at that photo'.

By 4 August the young recruit, so he wrote to his mother, was heartily sick of guard duty. 'I am that sleepy I can hardly stand up…we are the only company able to do guard in camp now, and we have one night on and the next night off.' He also advised her, 'There are all sorts of roumers about the camp as to when we are going' but 'we are not going strait to Egypt now as we were at first.' As the troops rehearsed for their farewell parade through Hobart, the young sentry watched his fellow recruits 'march out of the camp. First there were the light horse & Artillery then the band and last of all about 600 foot soldiers. Infintry, Engineers etc there were 900 in all.' On 12 August, with their departure date looming, Alec apologised that he was 'so busy fixing up our affairs, getting regimentals numbers etc that we have not much time to write . . . We have just got orders to parade in full marching order this morning so I suppose I will have to cut this note short and get my kit ready.' He added, 'I wish Dad or Mac or someone could get down to see me off by Monday's boat but I don't suppose any of you could very well manage it.' In his next letter he pressed his case: 'We are leaving Claremont on next Monday so will have one more Sunday in poor old Tassy.'

Alec's appeals were answered, although not by his father. Sam, Estelle explained, was 'always very emotional and so was unable to go down to Hobart to see off his eldest son — perhaps waving him goodbye for the last time. He simply could not do it.' His mother, however, was determined that Alec would have someone there to wave goodbye to, so she travelled down to Hobart on the long, slow overnight train known as the 'Midnight Horror' to farewell her first son. They had always been close. In later letters he would address her affectionately as 'dear old Darling'. In Hobart Marian stayed with her brother-in-law, Harry Pybus, who met her at the station and 'was a tower of strength'. She visited Alec at the Claremont Camp on 15 August, much to his delight as he immediately wrote to his father. 'I showed Mum all around the camp. I explained to her all the trenches and rifle pits and took her up and showed her all our trenches so she will be able to tell the boys what the trenches are like. We have got a picture show in camp now.' With equal enthusiasm the letter reports on a rather less decorous highlight of the soldier's life: 'We had a real old brawl in our hut on Friday night, 5 fellows came in a bit drunk and started pitching in to some of our fellows. About 10 of our chaps got up and gave them a jolly good hiding.' But the boys had soon licked their wounds and scrubbed themselves clean in time for a last group photo session. The high spirits may well have reflected the most important news buried in this letter — 'we leave for the boat tomorrow'.

Marian and Uncle Harry marched alongside Alec as the 8th Reinforcements paraded through the streets of Hobart to the docks where the troop carrier was waiting to take her son away. Harry's own younger boy Reggie, who tagged along, declared with dismay when he saw the kid soldier, 'He's too young to go to war!' Fighting back tears (Estelle would recount), Marian's 'sorrow was mingled with pride as she watched her first baby walk up the gangplank and sail off to war'. The ship carrying the 8th Reinforcements set sail from Hobart bound for the Port of Melbourne, and Alec was sick all the way. In Melbourne the Tasmanians disembarked for Broadmeadows and another brief, intensive training spell before boarding SS *Kyarra* — bound for Alexandria.

As the daily newspaper reports confirmed, more troops were desperately needed at Gallipoli, and they had to be better trained. The bloody battles of early August were almost as devastating as the landings back in April. On 7 August hundreds of young Australians were mown down like a field of wheat as they tried to capture Turkish trenches in a futile charge across a narrow finger of open land called the Nek. Unmounted troops from the Light Horse had been ordered to advance en masse into the Turkish guns. Against the decisive new weapon of this war, the machine gun, they could not possibly have succeeded. Australia's official Gallipoli historian and war correspondent, Charles Bean, horrified by the slaughter, compared it to asking soldiers to charge across a tennis court towards enemy troops arrayed along the back line firing machine guns at them. Two days later Australian soldiers of the 1st Brigade captured the strongpoint known as Lone Pine in one of the bloodiest actions of the campaign. They may have killed as many as five thousand Turks, but gaining those few hundred yards cost more than two thousand Australian lives. As it turned out, this would be the last significant victory achieved by the Expeditionary Force at Gallipoli. Efforts to break out from Anzac Cove and to capture obscure strongpoints such as Chunuk Bair, Hill 971 and Hill 60 failed; the campaign settled into the kind of static trench warfare that characterised the continuing murderous stalemate on the western front.

Some of these stories, eventually appearing in the Melbourne *Age* and Adelaide *Advertiser*, might well have accompanied Alec and his fellow recruits on board the *Kyarra*. Still, to Alec, 'It was all a bit of an adventure.' He did not know or care how long he would be away. After a parade on deck on 23 August Alec wrote to his mother, 'I don't know where I am going but I am on my way to either Egypt or England. I suppose it will be Egypt.' He promised to 'post this at first port of call. I suppose that will be Fremantle or Colombo. We are in the Great Australian bite now and the sea is pretty ruff.' Alec told how, perhaps inspired by Kitchener, 'We have all got orders to grow Mustaches. I will send you my photo as soon as I get to Egypt or where ever we are going and let you see how I look with a Mow,' but 'if the sea gets any ruffer I might get sick and not be able to wright till we pass Fremantle.' He wrote to his father the same day. 'There is about a thousand men abord the boat but only 50 or so are Tasmanians, but we have got the best boxer in our lot. I reckon I will be quite a pug when I land in Egypt as we have the gloves out every night after tea if the sea is calm enough to let us.'

On 28 August, in the last letter from the *Kyarra* to be posted in Australia, he announced, 'All our letters are under cencor now and we can't say anything at all even the name of the ship or the date so I am writing this & will give it to somebody on the wharf to post for me.' So far, he reported, 'We have had a pretty good trip except when we were crossing the bite, it was very ruff then, some of the waves came right over the bows of the boat. It looked very pretty at night to stand on the top deck and see them break right over the bows.'

A couple of weeks later, in a letter that would itself be officially screened, the country boy confided naively how he would trick the censor and disclose what he believed was to be their first port of call. 'We will soon be in [word blotted out]. I suppose the Cencor will cross Columbo out but I have written it pretty thick so if you hold it up to the light you ought to be able to read it.' They had 'just crossed the line', an event marked by much ceremony, including a boxing competition, and 'my word the boys would have loved to be there'. Next best was 'the pillow fight': 'there was a greasy pole across a big tank and a man on each end with a pillow. They got about half way through with it, the water looked so nice and cool that most of us jumped in and had a swim.' Life on board, Alec declared, was 'not so bad', although the food was not up to his mother's standards, Alec wrote to his kid sister. Soon, he announced, he would be in India, and if he got ashore there he would try to buy her a present. 'You would like to be on board the boat and see the flying fysh they are blue with wings like a bat, jump out of the water and go for a fly. One flew through the port hole while we were having tea the other night right on to the table, and a fellow got it and put it into a bottle with methelated spirats and sent it home to his Mother for an ornement.' Alec had been getting in some combat drill — both armed and unarmed. He wrote to his father, 'I have only had two fights on board. I got a good hiding once and gave another fellow a good hiding the second time but got my face cut about a bit. I have done a good deal of shooting with my revolver on board. Nearly all the boys on board have got one but none so good as mine.' He anticipated that their journey would soon be over. 'I suppose we will be in Egypt or India or somewhere by the time you get this.'

Late in his life Alec would remember the trip with pleasure. 'There were over 1000 men on the ship, and hammocks were slung so close together that you could touch your next-door neighbour if you put your hand out. And yet I never had a quarrel or a disagreement all the way over — five or six weeks.' The voyage provided Alec with the last real contentment he would experience for many months.

The Campbell brothers (*left to right:* Angus, Alec, Colin and Mac), *c.* 1913

AUSTRALIA

...USTRALIAN MILITARY FORCES.

AUSTRALIAN IMPERIAL FORCE.

Attestation Paper of Persons Enlisted for Service Abroad.

No. _2931_   Name _CAMPBELL Alex William_

Unit _15th Battalion A.I.F._

15th Battalion   Joined on _3/7/15_

Questions to be put to the Person Enlisting before Attestation.

1. What is your Name? ... ...   1. _Alex William Campbell_

2. In or near what Parish or Town were you born? ...   2. In the Parish of _____ in or near the Town of _Launceston_ in the County of _Tas_

3. Are you a natural born British Subject or a Naturalized British Subject? (N.B.—If the latter, papers to be shown.) ... ...   3. _Yes_

4. What is your age? ... ...   4. _18 5/12_

5. What is your trade or calling? ... ...   5. _Clerk_

6. Are you, or have you been, an Apprentice? If so, where, to whom, and for what period? ... ...   6. _No_

7. Are you married? ... ...   7. _No_

8. Who is your next of kin? (Address to be stated)   _Mother Mrs Marian J. Campbell Mary St Invermay Tas_

9. Have you ever been convicted by the Civil Power? ...   9. _Yes Rang without a light_

10. Have you ever been discharged from any part of His Majesty's Forces, with Ignominy, or as Incorrigible and Worthless, or on account of Conviction of Felony, or of a Sentence of Penal Servitude, or have you been dismissed with Disgrace from the Navy? ...   10. _No_

   St Louis 92.B

11. Do you now belong to, or have you ever served in, His Majesty's Army, the Marines, the Militia, the Militia Reserve, the Territorial Force, Royal Navy, or Colonial Forces? If so, state which, and if not now serving, state cause of discharge ...   11. _Yes 3 Years_

12. Have you stated the whole, if any, of your previous service?   12. _Yes_

13. Have you ever been rejected as unfit for His Majesty's Service? If so, on what grounds? ...   13. _No_

14. (For married men, widowers with children, and soldiers who are the sole support of widowed mother)— Do you understand that no Separation Allowance will be issued to you after embarkation during your term of service? ...   14.

15. Are you prepared to undergo inoculation against small pox and enteric fever? ... ...   15. _Yes_

I, _Alex William Campbell_ do solemnly declare that the above answers made by me to the above questions are true, and I am willing and hereby voluntarily agree to serve in the Military Forces of the Commonwealth of Australia within or beyond the limits of the Commonwealth.

And I further agree to allot not less than two-fifths three-fifths of the pay payable to me from time to time during my service for the support of my wife, wife and children. _A.W. Campbell   A.W. Campbell_

Date _2/7/15_   _A.W. Campbell   A.W. Campbell_

Signature of person enlisted.

D.877/L.15.—C.562.   * This clause should be struck out in the case of unmarried men or widowers without children under 18 years of age. † Two-fifths must be allotted to the wife, and if there are children three-fifths must be allotted.

Alec's enlistment form, signed on 2 July 1915   (Australian Archives)

The kid soldier photographed in August 1915 at Claremont Camp, Hobart

Alec's favourite photograph, another studio shot from August 1915

Group portrait of the 8th Reinforcements (Alec sitting on the ground, third from left) before leaving Tasmania

CHAPTER 5

IN THE THEATRE OF WAR

'We landed yesterday, got into camp about 4 o'clock in the afternoon, had some tea and went to have a look at Cairo. My word it is a funny place, after being used to seeing all white people about, seeing black, brown, yellow and all sorts of people walking about in funny dresses.'

Disembarking in Alexandria, the fresh troops went straight to the AIF base at Mena Camp, outside Cairo, in the shadow of the famous Sphinx and the great pyramids of Giza. Once he had found his tent, unpacked his kit and completed the arrival formalities, Alec wrote home excitedly, 'We have got a half holiday this afternoon so I think I will go and have a look at the Pyramids. I will write and tell you about them as soon as I have seen them.' He recalled later with pride how he climbed to the top of one of the ancient monuments, but the Tasmanian country kid, used to lush vegetation, was vexed by the ever-present dust and drifting sand. 'If ever I hear anyone talk about sand when I get back, I'll send him out here to try a bit himself. You have sand in your dinner, sand in your tea and sand in the Ink you write with.' And the river apparently offered little comfort: 'The Nile looks a nice sort of a river, till you try and swim in it and a gentle large Crocidile chases you out.' Of his first impressions, Alec later wrote, 'I remember the surprise we got coming suddenly on a place like Egypt, just to see the bazaars, colourful streets and all manner of things that we had never heard about, and the strange dress of the people. I remember all those things vividly.'

Opportunities to explore his exotic new surroundings were limited, however, for the men were now put through the gruelling final stages of training. Set up towards the end of 1914 as a training and acclimatisation base for Anzac recruits, Mena Camp was run by tough, experience-hardened soldiers according to a regime that had become markedly harsher since the disastrous landings at Gallipoli earlier in the year. Soon after their arrival, the men of the 8th learned that they could be sent to the peninsula with the 15th Battalion at any time. Now they were interested only in news of Gallipoli, whether from newspapers or from soldiers returning from the front. And during September at the Mena Camp information crossroads, while they trained hard they heard plenty — mostly bad.

Those who had been living in the trenches around Anzac Cove since the April landings were now coming up to their six-month anniversary. Not that they had much to celebrate. For weeks now they had suffered through incessant rain, which made conditions in the slippery-clay, semi-flooded trenches even more miserable than usual, and dampened the spirits of the most cheerful among them. But the bad weather had not silenced the machine guns or rifle fire, or checked the bomb throwing. A deadly new Turkish bomb launched by a powerful trench mortar was doing great damage and had forced the troops on the beach to keep their guns mounted all day for fear of an imminent attack. Many bodies of men who had died during the August fighting had still not been buried. A returning Anzac said it was 'a most gruesome sight to walk along trenches where light horse bodies were lying on the parapet of the trench as one could see legs, heads and bodies of our men who died in the charge at the beginning of August and are still there'. The German airplanes that flew over the Australian lines on spying missions had proved impossible to shoot down with machine guns. And the Turks were getting more aggressive, sneaking down the cliff and into the Australian trenches to throw bombs. Meanwhile the irrepressible Anzacs on Suvla Plain in the north still found time for a game of cricket or the occasional football match whenever units were withdrawn from the line for a rest period. The 8th heard an unsubstantiated rumour from a soldier of the 21st Battalion about friendly exchanges between Turks and Australians, with the antagonists trading bully beef and jam for cigarettes — which one soldier on leave believed showed just how unnecessary this campaign was. The high command continued to send 'great stacks of provisions' to Gallipoli ahead of Alec's reinforcements. Change was in the air, though, for just before they left Egypt the newspapers reported that the controversial British commander-in-chief of the Gallipoli campaign, General Sir Ian Hamilton, had been withdrawn. A new commander was to be appointed.

After weeks of nervous waiting and listening to rumours, the 7th and 8th Reinforcements finally left Mena, clambered on a train north back to Alexandria and, on 18 October, sailed out. Five days later, after a stormy crossing, they steamed into the harbour at Mudros, on the Greek island of Lemnos, disembarked and marched to nearby Sarpi Camp. Recalling his excitement, Alec wrote later, 'At last on the 23rd of October 1915, I joined up with the 15th Battalion I had been waiting to meet on Lemnos. We were just a company on our own. There might have been some others, a few stray fellows, but I can't remember anyone in particular until we joined D company pretty well straight away. Our Royal 15th Infantry Battalion was part of the 4th Brigade.' He had reached the last staging post before joining the fight.

But it was on Lemnos that the reality of war truly hit home for Alec. A jumble of hospital buildings and tents overflowed with wounded men evacuated from the peninsula, debouched from a steady stream of hospital ships. While the medical staff did their best for these mutilated soldiers, the growing eruption of crosses in the makeshift graveyard proved how difficult it was to repair their shattered bodies. Ironically, the fresh men of the 7th and 8th

Reinforcements were now struck down by an epidemic of mumps and were quarantined until the end of the month.

While in quarantine at Sarpi, the new men heard first-hand what the Anzacs had been through at Gallipoli. The 15th were 'licking their wounds' after suffering severe losses in the savage fighting of early August. 'When we arrived on Lemnos,' Alec wrote later, 'they were still all talking about the big bang in August.' And with good reason. The Australian Light Horse had suffered dreadful losses in early August when they failed to take the Nek in a desperate frontal assault into the mouths of Turkish machine guns, and more than two thousand more men were lost in capturing the well-defended outpost of Lone Pine two days later. The 15th Battalion had also experienced a terrible blood-letting during their vain attempts to seize the high ground at Hill 971 and Hill 60. In fact, of all the battalions Alec might have joined, the 15th held the dubious honour of recording the highest casualty rates of any unit in the AIF at Gallipoli: the reinforcements would bring its strength up to just 13 officers and 453 other ranks (a battalion at full complement comprised about 1,000 men). As recorded by the battalion's official historian, Lieutenant T. P. Chataway, 'While to some of these men lay the honour of being the first to set foot upon the Gallipoli Peninsula, they had also been to hell and back.' Among the first ashore at Anzac Cove in April, men of the 15th had also been among the first casualties of the landings, like Cecil Rush, who was hit in the head by a shrapnel pellet just as his boat hit the beach. Others had been astoundingly lucky — like Private W. Spiers 'when a shell pellet hit his Rising Sun collar badge in such a manner that it closed around the leaden ball, saving his life and holding it securely in a setting which could scarcely be improved upon by a jeweller'. Private Wally Rose was hit in the right temple by a shrapnel pellet that 'passed through his head and he just spat it out of his mouth'. Fortunately, 'Royal Army Medical men nearby immediately compressed the temporal artery which had been severed, stopped the flow of blood and saved his life.'

Maverick soldiers like Percy Toft, who had taken part in the April assaults, delighted in telling raw recruits like Alec how, during a macabre game of cards on board the troop carrier the evening before they landed, he was told he would be the first killed because he was dealt the nine of diamonds — 'that much abused card with the ominous name of the "Curse of Scotland", and whosoever got it would be the first to lose his life'. But Toft survived that first ferocious firestorm on the beach and it would be the card dealer, Private Harry Byrne, who met his maker at the battle for Quinn's Post a short time later. Some veterans suggested that getting shot was not the worst thing that could happen. Marines among the advance parties claimed they had seen Turks killing wounded soldiers by crucifixion or 'hamstringing every wounded man who fell into their hands, so as to render such men unfit for further service'. As a result of such reports, the 15th had a code of mate killing, which laid down that 'should a man lie wounded and a retirement be ordered, his friend or the man nearest him would dispatch the sufferer', and this promise had been carried out at least twice — at Quinn's Post on 10 May and on Rahman Bair on 8 August.

Soldiers of the 15th Battalion had also been among the first to push deep inland on that fateful day, bounding up Shrapnel Valley 'to the point where they scaled the side of the gully, gaining the high ground of this narrow feature', then advancing into exposed Monash Valley. Proud veterans recounted how, despite the steep cliffs and heavy fire from above, these pathfinders 'fixed bayonets and cleared the ridges of the enemy'. Without support, and in the general confusion of the day, some of these gains proved untenable, and the survivors were compelled to withdraw to newly entrenched positions closer to the beach. It was an opportunity lost, for soon Turkish reinforcement would make such forward positions almost impossible to regain. The 15th had suffered heavy casualties, among the officers Lieutenant P. Gibson, in command of the Tasmanian section of the 6th Reinforcements, who had joined the unit only on

2 August and had had no time to get to know the area. The battalion's medical officer, Dr Luther, was shot in a subsequent battle 'while attending the wounded — who lay everywhere — with remarkable coolness', inspiring other soldiers to crawl out into no-man's-land under heavy fire to rescue their wounded mates. 'The transportation of the wounded to the beach was in itself a nightmare,' Chataway records. When there were no stretchers available, soldiers strung puttees across their rifles, creating makeshift slings, then humped their mates to the relative safety of the beach, 'sliding and slipping down the steep hillside with heavy shrapnel fire continuously bursting above them'.

The battalion's early achievements gained official recognition when Captain Jack Hill won the Military Cross and Colonel J. H. Cannan a commendation, but they had no shortage of brave soldiers. Alec and his mates quickly learned that they would not be expected to step forward for the more perilous assignments, since Sergeant Tom Dann and Private Fred Hanley had 'the incurable habit of volunteering for anything that spelt danger'. In some respects, conditions would not be so bad for the reinforcements. The Anzacs were now well dug in, piers had been built for landing supplies, and there were maps and even a few signposts to follow. Gallipoli had become comparatively civilised, and the new troops would not suffer the confusion experienced in April, when the battalion had 'platoons landed without an officer and totally disintegrated as they did not have the faintest idea where the front line was'.

But as Percy Toft (now a sergeant) had reported before leaving Gallipoli for his well-earned rest on Lemnos, life on the front line itself was still terrible. 'The conditions were vile, and the lack of water prevented the men even obtaining a wash. Some endeavoured to shave or wipe their faces with the little tea they were willing to spare. But the majority never shaved or washed. One headquarters signaller admitted the stain of blood from a wounded comrade remained on the back of his hand for over a month until he was evacuated with sickness ... The lice and the flies brought sickness in their wake and man after man fell victim to dysentery or enteric fever. Throughout the whole war there was probably no position held by British troops so nauseating and soul destroying as this Kaiajik Dere section of the Anzac line during August and September.' The 15th had been plagued by dysentery from the start, the first cases contracted from the shocking food they received on the *Australind* transporting them to the landings. One trooper recuperating at Lemnos who may have made an impression on Alec was Private J. W. Henderson, at 18 the youngest soldier in the battalion before Alec's arrival, who had lost his hearing when he passed in front of the mountain battery at Gallipoli as it fired.

The latest rumours on Lemnos were that the Anzacs were abandoning further costly offensives and accepting the hopeless stalemate. Unknown to the troops, the situation on the ground had been observed by a visiting Australian journalist, Keith Murdoch, who on 23 September (while Alec was at Mena Camp) sent a scathing letter of complaint to the prime minister in which he recommended that the government withdraw Australian troops. Visiting London later, Murdoch sent a similar report to the British Minister of Munitions, Lloyd George. Perhaps it became part of the evidence convincing the British to withdraw.

Apart from the outbreak of mumps after the reinforcements' arrival, Lemnos had been the perfect place for the battalion's well-earned break, and they loved it. 'The island was filled with pleasant things,' wrote Percy Toft in the battalion history, 'including grapes which were in season and plentiful. A monastery nearby where fresh eggs and butter could be bought and the monks were very kind. A Greek who sold bread that was delicious. Pretty villages that sold coffee and biscuits. Wells from which women drew crystal clear water. Steaming marble baths fed by hot springs and concerts where artists from the 4th Brigade performed. We also attended a wedding where one of the chaplains performed a marriage ceremony on the

Island, marrying Serg. Ernest Lawrence of the 1st Light Horse Brig. and Staff Nurse Clarice Daley of the 3rd Australian General Hospital.' Star turns at Lemnos were the short speeches, generally of about 15 minutes, delivered by the 4th Brigade's charismatic leader, Colonel John Monash. The magic of his oratory seemed to cast a spell over the men, and although Monash would never become a part of the men's lives at Gallipoli, as some active officers did, on Lemnos he touched their hearts in a special way. In the following years Monash would distinguish himself on the western front as an outstanding general and Corps Commander, participating in a series of decisive battles in France in 1918, including the 4 July battle of Hamel and the 8 August battle of Amiens.

The long-awaited reinforcements, led by 2nd Lieutenant W. J. Cooper and 2nd Lieutenant J. H. Wilson, arrived near the end of the veterans' rest break. That week at Anzac Cove, Charles Bean wrote in his diary that he believed 'there are more Turks in front of us than on August 6th and the Anzacs should put on a demonstration to find out just how many Turks there are in front of the whole line and how many reinforcements are needed'. Bean was pleased to read in the latest newspapers that on 27 October war enthusiast William Morris (Billy) Hughes had been sworn in as Australian prime minister and had vowed to boost the war effort.

Suddenly it was time to go. Their quarantine was over. All they waited on now was a break in the weather. But day after day the storms worsened, heavy southerly winds and gales battering the little island relentlessly. The whole time Alec had been at Lemnos the weather had been bad, as indeed it was at Gallipoli, where the veterans reported the coldest nights they had ever spent. To keep warm in the trenches, they tramped up and down the boardwalks wearing all their warm clothing inside their overcoats, yet they were still 'shivering like leafs'. When the winter took hold the blizzards could last for days without respite, and snow would blanket the ground for weeks. The volunteers from sunny Australia were certainly not looking forward to long winter night watches.

At last, on 31 October, the wind dropped and the 15th were told to prepare for departure that night. Alec wrote later, 'It was exciting. We had no idea what was going to happen. But I remember we were just excited and looking forward to getting going.' That evening they marched from Sarpi Camp to the harbour at Mudros, boarded the *Osmanieh* and sailed out into stormy seas. As recorded by Chataway, 'on the night of November 1 the sea was exceptionally rough and though the "Osmanieh" stood in close to land it was impossible to disembark the men owing to the difficulty of transporting them into the open boats in such a sea . . . So the vessel sought shelter in the small harbour at Imbros.' The little island of Imbros, 15 miles west of Anzac Cove, was used variously as a forward base, a rest and hospital camp, and a command centre during the campaign. 'The following night, November 2, the sea having moderated, the vessel again approached the coast and stood to, for the purpose of landing its men. When the sleeping men were awakened to go ashore one of the number asleep on the deck failed to answer the call, and it was discovered that he had been killed by a stray shot from the Peninsula that had lodged directly in his forehead.' This first unlucky death reduced the ranks of the 15th Battalion to 452 men.

The new men were on edge as they prepared to make a night landing on that famous beach. After all, Gallipoli had been at the forefront of their minds for six months. And now they were here, about to throw themselves into the fight. No white feather would be nailed to their door, and this was reassuring on one level. But now they had seen for themselves the shocking condition of the wounded soldiers on Lemnos and heard the alarming stories from the battered survivors of the 15th, not to mention that poor fellow shot through the forehead before they had even approached the beach. So the moment of truth was probably more frightening than exciting for young Alec Campbell, who only the previous November had been quietly studying in class at Launceston's sedate Scotch College.

CHAPTER 6

THE KID SOLDIER AT ANZAC COVE

'The Turks were shooting at us all the time as we landed. Even though they could not see us there was just a hail of bullets. The rifle fire was incredible really. One fellow in my boat was shot in the head and fell to the bottom.'

They still couldn't see a thing from the boat apart from intermittent artillery flashes that picked out a vague outline of cliffs, but surely they were not far from the beach now. A muffled cry from the bow and a soldier slumped to the bottom of the boat, his head hitting the side with a thud. They must be within sniper range. But how the hell could the Turks *see* anything? Alec's heartbeat quickened as he huddled low on the seat and water tossed by the oars lashed his face. Sitting ducks. They would need some luck.

Almost too soon the boat's bow ground onto the pebbly beach. 'Everybody out,' said the officer in charge. 'Come on, move it!' he hissed urgently. This was it. If Alec needed to steel his nerves, this was the moment for the Campbell war cry — *'Cruachan!'* He pulled his knapsack straps taut against his shoulders, tightened his grip on the heavy .303 with its cumbersome bayonet, hauled himself awkwardly over the gunwales and dropped into the icy water. Without conscious thought he bolted after the shadowy figures ahead of him up the slope of the beach to the cluster of dark shapes accumulating at the base of the cliff, wordlessly joining his panting comrades. Alec was 'safely' ashore.

Crouched under the comforting shelter of the cliff base, they regrouped and took their bearings. Anzac Cove. Unbelievably, thousands of seasoned Australian soldiers were at this moment lying — sleeping? — within a few hundred feet of them in burrows scooped out of the surrounding cliffs. Before he could pursue these thoughts the CO passed the order and Alec and his comrades scurried off.

They had landed at the northern end of the beach near the bluff known as Ari Burnu (where many Anzacs had landed on 25 April) or perhaps on North Beach itself, for it later became clear that they were now in the far north of the Anzac sector, making for Hay Valley at the end of the inland arm of Aghyl Dere, a steep gully running back from North Beach. Hay Valley was named after New Zealander Major Bruce Hay, Otago Mounted Rifles, who was killed there during the bloody action of 7 August, which the survivors on rest leave on Lemnos had spoken of. Overlooked by Bauchop's Hill to the west and Hill 971 to the east, the valley held the brigade headquarters of the 4th Australian Infantry Brigade, under Monash's command, and the 15th Battalion was part of this command. Hill 971 was a prize that had eluded the Anzacs (including the 15th) in the bitter fighting of 7 August. While the battalion's dugouts offered some protection, the Turks holding the high ground near the Nek and on Chunuk Bair had a clear view down the valley, and used this advantage to make life difficult for the Australians.

Early that morning of 2 November Alec was shown his dugout, briefly met his neighbours and unpacked his kit in the dark. He cautiously explored the tiny hole in the earth that was now his home, casting about for a level spot to sleep on and picking out nooks and crannies in which to store his meagre possessions. Finally he stretched out gratefully. Writing to his mother a few days later, he declared, 'At last we have reached our destination. We landed about 3 days ago under fairly safe conditions, all except one poor fellow who got shot through the head.' The official record confirms the safe landing after a delay due to exceptionally rough seas. But that first casualty upset Alec, as he admitted later. 'That was awful. I think it shocked me more than a lot of others I saw because it was the first one and he was hit in the head and killed, and of course a nasty mess. I remember that very well.' (Late in life Alec would claim that although he had assumed the soldier was killed, he heard afterwards that medics had saved his life.) To his mother he wrote, 'We are dug in to the side of a valley just at the bottom of the big Hill 971, which I suppose you are reading a lot about in Tassy.' The 15th were living in a series of dugouts cut into the hillside. After what he had heard about the western front, Alec was grateful for the relatively tolerable conditions he experienced at Gallipoli. 'On Gallipoli, trenches were not as deep and as unpleasant as the French trenches, because they were wider and more open and we could go down to the beach, although people got hit sometimes. But there was a track from where we were camped, and there was nothing to stop us going for a swim except stray rifle fire. The trenches were just ditches, with bits of shelters put over them where we could. And you kept in them as long as you could. You didn't like going out, because you were likely to get hit when you moved from place to place. But in the trench you were fairly safe, and you could see, as there were loopholes to shoot through.'

When dawn illuminated the scene that morning, Alec was stunned by his dramatic surroundings. He was in the middle of a series of sharply rising hills with rugged crests. One peak stood out high above the rest: fresh from Mena Camp in Egypt, the first troops who saw it named it the Sphinx. The first thought that struck most new arrivals was to wonder 'how the first troops that landed ever got over the hills and took up the positions we now hold', as one 1st Battalion Reinforcement wrote. 'Without seeing the country you could not realize the difficulty of the job. The trenches are only about 20 yards distance from the Turks in some places and bomb throwing is the great sport. They have special men trained as bomb throwers, and whenever there is a favourable opportunity they heave a bomb into the enemy's trenches. There are not very many getting killed at present, and I think life is just as dangerous outside the trenches as there are always stray bullets flying about from the snipers as well as shells from the big guns going overhead, but after a few days one gets used to it and nobody worries or thinks about any danger, but goes on with their usual work.'

Like all soldiers, Alec was given a range of duties, including standing sentry duty (keeping a lookout for enemy incursion), fatigues, running messages and carting up water to the troops. Since water carrying would become Alec's main duty, on his first day an old hand gave him a guided tour of the delivery stations. The water had to be collected down at the beach, carried along North Beach and the crowded Anzac Cove and up the main thoroughfare of Shrapnel Gully. Alec was shown the graveyard at Shrapnel Gully, which by then contained the bodies of hundreds of soldiers. As recorded by a 20th Battalion Anzac, 'It is a level piece of land about ¾ acre in extent, and it is really kept in wonderful condition. Laid out so well and the graves with all their different headstones, crosses etc. Some are very artistically finished, done in some cases by the brothers of the dead, others have simply a bottle with a piece of paper with the name inside.' Before the evacuation more than eight thousand Australians would be buried at Gallipoli. Among them was John Kirkpatrick Simpson, the legendary 'Man with the Donkey', who had brought many wounded down from the lines to the beach, and whom Alec's mates still talked about in the trenches. On this first tour Alec saw plenty of horrible reminders of earlier battles, too. There were, for instance, the bodies still unburied from the battle for Hill 60, which the Anzacs had attacked with great losses in August. 'I remember we went around the back of Hill 60, and there was a pair of legs sticking out from a bush,' Alec would recall. 'And I don't know why that impressed me, because later I saw plenty of things like that, but that sort of impressed me most of all. Gallipoli was not so bad for me from the firing point of view, although that was a bad enough experience.'

Once he started delivering his cans of water, Alec also began to meet old hands who had been there since day one. There was a special aura about these veterans. Having survived the first 24 hours, they had long since seen war at its worst. Landed at the wrong beach on that impossible mission, they had simply refused to say die. These men had developed a formidable reputation. Faced by withering fire from entrenched positions, many of them had charged repeatedly up almost perpendicular slopes at the Turkish guns above, securing and frequently holding shockingly exposed footholds in the hills above the beach. They had many deeds to be proud of and many heroes, like the famous Albert Jacka, in their community.

On that first extraordinary day in April a few determined Anzacs had succeeded in penetrating the Turkish positions and pushing further inland, before being forced to turn back or risk being cut off. Private Arthur Blackburn of 10th Battalion got past enemy positions, scaling heights past Legge Valley as far as Scrubby Knoll. Captain Eric Tulloch had got up onto Chunuk Bair; others reached Battleship Hill. From these heights they might have caught a glimpse of the glinting waters of the distant Dardanelles. *The Times* (of London) wrote of the Anzac landings: 'In the face of murderous enemy fire this bold race of athletes proceeded to scale the highest cliffs.' English poet John Masefield would declaim: 'The Anzacs were the finest body of young men ever brought together in modern times. For physical beauty and nobility of bearing they surpassed any man I have ever seen; they walked and looked like the kings in old poems, and reminded me of the Shakespearean line "Baited like eagles having lately bathed".' In the Boer War Australian volunteers had initially been dispersed among different colonial regiments. Gallipoli was the first time Australians had represented their country as a united fighting force, and they had done their young nation proud.

But those were the early days. Since the failed August offensive, all they had managed was to hold their position, maintaining the same precarious beachhead they had held since April — no matter what the Turks threw at them. They were still Anzacs, though. On 2 November, the day Alec landed, Bean wrote, 'The Australians here can be picked out by their faces — a little hard, but the strong, lined, individual faces which men get who stand and think by themselves. The Australian discipline is for orderliness — to get an operation through in an organized manner. The British discipline has a different reason — to make men go forward because they were told to do so.' And there was still plenty of fighting, for given the chance the Turks would have pushed them into the sea at the drop of a slouch hat. Alec remembered standing sentry duty one time when they were 'belting away at Turks all day through loopholes in the trenches'; and at night, 'sleeping in a cold damp hole in the ground. People were always getting hit . . . Oh yes, you realise what is going on when you're in amongst it . . . It might not be frightening, but it puts you on your toes.' But Alec was carrying water more often than he was fighting. 'Water was scarce and had to be carried up after it was brought to the beach in boats and put in the big steel lighter. Every day a detail was sent off from the line, from our Battalion, from D Company, and three of us would be detailed off to go down to the beach. There was no water on Gallipoli, except one well, but we were told it was contaminated. And so water was brought by the British ships and poured into a large steel tanker on the beach and we had to go down every day and carry two cans of water up to wherever our Battalion happened to be. The amount we got was limited because it all had to be carried. But I don't think we ever drank bad water. There was that water well, near the old fisherman's hut. But I never heard of anybody drinking water from it. We were not that silly!'

The water was treasured by his fellow soldiers, as a 21st Battalion Anzac confirmed in a letter home: 'The Autumn weather here is bonza. Every second day I have a shave; and then with the same water, I clean my teeth and wash my face. Sometimes it is a cupful; but sometimes it is less! About every second time, I get enough to wash my ears and neck. All the water is brought over from Alexandria, and then these poor coves have to cart it up from the beach, but as something went wrong with the water-ship we are now on half-rations.' The job may have appeared routine, but Alec would always be at pains to point out the risks involved. 'It was a fairly dangerous operation. People often got hit on the way up because the Turks were good rifle shots. Every day somebody was hit bringing water up from the beach. And that was at a time when the Turks were not doing too much shooting.'

As Alec carted his water through the trenches and past dugouts where soldiers were cooking, sewing or writing letters, he picked up the first rumours of evacuation. Rumour was meat and drink to the soldier, and as one 19th Battalion fellow said, the 'rumours of early termination of war which have started are of course not at all credited but they are rather amusing to the fellows'. A story Alec might have found more interesting grew out of an official circular on finding the best shots among the men, to be confirmed through target practice. The brass were apparently sick of the poor hit rate during attacks against the Turks.

On the evening of 5 November the Turks unleashed their first major attack since Alec's arrival. A 21st Battalion soldier wrote, 'At 9.05 Abdul gave a very fierce demonstration. We had to stand to until about 10 pm. Poor me, just my luck, lost all my sleep through him, and had to go on shift from 12 to 4 am.' Of the same action a 20th Battalion Anzac wrote, 'We had a little excitement last night. I was asleep at the time, 9 o'clock, and had to be awakened and get into my boots, grab my rifle and bayonet and get up to the guns. There was terrific rifle fire on our right, we think near Popes. Rockets were going up by the dozen, red, white and green. They give a splendid light floating for a mile or more. It kept up for about 1½ hours then died out so we went back to bed, and heard this morning that it was a Turk attack on Pine Ridge, but was repulsed.'

The same night, from the relative safety of his dugout, the water carrier wrote to his mother by the light of a slush-lamp (a tobacco tin filled with fat with a wick stuck in it). It is Alec's only surviving letter from Gallipoli.

> *... The Turks sent a few shrapnel shells out over our valley but luckily nobody was hit. We were digging a new trench yesterday & there was a young New Zealander in charge of us. He was talking to me, when he lifted his head up above the trench only a few inches [words blacked out by Censor] through the [words blacked out by Censor] after seeing that I can tell you I kept my own head pretty low.*
>
> *I have not had a letter for quite a long time now old darling, but I know you are writing every week so I will have a bunch of letters to get somewhere. Dont worry about my safety darling as it is quite safe as long as you dont pop your head up over the trench top. I suppose you are all getting on alright but I wish they could arrange a better mail system. We are treated pretty well out here considering the crowds of troops there are here to feed. Tell Angus that I met Frank Walsh's big brother Mat here the one in the red cross, the other one is in England on a holiday. And tell dad that a lot of fellows say Billy Hinman is in England too, but others say he is dead so you dont know which is right.*
>
> *Heaps of love old Darling*
>
> *Your loving son Alec*

Alec was much more affected by the death of the New Zealander than he let on at the time. 'I don't think you see the value of life at that early age,' he would recall. 'You see, it was almost a thing you expected. I did anyway. And yet when someone was hit it was shocking, especially when the man was near you. I remember one Engineer, a New Zealander, who was on duty fixing up this barbed wire business, and he was quite near me and the top of his head was blown off. I still remember that, gave me a nasty turn I suppose. But so many men were hit after that, and it became a usual thing to expect, you know.'

In Hay Valley the following day, as Alec's letter made its way down to the beach and an outgoing boat, a 4th Brigade comrade wrote in his diary, 'Two casualties in Archyl Dere from snipers, both dangerously wounded following the enemy shelling of Franklins post at 0900 but doing little damage otherwise.' On 7 November an Anzac not far from Alec's position wrote, 'The first thing I heard was a big howitzer shell going over the valley. Thank God it was one of ours. The next thing I heard was an explosion in the cook's fire. Someone had put a live cartridge in it and of course it went off. Where the bullet went to I don't know, but the Quartermaster who was down there getting my breakfast was wounded in the arm. I took him down to the dressing station and had it bandaged up.' Tension remained high right along the front. In another sector, a soldier recorded, 'There is a very deep gully in between our trenches that the Turks called the Gully of Despair, and very rightly too, as I think it would be very deadly for either side to attack in this particular position, unless it was done under cover of darkness, and then of course we are very much on the alert for an attack any moment. But we still have patrols go out at night, creep up as near as possible to the Turks' lines to get as much information as possible, and of course the Turks are up to the same game.'

Many of the trenches and dugouts were contaminated, as one Engineer observed: 'Found a safe dugout, but the only thing that worried me was the fact that the hole contained a smell. This morning I discovered that the place had been used for other purposes than sleeping. Anyhow, it won't kill us.' It may not have killed the men directly, but poor sanitation certainly contributed to the sick list. The flies, Alec recalled, 'were terrible and you had to knock them off your food with your hand or they would get into your mouth'. Alec remained well during the early part of November, but the bugs made life miserable for all the men and inevitably brought disease. 'Everyone had fleas and lice and many had dysentery.' Chataway confirms that, 'although the fighting from November onwards may not have been as severe as earlier, especially during August or April, there was probably more disease now than ever;

and a young soldier could still die from diseases as easily as from a bullet'. Countless Anzacs died from disease spread through the crowded dugouts and trench systems as a result of poor hygiene and sanitation. 'Wounds were common and sickness rampant; dysentery and yellow jaundice were still prevalent in the Battalion.'

On 7 November Charles Bean learned that Britain's Minister for War was on his way to assess the future of the campaign at Gallipoli. 'Kitchener has, we hear, left London on duty,' and 'Putting one and one together it looks very certain where Kitchener has gone.' Bean, of course, had also heard the rumours of a possible evacuation, but, so far as he knew, no decisions had been made back in London: 'we are still making preparations for staying — 40 bootmakers, for example, are due here' and 'it is all talk of deep digging at present.' Meanwhile some of the diggers had started thinking about Christmas. Knowing how long letters were taking to get home and how unreliable delivery was, they had begun to send Christmas greetings. A 2nd Battalion soldier signed off his letter: 'Wishing you a very happy Xmas. I only wish I could be with you, it is a long time since we had the last Xmas together and may be a long time before we have another as I imagine I will be stuck here in this freezing dugout.' On 9 November Bean recorded, 'Lord Kitchener is already in Mudros to-day and could visit any time.' Unaware of the imminent visit, Alec continued his water rounds. Another newly arrived carrier reported, 'Went on fatigue to the beach. Here we loaded cheeses, bags and ammunition, whilst the other fatigue platoon fetched the water for the Company. But we only had a mug full for drinking, all the rest goes to the cooks for tea and cooking purposes. We new arrivals are now as dirty as the old hands and as lousy, too. My first introduction to Padre McKenzie ("Fighting Mac") was behind the cookhouse, where he was stripped to his pants, counting the bugs in his shirt, and he called out his score at 47 lice for the morning's catch.' Gallipoli had a habit of breeding eccentric characters — like 'Clark the collector', for instance. A soldier from a neighbouring dugout explained in a letter home, 'There is one man here — an old hand named Clark — who has a most interesting dugout. It is stocked with Turkish souvenirs — rifles, letters, watches, badges, cigarette tins, personal belongings etc. all belonging to the Turks. He calls it his Museum, and its quite a smelly one, too, but he has a mania for collection and it keeps him happy.'

One of their main complaints was the quality of the food — or rather the lack of it. 'The only meat we had was stuff called Fray Bentos bully beef,' Alec recalled. 'That was a South American make of beef and it was dreadful stuff — fat and muck running through it. Fray Bentos was like greasy soup in tins. It used to melt. We also had biscuits, big heavy army biscuits. Oh, cripes, the biscuits were hard. You could hit them with an axe, I think, and you wouldn't hurt them! And sometimes if you soaked them in something they were better and they would soften then. But I think they were good enough food — they kept us alive. We had very little nice tucker. It might have been reasonably nourishing, but it was not very pleasant to eat. Food on Gallipoli was poor and there was no fresh vegetables or things like that, and so there was a lot of dysentery, a lot of sickness.'

The Turks attacked again on 10 November, this time against the hard-won Lone Pine redoubt. A trooper serving on the front line with the 23rd Battalion noted in his diary, 'Major Newcombe ordered us to dig in for they are expecting some big shells any day. Turks bombard Lone Pine with 11 in., 10 in. and 9.2 shells, wrecking our trenches completely. Casualties about 200 men, most of whom were buried whilst in the tunnels for shelter. Our Section is sent round to Lone Pine to help clear up the trenches. Had a very close call with bombs and machine gun whilst working there, but we came off safe.' Hill 971 was relatively quiet at this stage, but the risks remained real, as Alec would later recall. 'There were casualties from Turkish snipers and shellfire and the Turkish guns were very accurate with the shrapnel shelling. Their rifle shooting was also accurate. If you exposed yourself in any way you were likely to get hit. People were getting bowled over pretty often in our company. I suppose while I was there we had half of them hit. Even though the big August attack was over and it was mainly a holding operation when I was there, there were a lot of young fellows on the Peninsula who would be hit by the Turks.' On 11 November a soldier near Franklin's Post wrote, 'At 1130 the Turks shelled Franklins Post heavily, putting 25 shells into the position from W. Hills. No serious damage was done to the defence, and there were no casualties. Work proceeded within the communication trench to Franklins during the night. A post of 3 men occupied Sandy Knoll throughout the hours of darkness but no enemy movement was detected. About 20 feet of the sap was completed and in the bivouac there was a certain amount of work completed.' Alec's 15th Battalion were also kept busy. The same soldier reported, '40 men were on fatigue at the Aghyl Dere'.

On their return to the peninsula the 15th Battalion, with the 8th Reinforcements, had not gone back to the front line, which disappointed Alec but may have saved his life. One frontline soldier wrote home on 12 November, 'At last we have reached the firing-line. I'm writing this in my dugout, by the light of a slush-lamp. The noise overhead is something terrible at times. Everything will seem to be at rest, when suddenly some of the big guns on the ships will open up — and talk about noise, it is enough to deafen one. This morning was the loudest and biggest noise since we came here. One shell landed within 20 yards of our back sheds. They did rock it in. You can look over the parapet of your trench with the aid of a periscope and not see any movement, but if you put your hand up for a few seconds, you are lucky if you don't get a hole in it! As far inland as we can see, there are Turkish trenches; so it's going to be a long, weary way to Constantinople.' He had no shortage of inspiration, however: 'This is a very reasonable position. It is where Jacka (of Wedderburn) won his Victoria Cross.'

On 11 November Alec heard a new rumour about fraternising across the front lines. According to Charles Bean, 'We threw over some letters from Turkish prisoners saying they were well treated and some pictures of nice fat happy prisoners in Cairo,' and the Turks 'threw over two packets of cigarettes with the inscription

Prenez Femez avec plesir Notre herox ennemis'. The Australians, Bean reported, then sent over some bully beef but the discerning Turks 'threw back a message on a stick and stone saying "Bully beef non" so we threw some biscuits (good biscuits) and jam until they called out *"Fini"* and waved down their hands (all had heads up). Next morning same proceedings. Interpreter spoke to them from our lines. They were allowed to go over and get a pocket knife we had thrown over. But the third morning we had orders from above not to carry on.' Once the officers had ordered an end to the social exchange the two sides resumed trying to kill each other. Alec recalled, 'Yes, many of our chaps had talks with the Turks, and of course they couldn't talk English and we couldn't talk Turkish, but cigarettes and things were exchanged. I didn't see this personally, but I've seen some of the things that others got from Turks as souvenirs. The only Turks I had contact with in that way, to say anything to, were in a group of prisoners we held on the beach at Anzac. They were pleasant enough fellows and some of them had smatterings of English.'

By the night of 12 November Charles Bean was not the only mortal in on the big secret about the VIP visit set for the following day, and rumours were flying. Blissfully unaware of the significance of these rumours, let alone their personal implications, the kid soldier was about to be inspected by the illustrious Lord Kitchener — the face on the letterhead back in Claremont Camp, Tasmania, and on thousands of recruitment posters all over England. This unlikely encounter would be Alec's main wartime brush with fame. For of all the diggers that might have caught the eye of Britain's formidable Minister for War during his brief visit to Anzac Cove, fate — much to Charles Bean's annoyance — had picked out Alec's party of newly arrived Reinforcements with whom he should pause and speak. What neither the kid soldier nor any of his mates could have known was that the visit was part of a British government reappraisal of the campaign that would decide the fate of thousands of Australians clinging desperately to that pitiless beachhead on the Gallipoli Peninsula.

CHAPTER 7
MEETING LORD KITCHENER

'There was no drinking water. It all had to be carried up to the line by hand from a huge iron lighter which had been run ashore on the beach and was filled at night by water carrying ships. Food was not good, mainly tinned beef and Army biscuits. A lot of men went off with illness, mainly dysentery and yellow jaundice.'

Lord Kitchener, the most senior Allied leader to visit Gallipoli during the campaign, arrived at Anzac Cove early on the afternoon of 13 November. It was an event of huge importance for this community of soldiers, as he was undoubtedly the pre-eminent British commander associated with the First World War. Indeed, for many he was the face of the war. For more than a year he had gazed down grimly from posters throughout Britain enjoining her young men to enlist — and they had, in their hundreds of thousands.

He arrived, as witnessed by Charles Bean, escorted by the Anzac commander-in-chief, General Birdwood. 'The tall man walked up the pier (with the brilliant red band on his staff cap towering over everyone else) and he had scarcely reached the end of the pier when the men tumbled to it — and down they came to the edge of the beach and on to the beach itself. Men began to run from their dugouts above, hopping over the intermediate scrub and holes and heaps of relics of old dugouts. Then one of the men on the beach called for a cheer and the sound of cheering brought every Australian out of his burrow and scuttling down like rabbits. The tall red cap was rapidly closed in amongst them — but they kept a path and as the red cheeks turned and spoke to one man and another, they cheered him — they, the soldiers — no officers leading off or anything of that sort. It was purely a soldiers' welcome.'

Alec would remember being abruptly called out of his dugout. On hearing who the VIP was, his first reaction was worry. After all, it was only in July that, as a callow volunteer, he had written his first letters home on that letterhead dominated by Kitchener's unmistakable portrait. So far he had got away with his underage soldiering, but what if Kitchener should spot him and demand his real age? His heart beat faster at the thought. Once on the beach, he would later recall, 'I was really worried because we had all heard so much about this high-ranking British leader, and I thought he might find something wrong with us as Reinforcements. But he seemed friendly and nothing went wrong. I can still see this big tall bloke with stooped shoulders walking along in front of us as we stood under the big ANZAC sign on the beach.'

Some who were there that day might have recalled Kitchener's unflattering conclusion, after a visit to Australia in 1909–1910, that Australian troops could not be relied upon for any serious fighting. Now Kitchener spoke out, Bean wrote: 'The King asked me to tell you how splendidly he thinks you have done — you have indeed done splendidly, better even than I thought you would.' Alec would say many years later, 'And I remember Kitchener saying we were as fine a group of Reinforcements as ever sent.' The young trooper was 'as pleased as punch' to have passed muster under the scrutiny of the great British war horse. Bean, who had a better sense than Alec of the big picture, and who had hoped that Kitchener would meet old hands at the front line with 'real authority', was disappointed that their visitor would waste the time speaking with inexperienced reinforcements like Alec. During one part of the tour, Bean complained, 'every man he spoke to had only been here a few weeks'.

Among old hands and new, Kitchener was a hit. 'The soldiers', wrote Bean, 'would not have cheered many men — they would never have cheered Ian Hamilton like that, for all his kindness and gentle manners. K. is the sort of man every Australian admires — not a polished man but a determined one, an uncompromising worker. These men honestly and quite sincerely like his absence of display ... K. received a welcome which I doubt whether he knows the value. There are not many men that Australians would honour in that way.' After two and a half hours in the Anzac sector, climbing with his entourage to Walker's Ridge, Bully Beef Sap and Rest Gully before returning to the beach, Kitchener sailed away. The impressions he took back to London would help the British government decide to authorise a full evacuation the following month.

Next day, for all that, the Army deposited another large cache of supplies, including ammunition, shells and tents, at North Beach, close to Alec's position. The YMCA also set up a tent that served as a canteen, where they sold — miraculously — cakes. The beach was now a hive of activity, with gangs of Maltese labourers along with a large number of Gurkhas, 'dapper chaps, very like the Japs in features and stature and always smiling and skylarking'. On the 15th the shelling resumed. A frontline soldier from the 21st commented in his diary, 'Abdul gave us more than his usual quantity of shells today.' A field ambulance officer reported on 16 November, 'Plenty of shells flying about. There was a mob of fellas standing near number 2 outpost who were going to Lemnos for a spell. One of them said "It would be funny if we don't go!" Then a shell burst near them and cut one of them in half.'

Out of the blue, on 17 November the biggest storm since the landings hit Gallipoli. The wind built to gale force, until 'there was just one mass of waves lashed into foam'. The gale erupted into a storm that hammered Anzac Cove mercilessly. Bean wrote, 'You could see the breakers rolling in, white, three deep, all along the beach and throwing themselves over the whole length of the pier.' The waves became so powerful that they smashed one vital loading jetty, Walker's Ridge Pier, leaving nothing but the piles, like broken teeth. As the storm grew in ferocity, the water advanced up the beach right up to the Naval Transport Officer's door. Dead mules were washed up by the waves and shallow graves were uncovered in the sand. Bean noticed 'old barges half broken up sawing and bumping about like elephants dancing some slow side step on the water's edge', and he saw one man very nearly carried away by the waves. Fatigue parties shifted the stores further up the beach, but many ammunition boxes were half submerged and at risk of being lost. Alec's water delivery round was postponed, but he drew little comfort from that. After dinner the storm broke in torrential rain, Bean wrote, and 'trenches up to 300 yards long became a rushing stream three inches deep with the mud over my ankles'. Retreating to the beach, he saw 'seas that were still roaring in, a driver dragging the harness from two mules that had been shot (one dead, the other wounded) and a man who had been shot too'.

When dawn broke next day conditions were even worse, especially when the Turks resumed their shelling of the beach, which they did intermittently all day. All the dugouts, including Alec's hillside burrow, had been flooded and needed bailing. A 21st Battalion soldier wrote, 'The storm last night was such as I have never in all my life seen before, and hope never to see again. The wind was something terrible — it was quite impossible to stand up in it. I tried it and lost my hat. It did not simply rain, but came down in one gallon drops — or something thereabouts. In about 6 minutes all the valleys were filled with rushing volumes of water, and the hillsides looked just like immense waterfalls. Everyone was flooded out. Today I had to dig everything out from about 18 inches of slush. I was wet to the skin and had to stop so all day. The trenches are terrible and with all this it is bitterly cold and all the piers have been broken. We could see before the storm half a submerged trawler, but today it is no more.'

Ironically, despite the deluge, water supplies to Anzac Cove now came under renewed threat as most of the water lighters had been sunk. The men's ration was cut by half. When Bean asked Commander George Gipps how he thought they were going to get through the winter, Gipps replied despairingly, 'The winter! I think we're within two days of a disaster.' Even with the water collected during the storm, they lacked the fuel to boil it. Their food supplies, too, were running short, and they had no winter clothing. Yet the British government could still not make a decision on the future of the campaign. Bean would write with disgust, 'The British nation has not the brains to make war and the troops there were being sacrificed to that pure British incompetence.' In reality, the issue was academic at that point since, as he then noted, with only one pier standing they could not have evacuated with dispatch even had they wanted to.

The weather cleared fortuitously for a ceremony that had been eagerly awaited by many Australian soldiers — Sergeant Albert Jacka's VC presentation. Before a large gathering of diggers, Colonel Monash spoke briefly but stirringly, reminding the men of Jacka's extraordinary action at Courtney's Post. It was a big moment for the Anzacs. Jacka had been the first Australian soldier to be awarded a VC in this war, and had provided badly needed inspiration both for the demoralised troops at Gallipoli and for the people back home.

Towards the end of November Alec received his own reward — a pile of letters from home, including several from his brothers and sister. He told Estelle later that 'he read and re-read these childish letters from home over and over even though some had half a page taken up with big crosses representing kisses'. He had written that he was 'longing to hear such simple homely happenings as whether or not we were still having honey for tea', and homely letters was what he received. Angus wrote, 'We miss you very much, but I don't mind it so much when you are going to fight for country and king. Stell set the chimney on fire last night. Col and I got our muscles to work and soon put it out and when Dad came home instead of giving us the V.C. he gave us some nice cakes and a cup of hot tea and we went to bed. Stell said she put the fire out, but that was only a rumour, you know, for a little thing like her couldn't do anything but eat.' In her own letter, Estelle insisted her brothers failed utterly as firefighters: 'I nearly set the breakfast room chimney on fire last night and Colin and Angus could <u>not</u> put it out.' Other news was closer to the heart of the young soldier. Mac wrote, 'Dad shot a big fine roo the other day.' He hoped his brother 'got good tucker at Gallipoli and a good sleeping place'. In Alec's absence, the 14-year-old had taken his place in the family, being admitted as a special guest to his father's men-only club in Launceston — the Commercial Travellers Association.

By 21 November the supply situation at Anzac Cove had reached crisis point. A disgruntled 20th Battalion digger reported, 'Very cold weather and bad food. This morning one rasher of salty, stinking bacon and no tea. Midday, tea only, and at night we got fresh meat stew and nothing to drink. It is really awful to think that we have been established here for so long and are unable to get water and are being fed worse than in the hot weather. They have condensers lying on the beach for two months and they have just started to erect them, and at the rate they are going we might get water in plenty by Christmas. One has only to reflect on the management of affairs and he will soon conclude that the whole system is rotten to the core.' An even bigger problem was encroaching winter: the temperatures had dropped dramatically, and the men had still not been issued warm clothing. The situation, as Alec knew, would grow worse 'when the snow came and the cubby holes that we'd lived in were flooded out'. In a letter home, a 54th Battalion soldier wrote, 'If this is the beginning of winter, Lord help us in the middle of it. So far I've not taken off my cap, comforter, and scarf since I've been here and I only take my great coat off for a couple of hours in the middle of the day.' This prudent soldier had a small hamper 'put by for Xmas of a bottle of wine and a box of almond raisins and biscuits and it makes our mouths water every time we look at it. If we work it properly we might get some chicken as there are two tied up outside a "brass hats" dugout.' On 22 and 23 November, he related, 'Two cruisers and a destroyer plus a lot of land batteries poured shells into a section of the Turks' beloved country known to us as the Olive Grove, which contains several guns which annoy us. I don't think it was possible for anyone to live through that bombardment. Clouds of dust and trees flew about as salvoes from the boats hit it.' Inevitably the Turks struck back but 'were repulsed with heavy casualties, ours next to nil. Turks charged at Courtneys and were repulsed. Turks charged at Helles whole Division and repulsed with heavy losses. But the gun the Anzacs tagged "Beachy Bill" was active.'

Despite the talk of evacuation, and the critical supply problems, on 24 November a new group of reinforcements clocked in not far from Hill 971, making Alec feel like an old hand. To the amazement of most of the veterans, the new arrivals seemed pleased to be there. One of these 14th Battalion Reinforcements wrote optimistically, 'After getting ashore safely marched with assistance of a guide up to the left nearly 4 miles. It was a drag, all were pretty tired, and had heavy loads. We were lucky, were not even sniped at. We camped in a gully in the open that night and at Bde HdQrs. My word it was cold, my sleeping bag was invaluable and we are bivouaced in the gully, where we imitate rabbits and dig and dig in. The dugouts are wonderful, I have just had a beauty completed. We are not far from the famous Hill 971 and Hill 60 which you may have read about. We feed pretty well too, we get bread sometimes and meat. It is wonderful the different understanding between officers and men here, quite chums, a lot better and the discipline is better. A. Jacka V.C. is my Coy. Sgt. Major, I am great pals with him. He is a particularly decent chap, knows the game, and very modest. The adaptability of our chaps is wonderful.'

On 25 November the first steps towards the evacuation were taken, although no one at Gallipoli knew it. In London Lord Kitchener and General Charles Monro (Sir Ian Hamilton's replacement) had issued secret evacuation orders. Brigadier General Brudenell White was to draft a detailed evacuation plan for Anzac Cove. It was keenly understood that such a plan could succeed only if the Turks were given no advance intelligence of it. So, even as the Turks bombarded the beach all day, Allied guns and other equipment began to be stealthily withdrawn. None of the soldiers yet knew about the evacuation. Even on the front line soldiers interpreted changed orders simply as a new ruse to trick the Turks. A 19th Battalion digger wrote, 'We are keeping low and the rations are being drawn at night, so as to make it appear that we have evacuated our positions. The men treat it as a huge joke, and think it will not have any effect on the cunning Turks or their German officers. The ruse is to keep it up till the Turks make an attack, and then give them a surprise.' Meanwhile the weather continued to deteriorate. On 26 November a shivering Anzac from the 4th Field Ambulance recorded that 'the lightning was awful, it lights the place up like day and the thunder worse than ever I have heard, raining too. It was that dark that you could not see your own hand in front of you. I have never seen a night like it in Aust., cold chilled you to the bone.'

The next morning Alec emerged from his dank, ice-cold dugout to find the hillside under a blanket of snow. The thermometer had not risen above freezing point during the night and showed 7 degrees of frost. The tot of rum issued that morning would have been received by Alec with an enthusiasm rivalling that of his older comrades. A dispirited 8th Battalion Anzac grumbled, 'The first fall of snow fell to-night. We spent a cold, wet and miserable night. The ground was frozen. In our support trenches we have no overhead cover. Our clothes and blanket wet through and our equipment frozen stiff. I had to stand at my post for my 2 hrs at the entrance of the communication trench. The wind cut through me, whistling along the commun. trenches. My feet were very near frozen. The snow is a beautiful sight no doubt. We are past admiring scenery just now. We are on half rations, biscuits and cheese. How we hate the sight of those biscuits. When we are not being frozen to death in

New arrivals at the AIF's Mena Camp training base below the pyramids of Giza, Egypt

(AWM P01436.007)

After disembarking at Lemnos, Alec and his fellow Anzacs march to Sarpi Camp.

(AWM C00050)

Rest Gully, Gallipoli: Off-duty Anzacs await the big attack on Lone Pine,
August 1915. (AWM P00591.004)

Dugouts at Anzac Cove

(AWM C01129)

Australian dead in a trench at Lone Pine, captured after the bloody
August assault

(AWM A04013)

Rush hour at Anzac Cove   (The Illustrated London News Picture Library)

Anzacs at rest between attacks

(AWM A03869)

Alec's only surviving letter from Gallipoli, written three days after his arrival (note the censor's hand)

Troops march up
White's Valley to
relieve the garrison at
Lone Pine,
August 1915.
(AWM POO188.014)

Private John Simpson
Kirkpatrick, 3rd Australian
Field Ambulance, helped
evacuate many wounded
soldiers before he was
killed in action. (AWM JO6392)

Anzac water carriers

(AWM G01241)

Anzacs turn out to greet Lord Kitchener, 13 November.   (AWM H10354)

Hospital Pier after the storm of 18 November

(AWM HOO299)

A kitchen in the snow, 29 November

(AWM GO1263)

A 4th Brigade tent hospital   (AWM PO1116.036)

The Hotchkiss Gully hospital tent where Alec recuperated from influenza in November   (AWM COO680)

Guns being taken off the beach before the evacuation, December (AWM PO1436.004)

Wounded en route to hospital ships (AWM A05784)

Evacuating the wounded (AWM CO2679)

This 17 December cricket match on Shell Green, during which shells passed constantly overhead, was part of the ruse to conceal the Anzacs' imminent evacuation.

(AWM GO1289)

To convince the Turks they were staying, the Anzacs fired guns like this 3rd Field Artillery Brigade 18-pounder right up to the evacuation. This photograph was taken on 19 December.

(AWM P0046.041)

A burial at sea on Christmas Day en route from Lemnos to Alexandria AWM P0OO46.047)

the supports we are on Quartermasters fatigue making pack mules of ourselves carrying boxes of biscuits and petrol tins full of water and other stores. On the way to the beach we have to pass over the Headquarters dugouts. They are very comfortable. No wonder we common pack animals growl and use bad language.'

Despite the extreme cold, the following day, a Sunday set aside for cleaning, the 15th Battalion bathed. Chataway records, 'The troops awoke to freezing winds and a blanket of snow dumped by an overnight blizzard.' Nevertheless, Anzac soldiers at Gallipoli had developed the custom of sea bathing when they could, both to keep clean and to ward off disease, and 'by an unlucky coincidence the 28th November was also marked down as the Battalion's bathing day, and no blizzard was going to be allowed to interfere with that occasion. The men stripped naked though the temperature remained below zero all day. They also received from the cooks a quart of thawed ice and a strip of flannel per man, with which they proceeded to wash themselves'. Alec dived into the sea with the rest and briskly scrubbed his shivering body clean. Growing up in Tasmania, Alec was acclimatised to cold weather, unlike the men from warmer parts of Australia. Even so, this swim may well have triggered the illnesses that would soon lay him low.

Even as Alec and his mates bathed in the icy water, one field artillery officer noted, the snow continued to fall. 'We have had a real taste of the Gallipoli winter at last. Last night it snowed for hours and it is still drifting down this morning. All the trenches round are deep in snow and you can scarcely pick up any land-marks owing to the drift. It is bitterly cold even in this comfortable dugout. What it will be like to people less comfortably placed I do not like to imagine. If we can only get timber and galvanized iron to fix the men up with decent shelters for the winter, everything should be all right.' But it got worse. The next day shivering Anzacs complained, 'Freezing all night and all day. The coldest night and day I think most of us have experienced. The beach is in a terrible state, snow and ice on everything.' The conditions for the poorly clad Turks must have been even more intolerable. Charles Bean noted six desertions on the 28th, and at daybreak the next morning he spotted two more bedraggled Turks approaching the Anzac lines along the beach, carrying one kitbag between them.

Snow or no snow, the war went on. On the 30th, high above Hill 971 at Lone Pine, a frontline 18th Battalion Anzac reported, '3 officers and 18 men were killed and 8 officers and 59 men were wounded. Mostly all buried but very cold snow still on ground makes it difficult to dig graves.' The next day a 21st Battalion front-liner wrote, 'I feel very bad today. We got a terrible bombardment by the Turks. Casualties and damage are heavy.' At about this time a friend of Alec's named Pritchard was shot and killed. 'When you're young,' Alec commented later, 'you take those sort of shocks much more easily that you do when you're grown up, I think. He was hit somewhere on the forehead. But everybody did lose mates at Gallipoli.' Alec would always concede that with all the shelling, shrapnel and snipers, he was lucky not to be hit. At about this time, however, he sustained an injury that would haunt him for the rest of his life and would help shape his postwar philosophy.

As he told it, 'The fellow in front of me got shot and fell backwards into the trench, knocking me right over, which could have saved my life. He did not hit me, but he fell back and the rifle clouted me on the head. I was not wounded but I was hurt.' The injury turned out to be more serious than it looked, for it destroyed a particular nerve (the 'seventh' or 'facial nerve') in his cheek in front of the ear. In time, this would paralyse the muscles of the right side of his face and lead to a condition known as Bell's Palsy, which eventually prevented him from closing his right eye, smiling properly or showing his teeth. The attacks of paralysis came and went during his younger years, but as he got older the condition produced an increasingly unsightly facial disfigurement. As an old man he lost his right eye.

'You were aware of people getting bowled over pretty often in our company,' he would later remember. 'I suppose while I was there we had half of them hit — some killed, and some just hit. You could be hit on the beach, because shrapnel was coming out constantly. It would be an almost accidental hit because, where Anzac Beach was, you could not get at it, except from the sea, and the Turks didn't have the sea.' As a good marksman himself, Alec had a healthy respect for their opponents. 'The Turkish soldiers were good shots and they had sharp pointed bullets like the Germans had. I think these cartridges were more effective than our .303. They were newer, anyway. The .303 is blunt-nosed and is nickel-covered. The Mauser rifle is handier. I know several of our fellows used a Mauser when they could. You could often pick one up, and if you had some ammunition, you could use it. A .303, unless it goes through a vital part, does not kill you as a rule.'

With winter tightening its grip, the game was up for the campaign, and the smart money was on evacuation. As Bean wrote on 31 November, 'staying on here we should be fighting the winter which is playing Germany's game'. He knew that the British authorities 'haven't prepared against the winter; they haven't made a harbour; they now find they can not expect to land water and stores as they would have wished — and the condensor is holed'. Alec, irrepressible despite his injury, was looking forward to a transfer and 'getting into the firing line in France', where instead of carting water he could put his sharpshooting skills into practice. He thought evacuation would give him a chance to become a real infantryman. What he did not know was that the living conditions, exacerbated by the effects of that bathe he had taken in the freezing Aegean, were about to make him very sick indeed, and if he did not get off the beach very soon he might well be buried there.

CHAPTER 8

ESCAPE

'By December rumours were going about our future. Some said there was going to be another big attack, others that we were preparing to evacuate the place. By mid December it became obvious that preparations were being made to get out, and so it was. By the end of December we were gone.'

As winter made life increasingly intolerable, many Anzacs at Gallipoli talked about the possibility of leaving. In his diary, war correspondent Charles Bean jotted down some tactical ideas of his own, which included 'landing empty boxes ... on the beach, keeping up the appearance of men about the place, all men camped where the enemy sees our camps like Shrapnel Gully and Ari Burnu, leaving the machine guns in place until almost the end and then all evacuation to be done at night.' As he read the situation, 'if we decided to stay on without a superhuman effort to back us, the result will be disaster.' One 48th Battalion soldier wrote optimistically, 'Old Winter has now taken a hand in the campaign in the Dardanelles as it has been snowing all night and the ground between the trenches — a real no man's land held by neither Turk nor Australian — is covered with a beautiful mantle of white. The fantastically shaped hills are capped with snow with beautiful streaks of white running down their steep sides. Trees, bushes and shrubs are all weighed down with the snow ... The floor of the trench and the tracks are covered with slush, the snow having been tramped into the ground but, despite the fact that overcoats are wet, feet and hands are as cold as ice and boots covered with a thick mud everybody is wonderfully cheerful.' Despite the extraordinary resilience of the Anzacs, however, this perspective was not universally shared.

Alec had now been on the peninsula for a month, and the persistent frigid weather, his permanently damp dugout, poor food, rationed water and the generally unsanitary living quarters of the crowded community were starting to take their toll. In this environment, and with the incidence of sickness and disease increasing, it was only a matter of time before he himself would fall ill and would have to take his chances in one of the Anzac tent hospitals.

Despite the worsening conditions, fighting flared up again in early December. At Lone Pine, the Turks used 12-inch shells to blow up several trenches, 'killing about 100 officers and men as well as wounding 200 more of our fellows,' according to a frontline 2nd Battalion Anzac. 'Plenty of the men also now frost bitten . . . the weather playing hell with our men.' One soldier had had enough. According to a 4th Field Ambulance man, 'He shot himself through the foot half an hour ago. The general opinion is that he did it on purpose so as to get out of danger. He has broken the bones.' But no one was safe. One of the doctors in the hospital tent where the wounded man was taken 'was in the operating theatre and was just about to do an operation when a shrapnel shell burst just outside the tent and a bullet got him in the back and went into his heart. He made a motion as if to pluck it out and then just dropped.' A hospital visitor wrote, 'I went down to the hospital to see one of our chaps who was being sent away to the beach to join the hospital ship. While there I saw where a large shell came through the tent roof and entered the ground in the middle of the tent, but did not explode. The tent was full of patients. There are a lot of tents with big holes in the roof from shells.'

Alec's water-carrying duties were increasingly disrupted because of delivery problems at Anzac Cove. A soldier of the 20th complained, 'even though there was drizzling rain last night and all day there is still an awful shortage of water, with men offering 5/- for a drink and unable to get it. The little drop of tea we get once or twice a day is delicious.' Mail services were also interrupted after the tug *Gaby* foundered; of the 18 bags of mail on board from Australia, dated 14, 15 and 16 November, only four were saved. Alec was fortunate to have just received a package of letters from home, including one from Estelle with a charming studio photograph of her dressed in Campbell tartan that he would thereafter carry with him in his kitbag.

Between 4 and 6 December, an 18th Battalion soldier wrote, 'Turks again fired on us using about 100 shells and again on the 5th and there were shells flying around everywhere and some flew into the D.H.Q. and also blew the 16th C.C. Hospital to smithereens and blew sick and wounded men to pieces while they were waiting to go on board the Hospital boat. It was an awful sight to see. Legs and arms all over the place. Then a German Taube flew over today and dropped two bombs — one in our gully and one in the next. She also dropped numbers of steel darts (poisoned). I have one as a memento.'

By 7 December the freezing conditions were claiming many lives thus far spared by the Turkish bombardments. 'A number of men, including about 200 Gurkhas, have been sent to Hosp. from the Peninsula suffering from frostbite,' a 14th Battalion Anzac recorded. 'They are in a very bad way and many may not live through it. Two members of the R.N.A.S. were also killed here today when their aeroplane turned turtle in the bad conditions and crashed down.' Later that day a 27th Battalion soldier wrote, 'after it finished snowing we had it very cold and the snow froze and it caused a fair number of our men to get frost bitten feet, and a couple of them are bound to lose their feet altogether through it. When the snow thawed and the sun started to shine they started to take the frost bitten ones aboard the Hospital boats. There was a boat load of Gurkhas with their feet frost bitten. Many near dead from the cold. In dozens of places men were found in trenches sleeping frozen stiff with cold. Some dead on duty. I can tell you it is pretty rotten to see some of them. The Turks got on to our Hospital and pretty well wiped it out of existence with one of their heavy guns. Tentfulls of wounded and sick were killed and maimed.'

That week Private Campbell maintained delivery of the reduced water rations to the Anzac positions, trudging through freezing rain, snow, mud and slush day after day with inadequate covering and no dry clothes to change into. On the morning of 8 December, shivering uncontrollably in his miserable dugout under Hill 971, he realised he was sick. Since he was clearly not strong enough to cart water that day, he was escorted down to the 4th Field Ambulance hospital in Hotchkiss Gully, where he was admitted with influenza. This flimsy, snow-covered tent was just like any of the field hospitals that were struck from time to time by Turkish shells. But at least for the moment he was a little warmer and was sheltered from the foul weather.

Influenza was a serious, often fatal, illness in 1915, when doctors still knew little about how to control it. Just three years later the great Spanish flu pandemic would kill some 40 million people around the world, dwarfing the numbers killed in combat during the war. At least eleven thousand Australians would die of the flu by 1919, many of them war veterans. For Alec, this bout of flu was the first of a series of illnesses that would knock him out of the war, force his repatriation to Tasmania and plague his health for the rest of his long life.

At last Charles Bean received confirmation on the evacuation. 'A definite decision has been come to — we are to take everyone off the peninsula except those needed to definitely defend it till the last moment.' Meanwhile the fighting went on. A soldier of the 14th recorded, 'Our Artillery had a little practice at Jacko's expense this afternoon for a while and we blew up a Turkish position with dirt, sandbags, barb wire and a Turk or two going sky high and filling the atmosphere — we did give them a stir-up. It is amusing to see every one of our chaps put their heads over the parapet to see the shells land, then when the bombardment ceased, Jacko had a few shots and of course down came all the heads. Yet we take not the least bit of notice of the everlasting bang bang and I can tell you John Turk's index finger hangs on the trigger very lightly at night time. He wastes thousands of rounds of ammunition.' Later that day a field gunner wrote, 'Major Scott from Wangaratta was blown right away with a "Jack Johnstone" last week, it never left a single trace of him anywhere. We could not find anything of him. I feel quite confident that I shall get through all right, but should my time come I am prepared to face it.'

During Alec's third day in the field hospital the Anzacs went on the attack again. A 21st Battalion soldier reported, 'One of our battleships, two cruisers, two monitors and three torpedo boats stood out opposite us and gave the extreme right flank a terrible doing with all the largest high explosive shells for about three quarters of an hour. They used about 800 rounds. The latest rumour is we are to man the Lonesome Pine trenches. It was here that I had two very narrow squeaks — one from a shell which blew the whole of the earthwork from behind me and the other from a bomb which burst in front of me.'

By 11 December Alec was discharged from the hospital in Hotchkiss Valley and reported back to his unit. It was a good day to emerge from the relative security of the hospital tent, for there was no shelling at all, Charles Bean noting, 'The Turks were curiously quiet all day.' Next day Alec was back on water-carrying duties, which were more tolerable since the Turks had stopped shelling the beach. The weather was his main enemy now. On the day he rejoined the 15th, the evacuation was made official and he learned that his battalion was to be among the first to leave. Colonel Monash, commander of 4th Brigade, recorded the momentous news in his journal:

> *Like a thunderbolt from a clear blue sky has come the stupendous and paralysing news that, after all, the Allied War Council has decided that the best and wisest course to take is to evacuate the Peninsula,*

and secret orders to carry out that operation have just reached here. The secret is known so far to only a small handful of men and already we have stopped the further arrival of stores, mails, reinforcements, and munitions but the first thing to do is to secure as great a measure of secrecy as possible.

The operation of withdrawal is going to be every bit as critical and dangerous an enterprise as the first landing, and if the Turks were to get the slightest inkling of what was intended, it would mean the sacrifice of at least half our men. As it is, it will mean the sacrifice of some men, and of vast quantities of munitions and stores. At a conference of the commanders it was decided to put up the bluff that, owing to the severe winter conditions, it is intended to form a winter rest-camp at Imbros, and take the brigades and battalions there by turn. In this way we should be able in two or three stages to remove about two-thirds of the total army, leaving the remaining third to man the defences very lightly, and then finally to make a bolt for the beach, in the dead of night and into boats which will be in waiting. It is of course an absolutely critical scheme, which may come off quite successfully or may end in a frightful disaster. But orders are orders. I need not say I feel very unhappy and I am almost frightened to contemplate the howl of rage and disappointment there will be when the men find out what is afoot, and I am wondering what Australia will think at the desertion of her 6000 dead and her 20,000 other casualties.

Other responses were more emotional. An Anzac chaplain wrote:

Horror of horrors! We are to evacuate Anzac and Suvla. That is the movement that is taking place. If only fine weather lasts we are to be away by Saturday. I could cry. But what is the use? I must smile and cheer everybody up, but my heart is very sore, not for the evacuation itself, for I know this is best, but for all the valuable lives that have been lost here. The boys have done their job grandly and well. We are bound to leave many stores behind but nothing of any value in the

*way of munition. I do not know yet what part the Padres will take in
this affair but I am shifting to the 1st Casualty Clearing Hospital for
that will be the last to get away (if it gets away at all). The beach is
very busy and everyone is packing up. All gear must be moved from
the firing line at night so that Abdul does not get wind of anything
unusual. I have come to the conclusion that our evacuation is a wise
move and that in military circles our getting away safely will take
equal rank with our landing.*

On the appointed day, 13 December, oblivious to the strategic
and moral considerations weighing heavily on Monash and others,
Alec was instructed to complete his deliveries, pass his water cans to
relieving carriers, get back to his dugout and pack up his gear,
because that night the battalion was moving out. So, without
ceremony, and under cover of darkness, the 15th Battalion sneaked
away, and Alec left Anzac Cove and Gallipoli behind him. He must
have been aware of the significance of this retreat, although his
letters suggest that even now he saw it more as a transfer to the
battlefields of France than as a defeat. Alec had not been with the
first to land at Gallipoli, but his was certainly among the first units
to leave. The plan of withdrawal had been revealed only the
previous day. Chataway records, 'So on 13 December the 15th
Battalion filed out of Hay Valley under cover of darkness and
stealthily marched along the now familiar beach to the pier at North
Beach from which it was evacuated from Gallipoli, embarking just
after 7.30 pm on S.S. *Carron*.' The history reveals a 'great deal of
bitterness within the Battalion that the honour of forming the Anzac
rearguard fell not to the 15th but to other units. The disappointed
members of the 15th felt it had just been "ordered to fade away into
the night" almost a week before the final evacuation.' Their early
departure could nevertheless have saved lives, including Alec's.

Looking back towards Gallipoli and the lights of the little settlement he had come to know so well, Alec had mixed feelings. He had
not served in the firing line, as he had for so long dreamed he
would, but at least he had made a difference. As the lights retreated,

and the Gallipoli Peninsula was swallowed up in the night, he could not have imagined that with this image his war service, too, would be over. Nor could he know that the six weeks he had served at Anzac Cove would one day make him famous not only in his own country but around the world. Alec's head was full of other ideas, of course, and after a blissfully peaceful night rocked gently by uncharacteristically benign seas he arose early and made for the bows, where he hoped for a glimpse of Lemnos — for the island, in Alec's eager young mind, was the next staging post to France.

Those hoping for a short stopover at Lemnos would be disappointed. The battalion spent 'the next ten days in the cold, windy and exposed Sarpi Camp, right up till the 24 December, waiting for further orders'. Halfway through this wait the main body of Anzacs, whose withdrawal began on 18 December, started to arrive, and naturally they could not wait to tell the men of the 15th exactly how they had got away. Following the plan devised by General Birdwood's chief of staff, Australian Brigadier-General Brudenell White, the evacuation was a brilliant success. Over several successive days thousands of Anzacs and countless tons of matériel were removed under cover of darkness, with no loss of life.

From Anzacs in the main force on Lemnos they heard 'how deathly quiet the evacuation was once the navy guns stopped firing, because normally the big navy guns were blasting away at the Gallipoli shore.' Among the many ingenious ruses adopted by the retreating soldiers, they heard about the delayed self-firing rifles: the men would tie a kerosene can to the rifle trigger with string then set up a second can, filled with water, above the first; before leaving the trench the last man would carefully punch a small hole in the top can so that, long after their departure, sufficient water would have dripped down into the lower can that its weight alone pulled the trigger. Delayed explosive charges were laid in tunnels and saps. Escape routes through trenches and saps, along which sound-absorbing hessian bags were laid or the boards torn away, were lined with white stones to aid navigation in the dark. In the end, the old hands said, their greatest regret was leaving thousands of their mates buried out there, having died in a battle they could not finish. And the question they could not stop asking themselves was, what was the point of their dying, if we are just going to abandon the campaign by sailing away?

By 21 December every Anzac had been pulled off the peninsula. As Charles Bean observed, 'It was an extraordinary end to our fine history at Gallipoli. The Turks at last have now got it — the place they never could take — by our quietly leaving it in the night. And in the end perhaps, the greatest success we have achieved there is quietly giving it to them without their knowing it.'

With Alec's health further jeopardised by the miserable conditions on Lemnos, the medical authorities secured him a berth on the troopship *Ionian*, which left the island ahead of the bulk of the battalion, who were scheduled to sail on HMT *Ascanius* on Boxing Day. Alec disembarked in Alexandria on 25 December 1915 and was sent to a new camp allocated to the 15th at Ismailia. As he would later say, arriving in Egypt was the best Christmas present he could have had. It was nevertheless his first Christmas away from home, and he must have missed his family. They would be overjoyed to know he was safely back in Egypt and out of the war zone. Alec could only think, now for France and the real fighting.

CHAPTER 9
DOWN AND OUT IN CAIRO

'It was here that I became ill with yellow jaundice and then a very bad attack of mumps and Bells Palsy developed on the right side of my face. I spent some months in Egypt but was eventually invalided home.'

Ismailia, set up as a recovery base, meant rest and relaxation at last for the exhausted 15th Battalion, soon joined by the main body of Monash's 4th Brigade. 'For the battle-scarred veterans of Gallipoli, Egypt proved a blessing,' Chataway records. 'There, the urgency of time seemed non-existent for they now trod the sands of all time — lost in thousands of years or more of the world's existence. It was a period of great healing.' Although the underlying purpose was further training in preparation for joining the fight in France, in the event they 'only had a few parades of a trifling nature' and instead 'fought once more their battles and conjured up to their minds first one then another of the many friends who had gone west'. And they recovered as best they could. A few enlisted men died from wounds or diseases picked up at Gallipoli, Lemnos or since arriving in Egypt, although 'the death toll did not total double figures'. Nevertheless, with the big battles in France ahead of them these were losses the battalion could ill afford, especially since recruitment had fallen off in Australia with the news of the Gallipoli evacuation. The AIF needed every soldier it could get, including Private Campbell.

On 1 January 1916, however, Alec was admitted to No. 2 Australian General Hospital suffering from a bout of laryngitis. Out of the war zone, he was by no means out of danger, and he now began to pay the price of his brief but gruelling service. At 2AGH he was diagnosed with jaundice and transferred to a second hospital, Helouan, at Heliopolis, for further treatment. In a pattern that would characterise his months in Egypt, no sooner did he rejoin his unit at Ismailia than he got sick again and had to be readmitted to hospital. He would spend the next five months in and out of hospital in Egypt, before being invalided home in June. Alec recalled first getting sick 'after we'd left Lemnos and I was in Egypt in a camp. And from there I was in hospital in Heliopolis. I had four or five months in hospital on and off. I just got ill, I don't know how or why. I was very thin and weighed about eight stone, I think.' During this period he was treated for jaundice, scabies, head lice, mumps and attacks of paralysis to the right side of the face.

Much to his relief, Alec rejoined the 15th in time for their transfer, on 21 January, to a new base in the desert at Moascar. Alec was excited about the relocation both because of the new camp's exotic setting and because 'leave to Cairo was also frequent, and almost any man with a credit in his paybook or with friends to aid him was given permission to go'. On the day of the route-march to Moascar, Alec's family were alarmed to receive official notification of his first hospital admission with laryngitis.

Alec was well enough to celebrate his seventeenth birthday with his mates in the 15th at Moascar, although he would have been guarded about the particular anniversary being marked, since he was still one year short of the minimum age to wear the uniform, let alone fight overseas. Later that day they repacked their kits, for the 15th Battalion had orders to move camp the following morning. On 27 February Colonel Cannan, who had also been in hospital, resumed command of the 15th and immediately ordered them to break camp and entrain for Tel-el-Kebir, where they were to set up a permanent base 'near the site of Sir Garnet Wolseley's 1882 battle against the Egyptians just thirty-three years earlier'. Alec loved the weeks he spent in this 'wonderful big camp'. He was certainly among those souvenir hunters described by Chataway as searching 'the sands enthusiastically in the hope of unearthing a Damascus blade with jewel-studded hilt and gold-embedded scabbard' from the famous battle. Although this prize eluded him, he nevertheless unearthed enough trophies to send 'a box of things for Angus as he asked me to send him some for his Museum'. Apart from training exercises such as forced marches through the desert dunes, Alec would remember many diversions to amuse a high-spirited young man, including swimming in the canals, chatting and trading with the local Arabs, and of course visiting Cairo with his mates, where anything could happen. Alec was struck by the cosmopolitan nature of the camp. 'It was such a great big camp at Tel-el-Kabir and there were French and English and a conglomeration of troops — nearly all our allied nations were there.' Diverse companies of troops had arrived progressively following their evacuation from Gallipoli in January, and camps like Tel-el-Kebir became truly international.

With newspaper reports recounting the new Australian prime minister's visit to the western front, most of the Anzacs seemed to want to transfer to France. Billy Hughes was an ardent supporter of the Australian volunteer forces and was frequently quoted in the newspapers praising their fighting skills and calling for more recruits, especially after the battle for Verdun was joined in late February. On 7 March the first Anzacs from Gallipoli had reached Europe, eager to show their allies just how Australia's all-volunteer army could fight.

Alec enjoyed training with the 15th at Tel-el-Kebir. The camp was overcrowded and unhygienic, however, and disease spread like wildfire. On 19 March Alec again fell sick and was admitted to No. 4 Base Hospital at Heliopolis, this time with scabies. He therefore missed the 15th Battalion's three-day trek to Serapeum, which started on 26 March and turned into 'a gruelling march through the desert which was a severe test to the men many of whom were still weak from wounds received in Gallipoli'.

One luckless soldier of the 15th, who was attacked by a particularly aggressive camel during the trek, ended up joining Alec in hospital and so told him the story first-hand. 'What might have proved a very serious accident happened to Private Wally Eastment,' Chataway recounts, 'when he was travelling with the camel train carrying our provisions, as just when he passed one of the larger camels it seized him by the elbow with its teeth and shook him viciously. The native drivers rushed to his assistance but so severe was the bite that Private Eastment had to be taken to hospital and it was a long time before the unfortunate man fully recovered.' Alec learned later that he also missed 'the worst sand storms the unit was to experience while it was in Egypt'.

He had barely got back to camp after his latest illness before he fell sick again and was readmitted to hospital on 3 April, this time with mumps. Back at Tel-el-Kebir ten days later the young soldier wrote a cheerful, reassuring letter to his mother: 'Dont ever worry about my health Old Darling because I never felt so well as I do now.' He painted a colourful picture of life in Egypt, but ended on a sobering note: 'Our Battalion is camped on the old battle ground of Tel-el-Kebir, the place where the Bedouins broke the British square in 1882... Every day now we are expecting to leave for France so before you get this I hope to be in the firing line again.'

Despite this optimistic letter, on 16 April Alec was back in hospital suffering from 'an old fracture (mild)'. He returned to Tel-el-Kebir in time for the first anniversary of the 25 April Anzac landings. For weeks the men had discussed the best way of marking the occasion. Some of the 15th attended the big celebration held on the embankment of the Suez Canal. The occasion was treated, Chataway records, as 'a sports carnival for thousands of men who had one idea — to enjoy themselves thoroughly. Probably never in the history of the unit was there such a day. General Monash had ordered in his brigade the wearing of two ribbons, red and blue by all troops who had served on the Gallipoli Peninsula, while those who had served only in Egypt wore the blue ribbon alone. But the surprise of the afternoon was the arrival of the Prince of Wales, and his appearance to the troops resulted in a wild burst of cheering. Shortly afterwards, while thousands of naked forms were sporting in the water or sunning themselves upon the Canal's banks, another wild shout broke the peaceful scene and men disappeared under the water in all directions, for a woman had suddenly appeared upon the canal controller's ship. Naturally she soon left the carnival.'

The festivities evidently ended too soon for one particular private. On the evening of 27 April, in the third year of the war and two days after the first anniversary of the ill-fated Anzac landings, the military police in Cairo detained a wayward soldier from the 15th Battalion, who proved to be not only drunk but absent without leave from his camp. He was arrested and carted back to his quarters. Had they known that the miscreant was also an underage drinker (not to mention an underage soldier), they might have taken the matter further. As it was, the young man was reprimanded and advised that he would be hearing from the authorities. Sergeant A. A. Seefe, the humourless NCO in charge of the guard, was apparently oblivious to the significance of the celebrations. 'I was on duty,' he wrote in his Statement of Evidence, 'in the Esbekich District about 6.25 pm when I saw the soldier, Private Campbell, who was both drunk and Absent Without Leave. I conducted him to the Guard Detention Room and handed him over to the NCO in charge.' The incident resulted in a black mark on his record that would undermine any chances of future promotion but fortunately provoked no direct punishment, perhaps owing to his fragile health.

The temptations of Cairo exercised an understandable fascination for the kid from sleepy little Launceston, and many would have excused him for losing his head. Alec explained later, 'Egypt, and Cairo, were very exciting places for a 17-year-old who'd never really been out of Tasmania before. It was a fairyland.' In any case, for many Australians, who had seen their mates blown up in front of them at Gallipoli, all the rules had changed. Their lives could be hanging by a thread. They had heard how bad things were in

Flanders, and knew they would have a good chance of dying there
— so what the heck. Many Australian country boys lost their vir-
ginity in the back streets of Cairo, swapping a week's pay for their
first dubious experience, losing themselves in the city's fleshpots.
After what they had experienced, and after long months of enforced
male-only society, they would have been hard pressed to resist the
allure of the alleyways running off the bazaars, a world away from
the conventional behaviour drummed into them by their mothers
back in the sleepy country towns of their childhood. Some young-
sters would later admit to joining the Army only because once in
uniform they could buy a beer, a right otherwise denied Australians
under 21 years of age. With little to lose as they headed off for battle
and possible death, these soldiers developed a jaunty, cavalier
culture that egged on the reckless individual. Alec found Cairo a
'mesmerising experience, like a dream world that was not real'.

During May the men of the 15th were increasingly preoccupied
with the rumours of their next probable destination. 'When the
Quartermaster began to check over all our kit and withdrew one
blanket, various parts of Asia were suggested as the next scene of
action. This furphy was quickly dispelled when lectures regarding
our behaviour in France became the order of the day.' So it was
official — Alec and the 15th were off to France! It was exciting
news for Alec, who was fit and well again. He cleaned his special
revolver and army-issue rifle obsessively and tried to find out all he
could about France, which he had studied only briefly at school,
when he had rarely been paying attention. He had forgotten the
French words he had learned, which would surely not help him
win favour with any French girls he might meet in the villages while
on leave.

When the doctor conducting his medical examination eventually determined that the compounded illnesses listed on his casualty
form made him unfit for further service, Alec was devastated. He
had packed all his gear and in his mind's eye had already marched
with his Anzac mates down to the wharf and the ship for France.
Now they were going, and he was not.

Next day he awoke to this nightmare. On 31 May he watched the men of the 15th swing their kitbags over their shoulders and fall in for the last time on the camp parade ground. A few of his closer mates had commiserated: 'Sorry, kid. But don't worry, you'll get better soon and be on the next ship. See you in France.' Alec watched them march off to the trucks. Chataway notes, 'Packed to suffocating point in open trucks we were trundled violently down to Alexandria and embarked on SS *Transylvania* for our voyage to Marseilles.' Creeping back into his empty tent, Alec felt more alone than he ever had in his young life. Some of those men he had known since the previous July at Claremont Camp in Tasmania or had met, with the other Reinforcements, during training at Broadmeadows or on the voyage over; he had boxed and wrestled with them and beaten them at target practice; he had explored Cairo with them, survived Lemnos, landed at Anzac Cove and lived with them in those cold, cramped dugouts under Hill 971; he had carried water to most of them, had stood guard with them in the trenches; attended funerals with them. Together they had experienced the complex pain and relief of the evacuation and the frustration of that second, protracted stopover on Lemnos; together they had conquered the desert sands from their base camp at Tel-el-Kebir. Now they were gone. And he had been left behind.

He did not get better, and never did take that next ship. Perhaps that was as well, for the ill-fated SS *Transylvania* was torpedoed on her next run across the Mediterranean. Lucky Alec Campbell used up another of his nine lives. Left behind at the Tel-el-Kebir camp outside Cairo, however, a despondent Alec felt anything but lucky. There was still plenty for AIF soldiers to do in Egypt, of course. In early June the newspapers gave an account of the assembly of Allied troops bound for Palestine to fight against the Turkish and German occupying forces in that Arab region. They carried stories of how Grand Sherif Hussein of Mecca, with the support of an obscure British intelligence officer and Arabist who would soon become famous as 'Lawrence of Arabia', launched the Arab

Revolt to liberate the occupied territories. In a few months, General Harry Chauvel and the Australian Light Horse, in support of the Arab Revolt, would capture Beersheba, and in 1918 help Lawrence liberate Damascus. Alec, a good horseman, might have wished he had volunteered for the Light Horse. But with his medical report, he would have no chance of qualifying now, and no company wanted a sickly volunteer discarded by the Anzac forces who had sailed for France. Not surprisingly, the young soldier who felt so sorry for himself soon fell sick again, and by June Alec was back in hospital after further attacks of facial paralysis. Feeling keenly that this was no place for a good marksman who could have been a useful fighter in France, Alec became rebellious. The warnings he had received after his previous arrest went unheeded. The solace offered by the exotic sights, sounds and smells of Cairo reached through the windows of his Spartan, whitewashed hospital. On 16 June he escaped into the night.

Soon Alec was again stopped by the military police. Duly arrested, he was carted back to his hospital quarters and told to expect a court summons. On the appointed day he was charged once more with being AWOL and with 'breaking out of hospital'. He was cautioned that a further breach would find him behind bars rather than in a comfortable hospital or behind the flap of a dusty tent in Tel-el-Kebir. These offences, although minor, stained his army record. Promotion, like a transfer to France, was now out of the question. But in the third week of June Alec was served with a much more distressing sentence when the hospital tests confirmed the earlier diagnosis that he had contracted Bell's Palsy, and that his facial paralysis would not go away. The medical authorities recommended his total discharge from the AIF. The verdict debarred him from joining the fight in the terrible killing fields of Flanders and the Somme. Some might have been relieved by such a fortuitous delivery, but young Alec was not among them. On 23 June he was sent back to Tel-el-Kebir, where he was instructed to pack his kit and prepare for the journey back to Australia. That was it. There was nothing he or his mates from the 15th could do. They were in France, 'in the firing line'. He had a one-way ticket home. Short of a miracle, he had been knocked out of the war.

The following day the battered young Anzac boarded the *Port Sydney* at Suez and set sail for Australia. He had a few weeks to get used to his disappointment, because the ship did not arrive in Melbourne until 17 July. There was no army drill on this voyage; no point in practising with his revolver, let alone with the .303 they had reclaimed before he left Tel-el-Kebir; no exercises or boxing bouts with exhilarated young comrades. Just a shipload of other wounded and sick patients being invalided out of the war. Yet they were the lucky ones. Many of those sent on to Flanders or France were killed there. By the end of the war five times as many of his fellow Australian volunteers would die. While 8,709 Australians (many, like Alec, still in their teens) were killed at Gallipoli, 48,617 more died in the carnage of the western front.

Alec's voyage home was uneventful, apart from losing his kitbag containing the letters and photographs his family had lovingly sent him — the only tangible record he had of his time at Gallipoli. In Melbourne he stayed only long enough to organise passage to Launceston. He may have picked up a copy of *The Age* and read of the terrible first battle of the Somme, which began on 1 July, and in which so many Allied troops were slaughtered. It was obvious they needed a hand from trained soldiers like him. His heart wept when he later read of the 5,500 Anzacs killed on 19 July in a single day's fighting during the disastrous battle of Fromelles, when Australians were cut down by machine guns as they advanced across an open field — just as at the Nek on Gallipoli, before his arrival at Anzac Cove. Once again he was not there to help out. It must have been galling to read, on 31 July, Billy Hughes urging all young men to enlist to help win the war. But now Alec's only remaining military duty was to report, on arrival in Launceston, for a final, pre-discharge examination by the same medical authorities who had accepted him into the AIF the previous year.

At the end of August 1916 Private Alec Campbell, aged 17 years and six months, stood in the bows of the ship carrying him across Bass Strait, straining his eyes for a glimpse of the north coast of Tasmania. He hoped his family would be waiting to welcome him in Launceston. He longed for home. So much had happened to him since he had left Chesney 13 months before. For although even now he was too young to enlist, he had in the meantime trained as a soldier, sailed to the other side of the world, explored Cairo and climbed the pyramids, joined the famous 15th Battalion, landed and fought at Gallipoli, surviving weeks in a cold and wet dugout, served under Monash, met Lord Kitchener, participated in the historic evacuation, spent months in and out of unhealthy Egyptian hospitals, and twice been arrested by the military police for drunkenness and dereliction of duty. He had also, painfully, been discharged from the fighting force he had been through so much to serve. But now he longed simply for his first family meal at Chesney, and to slip back into his old bed in the room he had shared with his little brothers all those months ago. On the journey he had come to accept that his war was over, but he had given little thought to what would happen next. He had no intention of going back to that boring insurance company. His parents would tell him repeatedly that he still had his whole life before him. But Alec had been changed by his experiences, and he was not sure how he could start to live a normal life again.

The
LONG TRICK

I must go down to the seas again, to the lonely sea and the sky,
And all I ask is a tall ship and a star to steer her by,
And the wheel's kick and the wind's song and the white sail's shaking,
And a grey mist on the sea's face and a grey dawn breaking.

I must go down to the seas again, for the call of the running tide
Is a wild call and a clear call that may not be denied;
And all I ask is a windy day with the white clouds flying,
And the flung spray and the blown spume, and the sea-gulls crying.

I must go down to the seas again, to the vagrant gypsy life,
To the gull's way and the whale's way where the wind's like a whetted knife;
And all I ask is a merry yarn from a laughing fellow-rover,
And a quiet sleep and a sweet dream when the long trick's over.

John Masefield

CHAPTER 10
THE CARPENTER BUILDS PARLIAMENT HOUSE

'On discharge from the Army I was lost to employment as I had no training for any civilian occupation. I thought of farming of some kind and went to Flinders Island for about 3 months and worked mustering scrub cattle. I was employed by a drover named Rainbird.'

To Alec's relief, when the ship at last docked in Launceston the whole family was there to meet him on the wharf. The Department of Defence, he learned, had written advising them of the details of his return. After exchanging excited greetings, they set off for Chesney and a special dinner of his favourite dishes, during which Alec was deluged with questions and news from home. For more than a year Private Campbell had passed scarcely noticed in the large company of men, and he was soon exhausted by the solicitous attention. The prodigal son eventually excused himself, retired to his old bedroom and fell into a deep sleep, safe in the knowledge that no Turkish shell or sniper's bullet could reach him.

Awakening in the familiar surroundings, he knew in a deeper part of himself that his war was over. The final act, attending his discharge medical in Launceston, he performed on 22 August, when his service with the Australian Imperial Force was officially terminated and his file firmly closed. Some of the illnesses that had plagued him over the past months, however, could not be so readily shelved. He would carry the Bell's Palsy with him all his life. Indeed, for some time, Alec would remember, he was 'visiting doctors and in and out of hospital for every infection you could think of, and although I was officially discharged it was some months before I was finally free of the hospitals'. He 'did nothing for about four months. It wasn't terribly long, but I needed the rest.' For all the love and attention of his family, it would in some ways be a lonely time for Alec. Not many of those around him could have understood what he had been through. (A fledgling branch of the Returned Servicemen's League was opened in Launceston later that year.)

While he was recuperating Alec's spirits received an unexpected boost — a postscript to his war service. Out of the blue his parents received a letter from a Colonel Pleasant: it seemed that the kitbag he had lost on the ship home had shown up in one of the army's lost-and-found stores, and this aptly named officer had traced Alec through the letters from Chesney he had carried. The colonel wrote of how lucky he was to have such affectionate little brothers; of the much-prized photograph of nine-year-old Estelle dressed in Campbell tartan, 'he wished he had a little daughter like her'. Touched by his generosity, Marian sent their benefactor a copy of the photo along with a letter thanking him for going to such trouble.

Alec had learned to ride as a young boy at Cressy and had been for a few rides since his return. Towards the end of 1916 he had another stroke of luck when local horse owner Harry von Stieglitz, whose regular jockey was away, invited him to ride his horse Khyber in the Amateur Champion Hunter event at the Launceston Annual Show. Kitted out in his uniform, Alec rode Khyber for all he was worth, winning the race and much acclaim, including a story in the *Examiner*. Things were looking up. In early 1917, perhaps helped by his success at the country race meeting, he landed his first postwar job.

It was a widely held view that returned soldiers who found themselves at a loss could benefit from going bush, where through hard physical work they might better recover from their experiences. Sam, who believed in this form of healing, secured a job for his son on a country property on remote Flinders Island. Perhaps he hoped the isolated location might also help Alec cope with the unpredictable attacks of facial paralysis that caused him such anguish. Sam had travelled to the island in the course of his job. He knew Harold Jeff Walker, of Whitemark, principal farmer, shopkeeper and guesthouse owner in the tiny settlement on Flinders, where travellers were often forced to wait out bad weather. So Alec found himself once more outward-bound, this time on a small trading vessel that two days later deposited him on the tiny island. Harold Walker put Alec to work with his outstation drover, an old bushman called Rainbird.

As a bush drover on Flinders Island Alec rode through country almost as rugged as Gallipoli. The island cattle ranged free in the unfenced scrub, and it was the drovers' job to track and muster these animals into herds using blue heelers and stock whips before driving them to better fattening pastures or yarding them for market. It was, Alec would recall, 'fair dinkum droving'. He rode everywhere, camped out, cooked over an open fire, slept on his swag under the stars and swapped yarns with Rainbird. Alec enjoyed working with the horses in the bush, and in his solitude would recite Paterson's ballad 'Clancy of the Overflow', marvelling at 'the vision splendid of the sunlit plains extended' as he went 'a-droving' down the creeks on Flinders Island.

Sam's plan had been a success. Alec worked well, rebuilt his strength and put the war firmly behind him. Like many soldiers who had worked hard on the battlefield, the former water carrier proved to be very handy on the land. Since Harold practised mixed farming, Alec also gained experience mutton-birding and fattening cattle on unfenced land. But after three months on Flinders Island he became restless. Missing his family, he returned to Launceston, where he learned of the battle over conscription raging through Australia, notably in the staunchly anti-conscription working-class electorates of Launceston. The war had been going badly, and the chronic shortage of soldiers had prompted the government to promote conscription. Labor Party activists and left-wing unions spoke out against the war and clashed with those returned soldiers who sought to persuade voters to support conscription. Meetings were broken up when ex-soldiers scuffled with anti-conscriptionists, who in turn trashed the Town Hall and Trades Hall to disrupt scheduled pro-conscription meetings.

On the mainland, while Billy Hughes pressed for conscription, Catholic Archbishop Daniel Mannix spoke out strongly against it. Former Liberal prime minister Joseph Cook, who toured Tasmania as a conscriptionist, was howled down at meetings, as was pioneer feminist Vida Goldstein, who urged the government not to force young men to enlist. Tasmania's most vocal conscriptionist, Duncan Macrae, who had lost the use of his legs when wounded at Gallipoli and who became a popular platform orator, proposed that 'only those who had felt the blood of a comrade on their faces had a right to talk about conscription'. Macrae's conscriptionists carried the day in Tasmania, where voters supported conscription in both the 1916 and 1917 referendums. At the same time Alec learned of new slaughters in France, where thousands of Anzacs, including Gallipoli veterans he had known, had died in the battles for Bullecourt, Pozières, Passchendaele and Ypres. Later in the year, after the Bolsheviks pulled Russia out of the war, things got even tougher for the Allies. Europe seemed to be going mad, and Alec knew his mates in the 15th Battalion had their work cut out.

Determined that his son should not be caught up in the commotion in town, Sam found him a position as a jackaroo on a sheep station near Campbelltown called 'Streanshalh'. Sam knew the owner, Norman Nicolson, and persuaded him to train Alec in all-round property management so he could one day manage a property of his own. Nicolson gave him 'tea and tucker' and a bunk in the jackaroos' quarters and put him to work. Alec's main job was to ride through the paddocks and check the mobs of grazing sheep, ensuring that they always had access to water in the dams or troughs and had not become bogged or caught up in the fences. He would clip away the wool under their tails so they would not be fly-blown, cutting away the dags to keep them healthy. Alec enjoyed the work more than he had on lonely Flinders Island. He made many country friends and loved the Midland social life and sport, especially riding with the Midland Hunt Club. He became physically stronger, too, and for a while the paralysis disappeared.

In a letter home, Alec sketched out his new life enthusiastically: 'We have been busy this week and will be a lot busier next week. The lambing season has started now. Mr and Mrs Nicolson are going to Sydney for a little while, they are leaving tomorrow. Tell Dad that I did not get his letter till it was too late to answer it, the sample of nails he sent was no good. Mrs Nicolson asked me to thank him for his trouble. My word they are nice people down here. We had about a thousand visitors here this afternoon . . .' Alec jackarooed for more than a year in this idyllic country setting and was still at Streanshalh when the Armistice was declared on 11 November. He could feel proud of the small role he had played in the war, yet the activists who had fought so hard against conscription had started him thinking about the bigger picture: the cost of the Allied victory had been enormous, including 61,720 Australian dead. But people of all opinions could celebrate the end of this terrible blood-letting, and the Launceston community joined similar communities around the world in days of festivities, with impromptu parties in public parks and street processions led by returned soldiers — including Alec, who went to town for the occasion — and featuring service organisations such as the Red Cross.

By the end of the year Alec had left Streanshalh. There seemed little point in learning how to run a station if his family lacked the capital to buy a property. 'I could see that the land was not possible with the limited capital that would have been available to me.' His parents, meanwhile, had invested their savings in a new, ten-room family home, 'Karadi', in Trevallyn, Launceston, with french windows opening onto a wide verandah, a rose garden, a lily and fish pond, and a walk-in aviary with canaries, finches and doves.

A bush horseman who could ride anything, Alec soon became a sought-after jockey in the district. He rode as both an amateur and a professional steeplechase jockey, and won a string of races. In one amateur event, the Midland Hunt Club Cup at Mowbray, he beat his brother Angus, also an up-and-coming jockey, who was riding his own horse, Freeney. As on other, similar occasions, however, Alec's participation as an amateur was controversial, given his professional outings. He also raced a beautiful mare, bought from Arthur Faulkner, manager of the Connorville Estate. Sired by a thoroughbred stallion named 'Brilliant', he named her 'Brilliant Bint' 'because in Egypt the word for young woman was "Bint", which was one of many words Alec had learned while convalescing in Cairo hospitals', Estelle wrote. Like the camels he had ridden when off duty at Mena Camp beneath the pyramids, Brilliant Bint was hard to ride and, Estelle recorded, 'returned home riderless many times after getting rid of Alec while he was trying to teach her to jump in nearby paddocks, forcing the young rider to limp back home on foot. The thoroughbred also bolted once when the returned soldier took a girl friend Marjorie Balfe for a joy ride down Mayne Street, and by the time Alec pulled the horse up the terrified passenger sitting behind him vowed she would never ride with him again.'

While Alec and his siblings enjoyed the healthy air of this country town, the great influenza epidemic spread through the mainland cities. The scourge would claim the lives of more than 11,000 Australians, including some of Alec's comrades in arms, cruelly cut down on board troopships homeward bound from France. In Launceston 50 locals died of the infection in 1919, including their family doctor, Charles Irvine, who would have been more exposed than most. Already laid low by this virus at Gallipoli, Alec survived once more.

The following February Sam and Marian determined to celebrate the twenty-first birthday of their first-born with more than the usual sense of occasion, laying on an open-house dinner at Karadi for family and friends from near and far at which everyone toasted the young man who had already led such an interesting life. By now, though, he had begun to feel held back by his limited range of skills; it was time, he decided, to get some serious qualifications. An initial interest in accounting was thwarted by the lack of available subsidised courses, so the cash-strapped young veteran investigated other professional training options. For a while he could find nothing locally and thought he might have to go bush again. Fortuitously, he remembered his old Scotch College headmaster's encomium to persistence. He persevered. Finally he found a government training scheme for returned soldiers in carpentry that offered him entry into a long-term profession. He trained for a year as a car and wagon builder before finding work as a carpenter. This training was the first step down the long path towards self-improvement that Alec would travel all his life. Once he had mastered one skill he would select a new challenge, teaching himself along the way. He would no longer depend on the goodwill of a station owner, or retreat to some isolated bush property for fear of public attacks of Bell's Palsy. Rejecting self-pity, he seemed to use these attacks as a springboard to set himself greater tests. His daredevil streak saw him take up boxing again. 'Alec never responded negatively to his facial injury,' Kate, his second wife, would say. 'He just turned the other cheek, literally.' Family portraits taken during the 1920s suggest that (perhaps unconsciously) Alec tended to turn the undamaged left side of his face towards the camera. In Kate's view, having escaped death in the war, Alec acquired a special zest for life and a determination to try everything. Over the years, she said, 'he certainly developed greater self-esteem, will power, motivation and energy — physical, mental and sexual. And like many oldest children he never lost his sense of responsibility for himself and others.'

Many returned soldiers suffered torments during the early 1920s as they sought to put the horrors of the trenches behind them and fit back into civilian life. In some cases men who had not volunteered had taken their jobs. Pensions were hard to get. The government had set up a scheme under which 'soldier settler blocks' were granted to returned servicemen as a reward for their war service, but the blocks were often on marginal land that was hard for inexperienced or injured ex-soldiers to manage. Some displaced veterans hung around Launceston's parks. Many took to drink, drowning in self-pity, or (especially those with war injuries) developed a victim mentality. A few chose suicide. But for Alec life was looking up. Later that year he returned to Scotch College for the Old Boys' Athletics Carnival, and despite his small frame and war-weakened condition finished runner-up for the Old Boys' Perpetual Trophy, having come second in the 440 race and third in the 100 yard dash. He also began training seriously for professional boxing fights. Alec and his siblings, known as 'the Sporting Campbells', had enshrined a whole room at Karadi to their enthusiasms, with sporting pictures adorning the walls. The brothers (and even Estelle participated as occasional sparring partner) used it for boxing matches refereed by their father. Whenever the boys' upper cuts or left hooks looked like damaging the teen-aged Estelle, Alec's father would call 'time'. It was in this room that Alec learned the skills that would enable him to compete successfully in professional matches.

In 1920, during his carpentry course, Alec sparred with local professionals such as Algy Daniels until he was ready for the bigger rings of Hobart, where he fought in the bantamweight division, defeating all comers to become bantamweight champion of Tasmania. Completing his course at the end of 1921, he crossed Bass Strait to box on the mainland, earning his keep by working on building sites. Sometimes he fought as an amateur under his own name. As a professional he adopted the pseudonym Pat O'Cahan, after the Irish spelling of his mother's maiden name (O'Keene). He boxed successfully in Melbourne and around Victoria before graduating to Sydney, where he fought nationally against legends such as Striker Clarke, who went on to become Australian champion. A Sydney sportswriter covering the fight was clearly impressed by Alec's win against the heavier, more experienced fighter. 'Clarke had the very great advantage in height, weight and reach and looked big enough to eat Campbell,' he wrote. 'But Campbell is a greatly improved boxer since he was last seen in the National Ring, and both in foot work and head work he excelled last night.' Despite some heavy punishment, 'Alec Campbell took it all and fought back . . . Campbell deserved every credit for his showing against odds that would have knocked all the heart out of a less game fighter.' Alec retired in the mid 1920s with the enviable record of never having been beaten by an opponent of his own weight.

When not fighting, Alec 'built houses, carriages, and boats right around south-eastern Australia in capital cities and smaller towns in South Australia, Victoria and New South Wales'. The carpentry course had launched his career. He was making money from his new trade and enjoying the power it gave him to travel and be his own man. He returned to Launceston with 'a few quid in his back pocket' for Christmas 1922, in good time both for the family celebration and for the players' draw for the following year's football season. But something far more momentous now occurred that made the boxing carpenter come to his senses — or rather lose them completely. Alec fell in love with a woman who, he would always say, 'was so beautiful she took my breath away', and he knew if he could only win her hand he would have kicked the biggest goal of his short life.

It happened after an Australian Rules game with the Longford team at Beaconsfield, north of Launceston, when Alec and his team-mates called into the local Exchange Hotel for a well-earned drink. Across the bar his eyes met those of the publican's daughter, Kathleen Connolly, who had been watching the game and was now helping her father serve drinks in the country pub. Alec would always maintain it was love at first sight. Having introduced himself, the young footballer promised to return in more respectable attire if she would be kind enough to see him again. With his new-found funds from the mainland, he had bought himself a motorbike complete with sidecar — tailor-made, he thought, for dating. During 1923 he began courting Kathleen, his hopes rising with each date.

Alec was now 24 years old, Kathleen 20, going on 21. Tall and slim with fair skin, a strong, well-sculpted, animated and open face, and twinkling blue eyes framed by straight, jet black hair, she was a striking woman. One of six children, she had also experienced the best of two worlds, having grown up on orchards around her father's hotel and gone to school at St. Mary's in Hobart. She had always had her own pony and rode well. Naturally musical, she also played the piano beautifully. Alec had picked one of the most beautiful and intelligent women in the Launceston district, yet the precocious young man might also have picked a fight. Her father, Tom Connolly, was a fervent, tough-talking Catholic and a man of some power and influence. Tom Connolly had always been a man of property, running the popular Beaconsfield pub while owning several houses. An argumentative Catholic, he had a reputation for getting his own way. One of the jokes around Beaconsfield ran: Question: What is the quickest way to get to Launceston Hospital? Answer: Tell Tom Connolly the Pope is a bloody idiot!

But the Gallipoli veteran was a risk taker. As a professional boxer who had defeated every challenger, he was forceful and determined. As a man of the world who had no doubt tasted the carnal delights of backstreets Cairo, he was one of the faster young bucks in Launceston, and he delighted in taking the publican's daughter for rides in his fancy motorbike and sidecar. Since most Tasmanians still relied on horses, and even the local ambulance service had switched to motorised transport only that year, these rides must have made an impression on the relatively inexperienced Kathleen, who had worked as a shop assistant in Launceston and Hobart chemists, and whose biggest adventure to date had been crossing Bass Strait for a working holiday in Melbourne. Alec was also earning more money now. Wages had improved under the new state Labor government led by the self-made Joe Lyons, committed to helping the working man. The persistent suitor took Kathleen to the new Majestic Theatre in Launceston's Brisbane Street, to the Theatre Royal and to Saturday night dances at the Albert Hall. Here he would have put into practice Miss Amy Barnard's half-forgotten instruction as he waltzed the night away with his new partner. Although family legend claims she often danced with her brother Jack, who had a better sense of rhythm, once the new music of the roaring twenties reached Launceston the traditional steps were largely cast aside. Alec threw himself into the charleston, the syncopated rhythms of the jazz tunes of Charlie Jackson and shimmy-shaking to the most popular tune of 1923, 'I Wish I Could Shimmy Like My Sister Kate'. And with the arrival of radio, which soon began broadcasting the new tunes, he had plenty of opportunities to practise between the organised dances.

On their late-night trips back to Beaconsfield there were, of course, plenty of opportunities for wayside rest stops, where the well-prepared Anzac was sure to have picnic rug and thermos of hot coffee at the ready. Inevitably, after a year or so their luck ran out, or rather fate stepped in and made a decision for them. By the end of April 1924 Kathleen was pregnant. As good Catholics, the couple had no alternative but to confess all to their parents. Given the strict moral code of the fragile community, still licking its wounds after the war, this would not have been easy.

Fortunately, Tom Connolly loved big families and, seeing this development as marking the start of another branch of the family tree, he gave his blessing. Alec was handsome, with an honest and open face (at this stage mercifully free from the disfiguring effects of paralysis); he had a trade, always had work, came from a good family and was well liked around town; he was also a talented boxer and footballer, and had even served his king and country. Only a year earlier the Prince of Wales, during a visit to Launceston to unveil the town's new statue of his father, had congratulated the local lads for rallying to the mother country's cause. The *Examiner* had carried a lengthy piece on the Prince's remarks. Alec might even have mentioned to his prospective father-in-law that he had already seen the Prince of Wales in Egypt. At about this time, too, a war memorial to Alec's fallen comrades was opened in Royal Park. Perhaps Tom and Sam met and discussed the problem over a Guinness in the back bar at the Exchange. In any case, Alec soon did the right thing by the young woman he loved. Alec and Kathleen were married in 1924 at the Church of the Apostles,

Launceston, in a quiet ceremony of which there is no surviving photographic record. Officiating was Father Peter Adlum, who subsequently formed a long-standing friendship with Estelle. After a country honeymoon on the motorbike the newlyweds returned to Alec's parents to await the birth. Relying on wages earned from Alec's casual building work and some small savings, they slept on the enclosed verandah at 20 Claremont Street, which would be their first home as a married couple. Here Kathleen enjoyed the support of Alec's mother, Marian, the vastly experienced mother of five.

The marriage, a fine blending of Scottish malt and Irish stout, brought together two extraordinary individuals who would achieve much over the next 30 years. Indeed, they and their offspring would become almost unrecognisable to those they would leave behind in Launceston. Their first child arrived later that year, on 30 December, and was named Caithlean Estelle but nicknamed Sam (after her grandfather) by family friend Dr George Clemons, who delivered her at Launceston Hospital.

In 1925 Alec worked as a carpenter on building sites around Launceston, using his mainland experience to secure work. At a time when all trades had become unionised, he joined the Amalgamated Carpenters and Joiners Union. Inspired by the apparent success of the Bolshevik Revolution in Russia and the foundation of the Communist Party of Australia in 1920, a new spirit of radicalism had begun to move Australian workers — that year the Seamen's Union shut down ports around Australia to win better pay and conditions. Initially Alec found sufficient work on new local building projects such as St George's Church in Invermay Street and the new post office in Cameron Street. Still, they were lucky that Marian was there to help out, because late that year Kathleen became pregnant again. Another girl, Cressey, was born in June 1926.

It was the year of the General Strike in Britain. Local unions were becoming more militant, and strikes were on the rise. Conservative Launceston employers, who disliked this new mood, reacted by making it harder for tradesmen to find work. With the closure of local mines, Launceston's economy began to slow, while competition for jobs increased. Now with three new mouths to feed, Alec for the first time understood personally how much tradesmen depended on the whim of employers. His growing family responsibilities alerted him to the value of the unions. Economic conditions in Launceston worsened. More factories closed and more unions struck. Alec needed to earn more money. He had read of a building site in a paddock somewhere between Melbourne and Sydney, where the federal government was setting up the new national capital, to be called Canberra, and where builders, carpenters and tradesmen were needed. So in the winter of 1926 Alec, along with Kathleen and their two babies, crossed Bass Strait, traded the motorbike for a T Model Ford and drove cross-country to the site. The young family moved into a camp in the bush where the new capital was being built. He was especially pleased to learn that building unions had negotiated basic wages, and he immediately joined the Builders Workers' Industrial Union. It was a year of national strikes led by the Seamen's Union and the Waterside Workers' Federation (the coal and timber workers' unions walked out the following year). The newspapers carried reports from Britain of the working-class struggle to win better wages and conditions. The lessons learned during the General Strike were not lost on Australian unions, who the following year established the Australian Council of Trade Unions to protect the rights of workers.

Alec worked as a carpenter on the construction of Parliament House and on homes to accommodate the future residents of Canberra. With his experience working on foundations, walls and roofs on building sites around South Australia, Victoria and Launceston, Alec was a highly valued tradesman, and he was in his element. He found himself working round the clock while Kathleen looked after the children in the nearby tent village. Naturally, with such a large-scale project, mistakes were made. Once he was working with a group of Finnish builders who spoke no English but loved pouring concrete at speed. One day in their enthusiasm they poured concrete down a chimney before Alec could explain the need for the plumbers to first install the fluepipe, with the result that the entire chimney was filled with solid concrete. Alec would often wonder how the proud purchasers of the new house would react when they first tried to light a fire in that chimney.

On 9 May 1927 Alec and Kathleen, with Sam and Cressey in tow, attended the big opening ceremony for Parliament House at which the Duke and Duchess of York officiated. From the paddock opposite the entrance they watched the royal couple arrive by motorcar to a red carpet welcome before disappearing into the grand new building, heard the great opera singer Dame Nellie Melba sing the national anthem on the front steps and enjoyed the refreshments provided for the workers. With ambitious plans for the new federal capital, more work was promised, but Kathleen was now heavily pregnant again. Along with other workers and their families, they had only a rented tent for shelter. Conditions in the open paddock were not as bad as Alec's dugout under Hill 971, but even here water was a problem, and with only one tap between a number of tents and hole-in-the-ground toilets shared with other workmen's families, life was hard for Kathleen. The blowflies were terrible and the extreme heat in summer and bitter winter conditions compounded their hardships. Alec had heard that a number of new factories were to be established in Launceston for the manufacture of car parts, knitwear, locks and even tennis rackets made from Tasmanian timber. Woollen mills were also planned, and carpenters were needed to build these premises. Launceston was evidently booming. They decided to head home.

Alec drove their unreliable Model T back down the rudimentary backcountry roads to Melbourne, where they caught the ferry to Launceston. Back at Claremont Street they took up their old quarters in the enclosed verandah, where Marian helped Kathleen prepare for the birth of her third child, Gregor (always called Greg), who was born on 25 September 1927. The family was now far too large to camp out on the verandah, so they spent what little they had brought back from Canberra on renting a cottage in Doolan

Street, Invermay. By now most of the carpentry jobs had been taken, so to help pay the rent the adaptable Alec took a temporary job as a conductor on the Launceston trams. Between 1927 and 1931 Launceston Municipal Transport expanded its service from 26 to 29 trams (including three bogies). Since these bogies had to be built locally, Alec hoped for a vacancy in the workshops. The new trams were to be in regular service by 1931, so he thought it would only be a matter of time before a tradesman of his experience was needed. The local government was also duplicating lines and extending network services and route mileage every year.

By chance they were back in town for one of its biggest public events in years as air ace H. J. 'Bert' Hinkler, a pioneering aviator who had served in the Royal Flying Corps during the war, dropped (literally) into Launceston. Fresh from his triumphant solo flight from England to Australia (he was the first flyer to achieve this, and did so in a record time of 15½ days), he landed at Elphin Show-grounds, where Alec, Kathleen and their three children were among the 10,000 spectators gathered to welcome the hero of the skies. This event was the earliest childhood memory for Sam, then four, who would recall they were so inspired by the airman that Alec named their next high-flying rooster after him!

In 1928 Alec and Kathleen had their best stroke of luck to date when her brother Jack gave the young couple £20 to put down on their own house. Jack, who was still single, had been cutting cane in far north Queensland and had returned to Launceston with a fistful of banknotes. Losing no time, Alec and Kate bought a house in Kings Meadows, on the outskirts of Launceston. It was still a rural area then, with open paddocks, cows, horses, fowl yards, orchards and vegetable patches. Surrounded by poultry and dairy farms, the house was a perfect place to bring up a young family. The deposit of £20 was a quarter of the full price, so they were already well on the way to owning their first home — a goal strongly recommended by Kathleen's parents. They called the house 'Glen Roy', after the farm in Cressy of which Alec had such happy childhood memories. Alec himself was healthier than ever, the Bell's Palsy troubling him little in these years.

Since he now had a mortgage to pay, he used his Tramways contacts to secure a permanent job. With no vacancies in the Tramways workshops in Howick Street, he sought a transfer to the much bigger and safer state rail authority, the Tasmanian Government Railways, and found work as a car and wagon builder in the Launceston Railway Workshops. Owned and operated by the government, the TGR in 1928 offered the kind of security they needed with a growing family and a mortgage. Sam remembers her father's advice that the securest jobs were with the government, because they tended to last no matter how bad times got. It was advice that she and others among their children would themselves later heed.

Alec and Kathleen were fortunate not to have bought in the low-lying town centre, which along with many other areas of Tasmania was badly flooded in 1929. When the Tamar River rose dramatically, the post office rang its bell to warn the townspeople to evacuate, but thousands were trapped. Emergency services helped 4,000 people to safety, housing them in temporary shelter until the floodwaters subsided. It was the worst flood in the town's history, with more than 1,000 Launceston homes wrecked, although a relief committee would raise a remarkable £116,000 to help during the crisis. With the railway workshops submerged, Alec found himself temporarily out of work. Like many other, similarly affected families, the Campbells were issued flood relief food coupons, and until the workshops reopened Alec volunteered for clean-up work. This local crisis would seem insignificant in comparison with the troubles ahead, however, for in 1930, following the previous year's Wall Street stock-market crash, the Great Depression hit Australia. One-third of the Australian workforce would lose their jobs, and many their homes, in the succeeding years. With three young children and a mortgage, and with Kathleen already pregnant with their fourth child, one 30-year-old temporary railway worker was about to enter the toughest period of his life.

CHAPTER 11
FIGHTING FOR THE POOR IN THE GREAT DEPRESSION

'I returned to Tasmania in 1927 and was lucky enough to get a job as a 'Car & Wagon Builder' in the Launceston Railway Workshops.'

The Great Depression would radicalise Alec, transforming him into a socialist union leader committed to political, economic and social reforms on behalf of workers. The difficulties he and Kathleen experienced feeding their growing family as the Depression deepened propelled him into the labour movement, and changed him forever. He had joined the building workers' union in Canberra in 1926. With the apparent collapse of capitalism in the early 1930s and the daily struggle of Australian workers to survive, he could see there was a lot more work to be done, and as a family man he himself had too much at stake to leave this work to others.

He secured his new job as a car and wagon builder with the Launceston Railway Workshops by joining the Australian Railways Union. From the outset he took an active interest in union affairs. With Alec earning the family's sole income, the resilient couple applied extraordinary levels of energy and resourcefulness. As each new crisis arose they worked out a way around it. Politically, Alec changed with the times, reassessing his values and re-educating himself in order to understand the economic and political crisis and to build a career based on addressing these problems. Kathleen rose to the challenge, growing with Alec and becoming a true kindred spirit. They made a formidable pair.

By December 1929 Australian economists were predicting a long-term slump. The federal government had relied on borrowing £30 million a year from Britain. Now it could no longer raise these loans, and without the capital injection, the newspapers predicted, the national income would drop by ten per cent. Export prices had already fallen on the world market, and as investment funds dried up, private companies began to go bankrupt. The election that year had ushered in the federal Labor government of James Scullin, who promised that he and his ministers 'would get right down to hard work and apply ourselves to the serious problems confronting the nation'. But despite Scullin's efforts (among other measures, Labor built protective import tariffs to record levels and took the economy off the gold standard), economic conditions worsened throughout Australia, especially in isolated and vulnerable Tasmania. Much of the state had been stagnating even before the Depression started. Since federation 38,000 people, representing one-fifth of the population, had left for work on the mainland. Now, as businesses went bankrupt in Launceston, commercial trading dropped by one-third. In November that year Kathleen delivered their fourth child, Mary — her first home birth — at Glen Roy. After a bad experience with Greg at Launceston Hospital, Kathleen had decided to have all future children at home.

One year into the Depression and the worst unemployment predictions had been realised, with 20 per cent of the workforce out of a job. Many turned to the government's newly established unemployment relief program, tagged the 'Susso', which provided basic sustenance. Two of Alec's brothers, Colin and Angus, lost their jobs and had to return to the rent-free family home, where they waited out the Depression. Colin would not find work again until he joined the Army at the outbreak of the Second World War. Many men went bush, humping their swag and chasing dreams as 'sundowners'. In

Melbourne the Labor Party and the union movement called meetings to launch an 'anti-starvation crusade'. In Launceston the labour movement held meetings at the railway workshops at Invermay, which became a hothouse of political debate where workers deliberated on the worsening social situation and argued over possible solutions. These meetings opened Alec's eyes to the ideas behind social and political activism.

Alec was lucky to have a safe job at the workshops. After the war Tasmanian Railways had 80 locomotives based at the depot. In 1921 the state government unveiled a plan to create a gigantic workshop to build both engines and carriages for Tasmania's growing rail industry, and the large complex of concrete buildings grew out of this idea. Built to the latest design, with a sophisticated roundhouse and rotating platform that could handle engines of any size, they were the largest railway workshops in the southern hemisphere and had an enviable reputation. They were also a local institution. For a skilled tradesman who loved working with his hands, helping to build carriages and fashioning decorative woodwork and trimmings for the exteriors and interiors gave Alec great creative satisfaction. Trained in motor body building, he also built the wooden frames for the carriages. He worked on a range of carriages and rolling stock including 'butter boxes', railcars, driver's cabins and trailers.

Already the home of Tasmanian unionism, the Launceston workshops became a cauldron of socialism as the new generation grappled with the implications of the Depression. With as many as 1,500 tradesmen concentrated in a single industrial workplace, there were plenty of opportunities to talk politics, debate issues, circulate union publications and other political material, attend mass meetings and shape new ideas. Through his membership of the ARU, a union with a proud tradition stretching back to long before federation, Alec was part of this political nursery.

In time he became an active member of the ARU, seizing every opportunity to teach himself about unionism in the new industrial world. He attended all the meetings he could and offered his services in administrative and organisational roles, initially helping with the ARU's strike for 'a sixpenny pay rise'. Typically, he used the union to pull himself up. In this he was part of a trend among ambitious workingmen of the time: John Curtin and Ben Chifley (Chifley came up through the ranks of the ARU-associated Locomotive Enginemen's Union) were two activists who had progressed through the unions and the Labor Party and would become prime ministers during the following decade. All this new activity evidently provided a health bonus too, since despite the heavier workload Alec was less troubled by attacks of Bell's Palsy or other illness during the thirties than at any other time in his life.

There was no shortage of issues to debate at the mass meetings at the workshops. The Labor government seemed not to know how to halt the economic downturn. (Scullin invited out a British financial expert, Otto Niemeyer, who advised him to curb spending, devalue the Australian pound and force the states to adopt a draconian 'Premiers' Plan' for getting through the Depression by tightening the public belt.) In Tasmania the conservative Nationalist Party premier, John McPhee, who had ousted Labor's Joe Lyons the previous year, also appeared to have few answers. With reductions in government spending, public revenue also dried up as fewer people paid taxes. Export prices for wool, wheat and other vital primary products had crashed to record lows, as had exports themselves. Tasmania's export prices fell to half their 1928 levels. Despite 'a large deficiency of railway receipts due to the depression itself', however, the government kept the railways going.

At Glen Roy Kathleen, now in her late twenties, with four children and another on the way, managed to put food on the table by working day and night, herself growing and making almost everything they needed. Alec's oldest son, Greg, insists it was his mother who really carried the family through these years. As Greg recalls, they ran their lives according to the ideas of English social philosopher William Cobbett, who advocated self-sufficiency in all aspects of life, and his father and mother referred constantly to this manual. It was just as well, as the Commonwealth Financial Emergency Act then reduced the maternity allowance for mothers — particularly those whose husbands were still earning. 'By now Mum was a dab hand at growing all the vegetables, fruit and potatoes in the garden and picked them when ready, young and tasty,' Sam recounts. 'She grew broad beans, peas, carrots, potatoes, blackberries, plums, and raspberries — absolutely everything we needed — and also milked the cow and made the butter, cream and also the bread as well as a range of jams. She could create soup out of anything. She also fed the chooks and collected the eggs and with Alec's help killed, gutted, plucked and prepared the chickens for the table. But the mammoth task was cooking three meals a day seven days a week for such a big family.' Without Kathleen's fruit and vegetable growing the family could not have made ends meet. This flourishing country home must have reminded Alec of his Cressy days.

'The bath was in a large shed out the back called the "Pig & Whistle" with a wooden floor and fireplace,' Sam recalls. 'On Saturday afternoons we jumped in one after the other using the same water from our tank, or to save time we bathed two and three at a session, sharing the soap that Mum made. I remember the bath was on legs and of very good enamel. On washday the copper was filled with water through a short length of hose and a fire was lit underneath with small kindling that Mum chopped up. All the clothes were put in with washing soda and pieces of soap. As the clothes slowly came to the boil we had to poke and prod them with a thick wooden poker to move them around and dislodge the dirt. The clothes were then dipped out, rinsed, blued and wrung out by hand before being hung out on the clothes line down the back paddock. It took mother all day to wash because one boiling was never enough. There was so much cleaning to be done too, as all the wooden floors had to be washed and the kitchen scrubbed with a brush and sand soap.'

With no money for a car, let alone petrol, Mary recalls, Alec 'went to work very early in the morning on the bicycle, and it was a long trip, about three miles and then back again at night. Launceston is a very frosty, foggy place and it must have been an unpleasant bike trip. He had to get to work early because he was a carriage builder, laying down foundations for carriages, and he used to come home with his fingers bleeding from the hard work, and Mum used to bathe his fingers for him.' Greg remembers him once riding his bike to the local hospital with a severed artery. 'Dad was killing our pet pig in the slaughter house for the table when the knife slipped, cutting his left wrist, and I remember the blood shooting out across the floor to the other side of the room. Dropping the knife with a yell, he ran inside, stopping the blood with his right hand and screaming for Mum. She put a tourniquet on his arm in ten seconds flat and he jumped on his bike and rode off to the local hospital to get the wound sewn up.'

'As a father,' Mary says, 'he was very enthusiastic. He was quite strict, never soft about anything. He wanted everyone to do whatever they were capable of, all of us, even in the Depression. Particularly with the boys — he wanted them to do what they were physically capable of. He was never sentimental. He was eager and conscientious and all those sorts of things, but he never sentimentalised. And in his spare time he always seemed to be building an extension to the house for the next child.' In tune with these fighting times, he 'took his gloves off the shed wall from time to time and taught workers at the Launceston Railway Workshops how to box. Back then boxing was known as the manly art of self-defence. There was a different attitude to boxing in those days. It was quite highly thought of and was taught at private schools. Dad gave up boxing on the professional circuit only because Mum made this a condition of their marriage.'

In addition to the fervent political discussions at work, Alec would talk endlessly at the kitchen table with Kathleen, who was clearly his intellectual equal. Sam remembers debates on such disparate topics as the life of Jesus Christ; the reasons why different nationalities, especially Germans, had different-shaped heads; and the relationship between the Indo-European languages and English. The children listened, spellbound, when Alec passed on the stories of their warrior forebears, the Argyll Campbells, that he had learned from his grandfather.

Kathleen's fifth baby, Jim, was born towards the end of the second year of the Depression, in November 1931. Despite the extra stress of another mouth to feed, Cressey remembers only the joy of each new child: 'The delight of a new babe in the family was always a highlight. There was a feeling of great expectation throughout the home, the nursing sister made frequent visits and she and Mum laughed and gently talked over a pot of tea and biscuits together. After the new baby was born in Mum and Dad's room, eventually all would be in readiness for our return and we would be taken one at a time into the main bedroom and Mum, smiling from the bed, would hold out her arms to each of us and give us a big hug and kiss and allow us to stroke the little black head of the babe in the bassinette beside her.' In financial terms, however, Jim could not have come at a worse time, as the federal government had just cut the basic wage by ten per cent. The ARU attended a national congress of unions called by the ACTU to fight the cut, but after heated debate the unions caved in, opting to accept the reduction. There was not much they could do about it in Tasmania, where the increasingly popular conservative premier was especially hostile to the unions, the Right was in the ascendant and support for Labor had dropped to an all-time low. The 1931 state election was about to provoke the most violent public confrontations in the state's history, as the pent-up emotions of both ends of the political spectrum were unleashed. It was all Alec could do to keep out of the conflict, and ultimately he did so only because his fellow Anzacs were targeted by the extreme Left.

The frustrations of the Depression changed the political landscape in Australia. Old groupings collapsed and new associations emerged to contend with the economic and social fallout. Galvanised by the apparent success of socialism in Russia, the Left formed communist fronts around the country, while some returned soldiers were drawn to militant splinter groups like the sinister New Guard. In Tasmania the 1931 state election campaign featured running battles between fascist right-wingers determined to defend a discredited status quo and hard-line communists, who sought to dismantle the capitalist system and replace it with a socialist state that controlled the means of production and would distribute goods and services to all according to their needs rather than their ability to pay. The 'Reds' attacked the old order, especially Australia's ties to imperial Britain, which was now demanding repayment of its loans. They also attacked Anzacs who had 'been stupid enough to serve this empire' at Gallipoli and in France. When the communists disrupted campaign meetings the right-wingers urged veterans out into the streets to teach them a lesson.

Alec was at an ideological crossroads. He knew he had to choose once and for all which side he was on. He had believed in the idea of serving king and country back in 1915, but he had been only 16 then, half his life ago. Since then, and lacking capital of his own, he had consciously abandoned the ambition of running a cattle or sheep station and taken up a trade. Most of his old army chums and employers were political reactionaries; his parents were themselves middle-class conservatives. But he had drifted away from his political roots, and the labour movement had served him well. He could not go back. He had learned so much through the union, saw how the capitalist system had failed working people, including two of his brothers, and was convinced that the time had come to consider the socialist alternative. Alec was never a communist, or even a sympathiser, but he saw the sense of socialist economic theory as opposed to the ideas of the extreme Right. That the means of production be kept in state hands, with the country's wealth distributed according to need rather than profit, seemed to him manifestly just and right. Yet as a returned soldier he was being called upon to stand with the reactionaries. His heart was with the Labor Party, but they were failing in Canberra (in the 1931 election they were to record their lowest vote ever). In the end Alec simply kept a low profile in this fight, distancing himself from the conservative Anzacs but also from the extreme Left, opting to bide his time until the union-based Labor Party could be rebuilt.

The bitterly fought 1931 state election was won comfortably by the Nationalist incumbent, John McPhee, after a campaign in which the communists disrupted many public meetings and ultimately sabotaged the Labor vote. The Right brought together a coalition of Nationalist and Country Party members supported by returned soldiers and church groups; the Left was represented by communists, the unemployed and the revolutionary United Workers' Movement, led by Launceston radicals William Daft and Adam White, committed to bringing down the capitalist system. The communists argued that capitalism would never solve the problems of´the Depression. The UWM formed a group called the Workers' Defence Corps, committed to attacking 'spineless unions' such as the ARU; blocking attempts by the government to set up 'concentration camps', as they dubbed the bush camps for unmarried men forced to work on government projects; securing 'real jobs' for the unemployed; and preventing employers from 'treating workers like convicts'. Staunchly working-class Launceston became a battleground, with frequent brawling between the polarised factions.

For Alec the conflict came to a head on Anzac Day 1931, when the communists led by Daft and White flew red flags from their headquarters and distributed revolutionary propaganda leaflets in which they attacked the monarchy, the capitalist system and those who had fought in the imperialist Great War. An incensed group of returned soldiers and military trainees, singing the national anthem, marched on the headquarters, tore down the red flags, seized the leaflets and attacked the communists. A week later, when the communists marched through Launceston watched by 2,000 spectators, 300 returned soldiers waded into the column, tearing up the leaflets that attacked 'subservient soldiers' who had 'served the Empire and its capitalist arms manufacturers' in the war. The communists later vandalised trees planted in memory of fallen Anzacs and desecrated plaques and memorials to the war dead. It was too much for Alec.

After listening to the heated discussions at his workplace during the election campaign, Alec decided he needed to learn more about the competing economic theories behind the street fighting. The decision was vintage Alec Campbell. He joined the fledgling local Workers' Educational Association, where he and Kathleen would attend classes for years. Founded in Australia by Albert Mansbridge during the First World War, the WEA provided self-improvement classes for the working class. By the 1930s it had learning centres in all states run through extramural university departments. Alec and Kathleen were in good company. The Tasmanian association was led by educationist William Judd and supported by visiting academics including economists Douglas Copland and James Brigden; biologist Theodore Thomson; H. H. Scott, the curator of the Queen Victoria Museum and a versatile lecturer in the natural sciences; and Archibald Meston, an educationist who laid the foundations of modern historical research in northern Tasmania. Diverse future leaders in Launceston and the state owed much to these lectures. The WEA also set up a Field Naturalists Club for guided outdoor excursions, a Microscopical Society in which amateur scientists conducted experiments; a royal society; and literary groups that met regularly to read plays and stage amateur theatrical productions.

Alec was such a diligent student, especially of economic theory, that before long he became a tutor and later a lecturer and essayist for the WEA. He bought a copy of Marx's *Das Kapital* to discover for himself the fundamentals of socialist economics. 'Dad used to do a lot of lecturing,' Mary says. 'Mum used to write WEA courses and articles and short stories. Dad also used to give talks to the WEA — they were both very active. Dad was not a fist thumper but was exceedingly charming. He had amazing charm! Their political ideas were fairly radical, compared with what people feel about unionism and education now. I think they thought education was the answer to everything. But he was not abrasive at all.' Alec toured Tasmania to assess the demand for WEA centres in other parts of the state. He also organised and conducted classes at the Launceston Trades Hall for his fellow unionists. This educational work provided the grounding for the economics degree he later gained from the University of Tasmania.

In 1932, however, the political pendulum swung further to the right at the very time Alec was embracing the political theories of the left. Nearly one-third of the labour force had now lost their jobs, and the voters had taken a right turn in desperation. Former Labor premier Joe Lyons, who had formed the new right-wing United Australian Party, had defeated Scullin's federal Labor government. Having supported Lyons as Labor premier, Alec never forgave the 'turncoat' for deserting the federal Labor Party, neither could he respect Lyons' conservative policies at a time when the Right was becoming more extreme. At the grand opening of the Sydney Harbour Bridge the fanatically anti-communist New Guard carried off a propaganda masterstroke. As Labor premier Jack Lang was about to declare the bridge open, an active New Guard member, Captain Francis de Groot, burst on horseback through the crowd and sliced through the official ribbon with a cavalry sword 'in the name of decent citizens of New South Wales'. Subsequently the conservative Governor, Sir Philip Game, sacked Lang when the premier refused to pay back the interest on state loans from Britain. Returned soldiers were urged to join 'civil patrols' to round up communists. To Alec and his ARU colleagues it must have seemed that Australian democracy itself was under threat.

Now in the fourth year of the Depression, with Alec's reduced wage and the maternity allowance cut still further, Kathleen found she was pregnant again. But the day before Anzac Day 1933, a month after their sixth child, Geraldine, was born, Alec received good news at work: he was to receive a partial restoration of wages from the TGR following a federal Arbitration Court decision in May, and there were promises of more to come. The worst of the depression seemed to be over. There were even new opportunities for thrifty shopping when Tasmanian-based C. J. Coles, who had started his grocery business in Wilmot in 1910, opened a store in

Launceston that year. In the preceding years, with few people able to afford train travel, the railways had been progressively run down. Many of the older engines should have been scrapped a decade before, and a serious shortage of locomotive power was imminent. The increased wages bill ironically only made it harder for the railways to make a profit. Private trucks and buses and the improved road network offered faster, more flexible alternative forms of transport and delivery. Alec joined a committee of the TGR and ARU to rebuild and revitalise the railway network through tourism.

In 1934 the basic wage was restored in full, with a further increase promised as the recovery continued. It must have seemed a miracle to Alec and Kathleen, now feeding six children. They had brought their growing family through the worst economic collapse in Australian history. Unlike his brothers Mac and Col, the adaptable survivor was never out of work during the tough times of the Depression. For the past four years Alec's brothers had earned no more than pocket money by breeding dogs and horses in the next paddock. 'But everyone was poor in the Depression,' Mary recalls. 'We all went around in bare feet, and Mum used to make blankets out of old clothes. We wore clothes made out of recycled material and used flour bags sewn round the edges for tea towels. Yet whenever people came to the door selling things Mum would give them a cup of tea, as everyone was poor. Everyone knew that the Depression was on and none of the houses were painted and everything was very drab. But it was the Depression that made Dad very conscious of social justice. The Depression seemed to him so unfair — it turned people like him off capitalism. They assumed that capitalism had failed and they were looking for something new, something that wouldn't fail.'

It seemed to Alec that he had after all backed the right political horse for the long term. The Depression, right-wing political control and extremist movements of all persuasions seemed to have blown away like puffs of cloud, at least in Tasmania. Following a hard-fought campaign in which Alec and Kathleen were actively involved,

Labor won government under the dynamic and imaginative Albert Ogilvie, ushering in a long period of continuous Labor government in the state. In time Alec would throw himself into this work too.

He now earned the same as he had before the economic collapse of 1930 and could put more food on the table at Glen Roy. He also benefited from the first minor 'prosperity increase' loading on the federal basic wage. TGR revenues grew further after the federal government introduced legislation enabling more overseas passenger liners to visit Tasmania. With TGR's support, the Ogilvie government created a state tourist bureau, opening offices in all mainland states aimed at attracting tourists to the island. They also introduced a scheme to encourage school excursions by rail. One of Ogilvie's ministers, Robert Cosgrove, began meeting with the ARU in 1934 to discuss rail transport for unemployed men still experiencing the impact of the Depression.

It had been years since the family had had money for anything besides food necessities, but in 1935 they could at last afford a holiday. With this day in mind, Alec built his first boat, a Snipe dinghy, for a trip through the waterways near Beauty Point. It was a holiday worth waiting for, Mary recalls. 'He loved building, and the tools he used, and just the experience of building something. So he built this boat in the old shed out the back. He found the keel when we went up the bush and found a big she-oak that had a good keel in it. And he cut that down and brought it back and made it into a keel. Then we got a holiday cottage, just a sort of shed and we used to swim and play in the sand and that sort of thing, have ice creams. Dad was great on holidays, fabulous fun. He used to play with us, teach us to swim, go for walks with us — whatever else we used to do. We didn't do anything very sophisticated.' Alec used life as a teaching experience for his children. Cressey remembers her father insisting on rowing all nine of them in the dinghy up the Tamar River to the heads to show them where it flowed into the sea. 'Mum kept saying, "You can't do it on your own. There are too many of us. The tide will come back in against us. You'll kill yourself. Let's get

out and walk," but Dad just kept on and on rowing, saying he had
to finish the job, and after about five miles we got close enough to
have a look and he proved his point. If you start something, you've
got to finish it. Mind you, his hands were raw and bleeding, with
flesh peeling off.' He also taught them honesty, Cressey says, by
leaving a money bag on a nail behind the kitchen door for all of
them to put their pocket money into to be spent on holidays. 'And
despite the Depression, and none of us ever having any money,
nobody ever took money out of that bag. So when we got to Beauty
Point we all shared it equally. Dad and Mum gave us a really lovely
childhood.' Later that year the state governor, Sir Ernest Clark,
visited Launceston to open the new Pioneer Avenue, with trees
dedicated to early settlers such as Donald Campbell and James
Brumby. The governor planted the first in an avenue of trees down
the highway that would eventually link Launceston to Hobart. Alec
and his family took the opportunity to celebrate their pioneer
forebears and Scottish heritage.

In 1937 a poliomyelitis epidemic crossed to Tasmania from the
mainland, and to cope with the crisis the government fast-tracked
the building of the Queen Victoria Hospital. Alec and Kathleen were
determined to keep their six vulnerable young children isolated
from other children who might be carriers of the highly infectious
disease. With their usual keen survival instinct, they sent the
children up to a cottage at Beauty Point, keeping them away from
school until the worst of the crisis was over. It proved to be a wise
strategy, as some of their neighbours' children contracted the
disease and were affected by it for the rest of their lives.

Alec had begun putting in more time with the ARU, which had
helped carry many of its members through the hard times. He took
on secretarial and administrative work, all the while grooming himself for higher office. This increased the workload for both parents,
since it also meant that he spent less time at home. Often he would
get home late at night after a long evening meeting, and this left the
already hardworking Kathleen with more and more on her plate. By

the end of 1937 he was helping the union president handle the day-to-day log of claims, formulate policy and run the union. It was a good apprenticeship, but it meant he was working longer hours than ever. In order to spend more time at home, Alec began bringing his fellow unionists home for dinner, and this had the added benefit of acquainting Kathleen with the political issues of the day.

With the railways themselves under increasing economic threat, the work was critical. Since the Depression had lifted, the popularity of road transport had soared and the ARU had many jobs to protect. Freight loads were still much reduced since so many industries had gone out of business, and private trucks were hauling far greater loads on the improved roads. Although tourist numbers had increased by more than one-third since 1934, the railways were still languishing. Crises such as the polio epidemic (which had halted excursions by schoolchildren) and a damaging coal strike had further undermined profitability. Losses sustained by Tasmanian Railways were 30 per cent higher than when Alec had first joined them. It looked like the heyday of rail was over, and Alec's future did not seem as bright as it had. That year he helped fight for the railways' survival, working on a review of the sector initiated by Premier Ogilvie.

With six children under 15 years of age, Alec's job at TGR and his union work, and Kathleen's daunting domestic responsibilities, not to mention their WEA and other interests, they had never been busier. Nevertheless, in July 1938 they learned that Kathleen was pregnant again. This 'afterthought' child could not have arrived at a more frantic time. By the following year Alec would be running one of the most powerful unions in the state, as well as the Trades Hall Council. And then war broke out.

CHAPTER 12
PRESIDENT CAMPBELL ENTERS POLITICS

*'I was interested in the Railways Union and became President in 1938–39.
I was also interested in the Adult Education Movement and organized
classes at the Launceston Trades Hall.'*

In 1938 Alec got his first major break in the union movement
when he was elected for a two-year term as president of the
state council of the Australian Railways Union in Tasmania. He
now led one of the most powerful industrial organisations in the state
at a time of great political tensions. It would have been a demanding
job at any time, but it would become even more challenging when,
halfway through his second year, war broke out.

Founded in 1886 in New South Wales, the ARU was one of
Australia's oldest unions and by the 1930s had grown into one of the
largest. Historically, the railways had been used as a vehicle for
spreading unionism in the bush. Former engine driver Ben Chifley,
who had been groomed in the locomotives subdivision of the union,
already played a key role in federal politics. With its stranglehold on
rail transport, which still dominated Australian communications in the
late 1930s, the union was very powerful both on the mainland and in
Tasmania. It was also politically radical: during the Depression some
members had advocated the revolutionary overthrow of the capitalist
state. Like the Seamen's Union, the Shearers' Union and the Waterside
Workers' Federation, the ARU had a proud tradition of helping shape

public policy, and of winning better pay, terms and conditions for its members through negotiation or, when necessary, direct action. There was little an employer, or the government for that matter, could do if the ARU decided to bring the nation's trains to a halt. The union harboured more than its share of socialists and communists, and was strongly anti-war. Deregistered following the great railway strikes that began in Sydney in August 1917, the ARU was reborn in 1927, and in the 1930s it was still a hotbed of radicalism, and factionalism.

Known as a reasonable, fair-minded man who could mediate between factions and arbitrate according to the merit of each case, Alec was elected as a moderate. He had developed an outstanding ability to work with people and get on with them personally, and it was the respect he had gained in this role that won him the numbers to swing the election. A milestone in his own career, the election results also indicated that his socialist views were in line with those of the ARU membership. Through the WEA he had learned to put a compelling case for the advantages of state owner-ship and a centrally planned economy. With his election to office he also consolidated his personal political philosophy, for he was now publicly embracing views very different from those of his conser-vative father. The step validated the direction he had taken since reaching that critical turning point during the 1931 state election. The evolution of his political views was consistent and irreversible. As a union colleague put it laconically, 'the thought of voting any-thing else but Labor would have made Alec choke on his potatoes'. Since returning from Gallipoli a battered, poorly educated young man, he had gone through a series of personal transformations, his thinking and beliefs shaped through experience in the skilled trades, the hardships of the Depression and his union work, and through his adoption of Labor Party philosophy and self-education. On a personal level, accepting this high-profile public position also demonstrated that he no longer feared a recurrence of Bell's Palsy, which had bothered him little for some years.

The debates at the Launceston Railway Workshops, together with the traditional Christian and moral values he had absorbed as a child, had taught him the importance of community, social responsibility and putting the needs of others ahead of his own. What he had since learned of socialist economics and political ideology prepared him for union leadership. In political terms, as other self-educated union leaders like Curtin and Chifley had talked of in the Labor Party, he had seen 'the light on the hill . . . that beckoned towards the golden age . . . where the poor and disadvantaged would be cared for through the equitable distribution of all the resources available to a plentiful nation like Australia'.

Alec's first job as president was to join with other ACTU-affiliated unions in negotiating a 44-hour week, a reform that would improve the working lives of thousands of workers. (That year the union movement in New South Wales won an even better deal — a 40-hour week for some coalminers.) Alec organised and chaired meetings, set agendas and saw that the union was run democratically. He also had to process the evolving log of claims, negotiating with the TGR on benefits for the sick, pensioners, the disabled, and widows and orphans. His sympathy for union members seeking to overcome disabilities, and for the less fortunate who simply needed help, sprang from personal experience, which made him especially well placed to negotiate on their behalf.

His task of reconciling right and left factions within the ARU was a demanding one. Alec ensured that each faction had its representatives in important positions in the union. One of his most militant executive members was Bill Morrow, whom he appointed secretary. A controversial loose cannon, Morrow believed the Bolsheviks had created an exemplary model for socialism, and under Alec's leadership he asked that the union raise funds to send him to the Soviet Union on a study tour. Unsurprisingly, right-wing members were appalled by the prospect. In the event, the trip never happened, both because the rank and file failed to contribute sufficient funds and because of the impending war. Morrow further upset ARU members when he launched an appeal to cover production costs for a CPA-run daily newspaper, then attempted to form an alternative, socialist Industrial Labor Party in Tasmania based on the communist-dominated New South Wales Labor Party. Although never a member of the Communist Party, Morrow would be incensed when the CPA was outlawed in 1940 by the Menzies government.

Alec needed all his diplomatic skills when Morrow attacked Premier Ogilvie at the Labor Party conference after the premier refused to give TGR workers higher wages and then called for an increase in defence spending in response to the threat of war in Europe. Ogilvie wanted 'enough fighter planes to make Australia's skies black with defending aircraft'. Morrow attacked the premier's proposal so immoderately that he was expelled from the state executive of the Tasmanian Labor Party (by 112 votes to 16). And this was Alec's union secretary! Nevertheless, when he sought public office two years later, it was Bill Morrow he chose as his running mate. Neither was elected, but Morrow later gained a place in the federal Senate, where he continued to promote radical causes. After Mao's communist revolution in 1949, he visited 'Red China' and became secretary of the Australia–China Friendship Society. His biography would be aptly titled To Fly a Rebel Flag.

In 1939, at a meeting of union representatives, the popular ARU president was also elected to the prestigious position of President of the Trades Hall Council, a position usually held by the leader of a key union who had made a significant contribution to the cause of unionism. The THC served as a regional, de facto ACTU responsible for all unions in the northern half of Tasmania and answered to ACTU's state branch in Hobart. President Campbell, who still got about on a bicycle, had to coordinate the activities of all the unions, convening meetings, writing reports, and mediating in disputes between unions and employers. According to fellow ARU unionist Ralph Taylor, Alec was elected because he had the most merit, great standing in the community and great personal integrity. The role was normally rotated between unions to give different Labor factions an opportunity for leadership, but electing the ARU president would also have been popular because of the ARU's solid power base in Launceston. With talk of war, and the logistical importance of rail transport in any war effort, the ARU had never had such influence. Neither had Alec been so challenged. Mary would remember 'all the big political dinners at home. We kids had dinner and then we went into the lounge room, where there was a fire, and we stayed there while Mum and Dad had their dinner. And we were not allowed to argue because if we argued it interfered with Mum and Dad's dinner with unionists and members of parliament and all sorts of fancy people. We were told to behave ourselves very well while they had these big political dinner parties. But we'd hear laughter and sounds of enjoyment! And Mum was a terrific cook, a fabulous cook, so an invitation to one of Mum's dinner parties was very sought after. The people that came included premiers and trade union leaders. They were all Labor Party dinners. Other times they would just pop up to see Dad and Mum and have a cup of tea or whatever. And Catholic priests were always keen to come to our house, where they would get a good feed!' It was not long before Alec and Kathleen, ardent socialists who had become disillusioned with the Catholic Church during the Depression, broke with the church completely. It was a wrenching decision but essential, they believed, if they were to move forward.

In April that year the UAP prime minister, Joe Lyons, died of a heart attack. Although this event did not itself overly concern Alec, who had never forgiven Lyons for his betrayal during the Depression, his replacement by the more conservative lawyer Robert Menzies was a source of deep unease. Menzies' dictatorial approach had already alienated the unions. As attorney-general in 1938, he had fought successfully against the waterside workers who refused to load exports of pig iron bound for the military dictatorship of Japan, which had already invaded and subjugated parts of China. Fearing that the militarist Japanese could use the iron to make munitions directed against Australia, the unions had attempted to stop the trains from delivering their potentially deadly cargo to the wharves, where watersiders took up the industrial action. Menzies had responded by threatening to invoke the Crimes Act, jail unionists and bring in the Army to complete the loading.

In his official capacities as THC and ARU president and as a concerned individual, Alec, with Kathleen and many of their unionist friends, took to the streets of Launceston to protest against the pig iron shipments to Japan as well as the plan to introduce conscription without a referendum. Alec addressed hastily called public gatherings from the back of a union truck. He also supported a visit by Sydney-based pacifist, political activist and feminist Jessie Street, who spoke to Tasmanians on the dangers of the Menzies government's foreign policy. Even Alec's older children wrote, printed and distributed pamphlets against the pig iron shipments. 'Dad and Mum used to do a lot of campaigning against Menzies' war policy,' Mary recalls. 'They used to drive one of those converted trucks along to a street corner somewhere and the speaker would jump up on the back and start speaking, and then people would gather round. They didn't have definite meetings. But he did campaign for Jessie Street. My brother and I put leaflets in letterboxes just before the Second World War about sending pig iron to Japan.

'He organised a big peace movement locally. Jessie Street then got in touch with him from Sydney to ask if he would help her organise a street campaign. And Dad organised that from the back of a truck that went around the streets, and Jessie Street used it as a platform. I think he was very impressed by her. They got to certain points in the town and people would gather to see her. It would be like having a soapbox. He always said war was dreadful and he always campaigned for peace. He never told us any anecdotes about his war. He actually respected the Turks as soldiers. But pacifism was quite an active thing in those days and he campaigned for it. Dad made so many speeches and wrote scores of letters. But once it was obvious that the Second World War was going to start whether they liked it or not, he became a very good worker for the war effort. He and Mum were not pacifists through the war.' Three years later, on 19 February 1942, Japanese aircraft bombed Darwin using munitions that might well have contained Menzies' pig iron.

Under the growing threat of war Alec worked even harder. In June 1939 the relationship built up between the ARU and Ogilvie's

Labor government was severed when the premier died of a heart attack aged just 48. After a period of uncertainty Labor resumed government under Robert Cosgrove. Alec met and soon built up a rapport with Cosgrove, who would remain in office for more than a decade and would employ Alec both during and after the war.

As ARU president, Alec had to keep up with international developments as well as state and federal policy. With mounting anxiety he watched the war clouds gather around the world. In Europe the reactionary and fascist forces of old Spain had risen against the democratic second republic, and Italy's fascist leader, Benito Mussolini, had signed the Rome–Berlin 'pact of steel' with Nazi Germany, whose troops had already occupied the Rhineland. Hitler took Austria and Czechoslovakia in 1938, and now threatened Poland and Russia. In August 1939 Stalin, militarily unprepared to face the might of the German war machine, signed a ten-year non-aggression treaty with Hitler. Democratic Europe now faced a threat far greater than that posed by Germany's militarist state 25 years earlier. Compulsory military service for Australian workers seemed inevitable. The federal government had already organised national registration of all men of fighting age.

Alec's worst fears were realised on the night of 3 September 1939. It was just after dinner, and the whole family were listening to the radio show 'Lux Theatre Hour', when the broadcast was suddenly interrupted. 'We were all gathered around the big radio set,' Mary recalls. 'Mum knitting, Dad fashioning some piece of wood with a knife and the kids on the floor reading and playing, when the Australian prime minister came on and said Australia was going to war against Germany.' Menzies famously announced, 'In consequence of the persistence by Germany in her invasion of Poland, Great Britain has declared war upon her and, as a result, Australia is also at war.' Next day the *Examiner* confirmed the gravity of the news in a report that dominated the front page, displacing the advertisements that normally filled it.

Under these drastic new circumstances, Alec had to ensure ARU policies were also in the nation's best interest. The second year of his presidency would be packed with challenges, especially since he still also served as president of the Launceston THC. The conservative government in Canberra was at ideological odds with Tasmania's Labor government and with Alec's own principles, but with fascism now threatening peace from Europe to Asia, Australians of all political persuasions were asked to set aside traditional quarrels and pull together. There were still the everyday domestic issues, of course — the usual log of wage claims, overtime issues and the like — but now the ARU also had bigger concerns. In 1940 the union formally voted to set aside all internal factional differences and get behind the war effort.

During this fateful year Hitler occupied much of western Europe, including Holland, Denmark, Norway, Luxemburg and France, where the speed of the German advance forced the British to evacuate an army of 330,000 troops from Dunkirk, in northern France, in an operation that seemed almost as miraculous as had the Anzac withdrawal from Gallipoli in December 1915. When the Luftwaffe sent wave after wave of fighter and bomber aircraft across the English Channel in preparation for a land invasion, only the determination and heroism of the RAF's fighter squadrons won the day for the Allies, but it was a close-run thing. Once again, as in the dark days of 1915, Britain needed help from Australia, and Australian volunteers began stepping forward with the same enthusiasm as the volunteers of Alec's 8th Reinforcements before them. Among these volunteers were unionists and workmates from TGR and the sons of Anzacs who had served with Alec a quarter of a century earlier. Some asked his advice on whether or not to enlist — after all, he had been 'in the first one'. They trained at camps like Claremont, where Alec had begun his journey in 1915. These new recruits formed the Second AIF and, like Alec, sailed for Egypt, where they would once again train at Mena Camp under the pyramids. Reports of these arrangements must have revived some poignant memories for the Gallipoli veteran. At 41, Alec himself had no thoughts of enlisting. Having worked as a skilled tradesman and become a committed unionist, socialist and Labor voter, he had long since changed his views on war, and for many years considered his volunteering for Gallipoli had been a mistake. Indeed, as he walked past that famous 1915 photograph in his daughter Mary's home in his twilight years, he would be heard to mutter, 'Oh, what a foolish young fellow I was'. As president of the ARU he supported the Labor Party policy of opposing conscription for overseas service.

In any case, with the increasingly critical role to be played by the railways in the war effort, Alec now had his hands full at home. That year he helped to create a special new division at the LRW for war production. Boosted by war-related orders, Launceston industry was now thriving.

Alec also had to absorb the brave new world being built on the home front. Under the punitive National Security Regulations, all Germans (and then Italians) were arrested and interned as enemy aliens, and price controls and censorship laws were introduced. Conscription for home defence was introduced for all eligible men, including many of Alec's workmates. Given her extraordinary skills and experience in growing and preparing food and other essentials for her family, her leadership role in the WEA and her unflagging community spirit, Kathleen might have been tempted to attend a meeting of local women convened that year at the Anzac Hostel in Launceston to establish the Women's Land Army. In the event, she had another priority — in April 1939 her seventh child, Deirdre, was born.

As the war in German-occupied Europe became grimmer, the Commonwealth government adopted special wartime powers to take even firmer control of Australia's resources, production and people, and set up a manpower coordinating body for which Alec would eventually work. The federal government banned the Communist Party, and pressure was put on the ARU to line up with the government's 'win-the-war policy'. In spite of these developments, Australian public opinion was moving back towards the left, and in 1941 Labor leader John Curtin supplanted Menzies, who had resigned after being discredited over various foreign policy miscalculations, including his earlier support for Japan. Curtin was Alec's kind of man and his accession vindicated Alec's socialist beliefs. The union leader was now in perfect accord with both federal and state leaders. As Curtin's biographer Geoffrey Serle wrote, 'Curtin was a product of the Victorian Labor movement, a radical socialist internationalist, who while still young won enormous respect and affection from his colleagues, especially for his conduct of the 1916 national campaign against conscription for military service overseas.' He had also been a leading unionist, a member of the Australian Journalists' Association and editor of the union newspaper the *Westralian Worker*. Like Alec, he had been a keen self-improver: he too had educated himself in socialist economics, read widely, become a pacifist and run a trade union. Also like Alec, he had very good people skills and many friends among grassroots unionists and Labor Party members.

In Launceston Alec had the task of persuading the THC and the ARU to get behind the City Council's defence project to construct 48 reinforced concrete, pillbox-style air-raid shelters in response to the increasing threat of Japanese attack. News from the war continued to look bleak. In June 1941 Hitler overturned the non-aggression pact with Stalin to launch a massive invasion force against Soviet Russia, which declared war on Germany shortly afterwards. In December the Japanese air attack on the US naval base at Pearl Harbor, Hawai'i, brought the United States into the war. Despite the dire circumstances, the entry of these two great powers, with their massive resources, was an encouraging development for the Allies over the long term. Alec, who had never hidden his scorn for the British (a holdover from his experiences at Gallipoli), would have been pleased to hear Curtin announce that Australia would henceforth be aligning itself more closely with the United States in the war against Japan rather than with Britain, preoccupied by events in Europe.

Having completed his term as ARU president, and nearing the end of his time as THC president, Alec took on a new mission. Following Robert Cosgrove's re-election, Alec was inspired to serve Labor interests at the local level, teaming up with Bill Morrow to 'right the wrongs' at home by standing in the Launceston City

Council election of December 1941. Given that Morrow was still politically tainted by his communist sympathies, Alec's decision to run with him demonstrated the depth of his own political beliefs. Their election platform clearly reflected his political and social priorities, emphasising issues such as affordable housing and electric power, improved sanitation, town planning, better wages and working conditions, and greater democratic participation in local government decision making.

ELECTIONS - LAUNCESTON CITY COUNCIL
Voting Day : |Thursday, December 11, 1941
For Civic Improvement and Progress
VOTE FOR THESE CANDIDATES

OFFICIALLY ENDORSED

BY THE

TRADES HALL COUNCIL

WILLIAM MORROW

ALEC. WILLIAM CAMPBELL

SUPPORT THIS PROGRAMME —

◆ Municipal Modern Housing with Cheap Rents to replace Slum Dwellings.
◆ Scientific Processing and Distribution of Pure Milk.
◆ Better Sanitation and Extension of Sewerage Services.
◆ Draining and Reclamation of Swamp Area.
◆ Reduction in Charges for Electric Light and Power.
◆ Incinerators for Destruction of Rubbish and Abolition of the Smoke Nuisance.
◆ Good Wages and Working Conditions for Employees.
◆ Restriction of Land Monopolies in City Area.
◆ Extension of Children's Playgrounds fitted with Modern Equipment for Health and Physical Fitness.
◆ Abolition of Star Chamber Methods—Meetings to be Open to the Public and the Press.
◆ Regular Meetings and Conferences with Ratepayers to discuss Public Questions and Receive Suggestions.

These Candidates are experienced in Transport Organisation and have Business Training. They will apply Modern Methods to your Civic Affairs.

REMEMBER — Every Owner and Occupier has a Vote — USE IT

THREE CANDIDATES MUST BE VOTED FOR — OTHERWISE THE BALLOT PAPER WILL BE INFORMAL

Vote for Alec William CAMPBELL
and William MORROW
Endorsed Trades Hall Candidates

We Recommend you to give the Third Vote to W. J. (BILL) GELLIE

Authorised by P. P. Pike, Secretary Trades Hall, Launceston and printed by Telegraph Printery Pty. Ltd., 63-65 Charles Street, Launceston.

As it turned out, neither was elected, although Alec received about 900 votes (compared with Bill Morrow's 400), confirming his personal popularity. Although his running mate was undeterred, Alec was so disappointed he never again stood for political office. Morrow's communist affinities may have undermined Alec's chances. Nevertheless, Alec's brief foray into local politics would pay a dividend. His progressive platform and relatively high vote caught the attention of government ministers in Hobart who badly needed experienced Labor leaders to help fight the war on the home front. Once again Alec would be asked to answer his country's call.

CHAPTER 13
MANPOWER AND THE WAR AT HOME

'When war broke out I was again borrowed to take charge of the Manpower Directorate in the industrial area of the west coast — from Burnie to Queenstown. My office was at Queenstown.'

Alec received the call from the state government in Hobart in early 1942. The minister for Labour and National Service, who was also responsible for the sub-department War Organisation of Industry, wanted Alec to work in the new Manpower Directorate created by John Curtin's federal government to control wartime employment in Australia. The minister, who himself answered to the federal minister for Labour and National Service, was responsible for organising the allocation of wartime resources in Tasmania and needed a proven organiser to take charge of the western half of the state.

Alec was flattered by the offer. He had not even contemplated signing on for combat as he had in the last war (although men in their forties were dropping their age in order to qualify for enlistment), but the opportunity to help the war effort at home by contributing his professional skills at such a high level was very attractive. It also came at just the right time. He had completed his term as president of the Launceston Trades Hall Council, had done all he wanted at the railway workshops and had no concrete plans for the future. His unsuccessful bid for election to the City Council had put an end to his ambition to work for local government in his home town. In a sense, this rebuff from the voters made getting out of town for a while seem appealing. Others were leaving too, including many women and children who were taking the council's advice and evacuating to the bush. The LCC had just completed construction of the town's air-raid shelters and had warned the community that Launceston could become a target for Japanese bombing, given its strategically important rail and industrial operations.

The council's predictions turned out to be not that far off the mark, as 1942 shaped up to be the blackest year in Australia's history. Japanese land forces were sweeping all before them in Burma, the Philippines and Malaya. On 15 February Singapore fell; four days later the Australian homeland came under direct attack for the first time when Japanese aircraft bombed and strafed Darwin, killing 243 people. Three months after this, on 31 May, Japanese midget submarines penetrated Sydney Harbour, sinking the naval depot ship *Kuttabul* and killing 21. A week later Sydney and Newcastle were shelled from Japanese submarines. The Curtin government was mobilising all material and manpower resources to defend Australia and requesting US support. The February attack on Darwin had proved Curtin right to focus on home defence. In the succeeding months the Japanese also bombed Broome, Port Hedland, Wyndham, Exmouth and Townsville. Despite Allied naval victories in the battles of the Coral Sea and Midway, many Australians feared a land invasion. Japanese forces were now pushing south through the jungles of New Guinea, only a few hundred miles north of Cape York.

The federal government strengthened its financial control over the states, imposing a uniform income tax collecting system to pay for the war and introducing daylight saving to improve the efficiency of the war economy. As THC president, Alec had had the task of interpreting Curtin's about-face on defence to rank-and-file members and persuading local unions to support Curtin's approaches to the US, rather than seeing his transfer of allegiance as a betrayal of Britain. Conservative political leaders wanted to continue supporting Britain in the war against Germany and sending

Australian troops to Europe, but Curtin maintained his position that Britain could fend for herself. He recalled the 6th and 7th Divisions to defend Australia. With the Menzies-led UAP and Country Party opposition attacking Curtin for disloyalty to Britain, the prime minister needed union leaders at all levels to mobilise support for his new defence plans. For this, Curtin needed the union movement to act as a single well-oiled machine.

The government's war mobilisation reflected what then seemed a very real possibility of invasion from the north. The task of the Manpower Directorate was to ensure that the economy was as productive as possible by controlling the labour market and regulating employment in areas most important to the war effort. As Curtin said the day after the fall of Singapore, 'It is now work or fight as we have never worked or fought before.' Enforcing the war measures was no easy matter for managers like Alec, for the new regulations were the most wide-ranging, intrusive and restrictive ever introduced in Australia. Some Australians were still not taking the war seriously, living their lives as they always had without contributing to the war effort. But the Act was unequivocal: 'The resources of manpower and woman-power in Australia shall be organized and applied in the best possible way to meet the requirements of the defence forces and the needs of industry in the production of munitions and the maintenance of supplies and services essential to the life of the community.'

Manpower, as the new agency was known, prioritised key strategic industries such as iron, steel, munitions and primary production, and controlled and regulated the labour supply. The balance was critical. If too many workers enlisted in the defence forces, the economy could be brought to a standstill, unable to supply sufficient food and other essential goods and services, let alone produce weapons and other vital war materials. Manpower determined which sectors (such as primary production) were vital to both the economy and the war effort. These priorities were enshrined in the government's 'List of Reserved Occupations', which was sent out to field staff like Alec. Ralph Taylor, who tried to enlist aged 15 in 1942 (a year younger than Alec in 1915), recalls being told he could not join up because he was needed on the railways, a reserve industry. 'A man we used to call "Burns the Bastard", who was the Manpower director for Launceston, came to our family home and directed me to go and live in far-away New Norfolk, where they wanted help running the railway station. I had no choice. I was manpowered to go.' Conversely, the local Manpower officer might direct a worker in a non-essential occupation to enlist in the armed forces so as to boost the defence forces. Later in the year, when Japanese troops started crossing the Owen Stanley Ranges in New Guinea and Curtin feared Australia was under imminent threat, the government beefed up the Directorate, mobilising the nation for 'total all-out war' by stepping up production in the most strategic industries and boosting manpower resources where the war effort needed them most.

From January 1942 the Manpower Directorate's secretary was the highly efficient Wallace Wurth, who after the war would offer Alec work in a related field. Although directed from its headquarters in Melbourne, the organisation operated through state, regional and local offices with field directors all over Australia. When Alec was appointed, Manpower employed 2,374 staff. The director and minister for War Organisation of Industry, John Dedman, reported to the federal minister for Labour and National Service. About this time Dedman called for 291,000 more men and 24,000 more women for 'the fighting services, munitions factories, shipbuilding, aircraft production and allied works'. Some who were 'manpowered' claimed later that Directorate officers cruised the streets in government cars in search of extra bodies. Citizens lived in fear of the knock on their door, or of being picked out at their factory, and being ordered to move to another town to work in a munitions factory or directed to enlist. Not long after the attack on Darwin 100,000 men were called up for full-time service. During the war Manpower transferred nearly 500,000 people from non-essential civilian activities to war industries. Dedman assumed such draconian control over people's lives that he was tagged 'Lumbago

Jack', 'the Minister for Austerity' or (after he advised citizens not to waste money and time celebrating Christmas) 'the Man Who Killed Christmas'.

As the war continued, Manpower's control over people's everyday working lives increased. As a down-to-earth workingman with a trade who had worked his way up through the ranks and had a proven record as an organiser, Alec was an ideal choice for this difficult new role. A skilled moderator, he knew how to persuade workingmen to do what was needed for the greater good of the community. Travelling around the district selecting men and women for reserve industries or recruiting them for the armed services, Alec would be in his element.

When Alec caught the bus to Queenstown to take up his new position he left Kathleen to wind up their affairs in Launceston. (In his first letter home he told her that the house where he billeted was so quiet at night without the children that he could not sleep.) Kathleen duly sold their beloved Glen Roy, auctioned the furniture and with her six youngest children and all their luggage climbed onto a bus headed over the rough roads to Queenstown 'on the wild west coast'. Sam, now 17, remained with friends in Launceston to finish high school, where she was one of the first girls to study chemistry. 'Most girls chose Domestic Science, but Mother did not want us to learn how to wash dishes and cut up parsley. Better to learn something we could think about while doing those chores, and this inspired me to go on to university and teachers' college and become a teacher.' Important though Alec's new job was, the move was a big wrench, putting a great strain on Kathleen, their marriage and, in different ways, every member of the family.

Queenstown was a desolate settlement then, a small mining town that had grown to service local efforts to extract minerals (mainly copper, but also silver, lead, zinc and gold) from the sur-rounding hills. The town huddled in a tiny clearing in wild bush at the base of rugged mountains some miles inland from the exposed coast, where the winds of the roaring forties, blowing across the Southern Ocean all the way from the Cape of Storms, whistled in every day. The hills, an unlovely, denuded range including Mt Owen and Mt Lyell, were already stripped to bare brown earth by the acid rain and sulfur fumes from past mining operations. Compared with the picturesque colonial town of Launceston with its classic colonial architecture and grand civic buildings, parks and fountains, the family's new home was ugly and depressing. It was also one of the most parochial and isolated communities in Tasmania.

Perhaps not surprisingly, then, despite his stimulating new job, Alec's posting to this remote, ill-favoured outpost undermined family harmony. Slowly they developed differences of opinion and different plans for the future. The war may have turned the world upside down, but for Kathleen and the children Queenstown seemed to be a backwater where nothing ever happened. 'We all thought Queenstown was such a dump of a place, and Mum hated it,' Mary, then 13, recalls. 'And after we had been there a while she feared us teenage children falling in love, marrying locals and being trapped in Queenstown as adults.' Only Jim, at 11, loved this exotic new world. 'We moved first to Strahan, which was the shipping port for the mineral exports, where we stayed in a big old house with plenty of room. There was lots of fishing, and the ocean beach with its enormous waves rolling in with the force of the roaring forties was a spectacular sight.' For Jim (who went on to become a university lecturer in biological sciences), Queenstown was an educational paradise. He began collecting minerals and rocks from the mines and 'spent many weekends with Dad and Ian Best, nicknamed "Besty" fossicking for gold'. One of his best memories was a family mountain climb: 'One hot day Dad suggested we climb Mt Owen, the most conspicuous mountain there. We walked right from the town itself and eventually reached the top to see the glacial tarn near the summit and the view across the King River Valley towards Frenchman's Cap.'

Alec's work went well enough. Broadly responsible for regulating employment in the region, his local focus was on assessing enlistment applications from mining, forestry and agricultural workers. Jim recalls his father 'performing this difficult task in a very amicable way, without upsetting any of the locals at all'. Mary remembers, 'As Manpower officer he used to interview blokes and make the decision as to whether they were allowed to enlist or not, or whether they were in a protected industry, and if not, he would change their job so they could be of more use to the war effort. Queenstown's copper mining was a strategic industry. People who wanted to enlist had to go and see Dad first. Also, during the war you couldn't just apply for a job — you had to be put into a job. They'd have to go and see Dad to see what sort of job they were allowed to do. It was very strange, very autocratic!'

In 1943 conscription was extended to include some military service overseas. During Alec's war Billy Hughes had twice failed to push through conscription. Curtin had no such difficulties. With the threat of homeland invasion, his decision to employ conscripts for 'home defence' (a definition that included New Guinea, where Australia had a protectorate, and that would later be further extended) was generally well received. Curtin's popularity actually grew: in the elections later that year the ALP increased its majorities in both houses.

At Manpower, Alec had to help find ever more men for the defence forces, which meant checking up on young men who were eligible but had not enlisted. Applying the tough new directives would require all his diplomatic skills. Of course, manpower needs depended on the progress of the war. By 1943, while more fighting men were needed to win the war against Japan, fewer were needed in Europe, where the Allies had at last turned the tide. After the German defeat in February in the epic battle of Stalingrad, Russia had begun to roll back the German armies on the eastern front; German and Italian troops surrendered in north Africa in May; and with Allied forces advancing northward from Sicily, Italy changed allegiance, declaring war on Germany in October. With the full engagement of the United States and Russia, the war in Europe was looking more hopeful. In the Pacific, too, the Allies had seized the initiative by the end of 1943, and there was growing confidence that US, Australian and allied forces would eventually defeat Japan.

In this new mood of optimism, Kathleen had started planning for their future in postwar Tasmania. She still hated Queenstown, and she now began putting pressure on Alec to leave the backwater and move, not back to Launceston, where they had cut their ties, but to the state capital, Hobart. He had demonstrated his worth at Manpower. She urged him to apply for work in Hobart, where all the state government offices were based, including Manpower and its parent department, Labour and National Service. As Kathleen pointed out, there would be much more to do in the capital, and it was time to get the children out of Queenstown. Kathleen was increasingly worried that Cressey and Mary, not to mention Geraldine, might get locked into the depressing and parochial community. Although Alec was happy in his work, Kathleen could see no future in the Manpower Directorate, which would be wound up at the end of the war. Mary recalls, 'Mum wanted Dad to move and persuaded him to apply for new jobs. She looked in the newspapers and found him the positions and often applied for them on his behalf. She was better at writing letters. Eventually they succeeded.' Alec's application for a transfer to the Hobart headquarters 'for family reasons' (which included access to better schools) was accepted. Through his connections with Cosgrove's Labor government he was offered similar work in the state capital, although at a lower level.

Kathleen travelled down first, finding them a house on Forrest Road, which she bought using the money they had received from the sale of Glen Roy to Kathleen's brother Jack, who had advanced them the deposit in the first place. Here they took up residence in their own home again. The children certainly liked it. 'The big weatherboard house was on a steep hill a little way from the foothills of Mt Wellington,' Deirdre recalls, 'set among apricot trees, a grapevine and honeysuckle, and an elderberry tree at the bottom of the garden that made a lovely canopy and that was wonderful to play under. There was a verandah with pink glass windows at one end, a large wood-lined kitchen/dining room and a little bedroom leading off it with windows that opened out on brass hinges to a view of the Derwent River. The hallway was large and dark, with a very shiny floor that my sisters used to polish by dancing around on big cloths to rub off the wax. My bed was a huge wooden box in the kitchen.'

Alec's new work was now largely administrative — easier but not as interesting as the Queenstown posting. The untamed west coast had been Alec's kind of country (he would revisit it when sailing around Tasmania in 1950). There was no doubt that the strong-willed Kathleen had got her way. The move had improved the situation for the family as a whole, but Alec now found himself a much smaller fish in a bigger professional pond, with less challenging work and a drop in status. While the war persisted, however, he was kept busy. The government still needed to regulate the economy rigorously and continued to maintain strict rationing of meat and other foodstuffs, keeping costs down through price controls.

In May 1945 the war in Europe finally ended. Two months later, just a month before the end of the Pacific war, John Curtin died at the Lodge. It was a sad end for a gifted, indefatigable war leader who had worked around the clock, despite failing health, to steer the country through the greatest peril it had ever faced. Like other true believers, Alec, who had worked as a small cog in the big wheel of Curtin's government, was distressed by the news. Like many, though, he was also relieved to hear of Curtin's replacement by a like-minded visionary, a man even closer to Alec's heart — Ben Chifley, a former railwayman and ARU member who, like Alec, had lifted himself up through attending WEA classes. On VJ Day, August 1945, the streets of Hobart thronged with revellers. From his office near the centre of town, Alec called in his family to join the spontaneous street celebrations and toast the end of the war. Did he recall how, 30 years earlier, his own journey to war had begun in these same streets?

The Manpower work continued well into the following year, and this gave him time to look for another position. His work had become increasingly complex, involving all sorts of new government regulations introduced under Curtin, such as banking controls and tax increases to pay for new social services that included unemployment and sickness benefits. Alec nonetheless fully supported these welfare provisions and the compassionate postwar reconstruction policies that were being developed. The success of Manpower's central planning, with its regulation of market forces, also reinforced Alec's respect for the basic mechanism of socialist economic principles, and he was keen to remain involved in this government work rather than returning to the Launceston workshops. But when the National Security Regulations and wartime manpower controls ended in 1946 it was time to move on. Fortunately, the Labor Party continued to dominate the political scene both nationally and at the state level, where his political associate Robert Cosgrove remained premier. So he approached his political allies in the government and before long secured a position in the Department of Labour and National Service as an employment officer in the Rehabilitation of Disabled Ex-servicemen's Unit (working from an office in the T & G building). His brief was to find work for disabled war veterans. Just short of fifty, Alec had secured a solid position in the public service. In time he would become Deputy Director of the Rehabilitation of Disabled Ex-Servicemen and his responsibilities would be extended to include civilian unemployed.

Alf Hagger, a colleague in the Department of Labour and National Service, remembers how Manpower secretary Wallace Wurth was keen to transfer their best officers to the postwar Department of Labour and National Service. Wurth knew of Alec's work on the west coast and recruited him, according to Hagger, 'because his curriculum vitae was so perfect. Alec had run Manpower in the west coast; had been a trade union leader, president of THC in industrial Launceston; had close connections with the Labor Party; had a true-believer's left-wing political philosophy, a heart of gold and a wide network of personal contacts; was an experienced and tough negotiator, and was a nice, laid-back, self-effacing bloke who got along well with everyone.' His personal contacts often impressed people. On one occasion, when Alf was sitting in Alec's new office, he asked him about a new policy the government was formulating on a particular issue. Alec said he would find out. Picking up the phone, he dialled straight through to the premier. 'Is that you, Bert? Yes, Alec here. Well, thanks, and you? Good. Well listen, Bert, I just wanted to know our position on this new rehab policy . . .'

Alec was also a no-nonsense straightshooter, Alf recalled. One night in Hobart, while they were sharing a drink in a popular Hobart pub, Alec was goaded by a fellow drinker: 'If you used to be a fair dinkum boxer, you'd agree to have a fight with me, wouldn't you. But I don't believe you ever were.' This went on and on, so eventually, just to shut him up, Alec agreed to step outside and promptly dropped the drinker to the floor of the car park with one well-placed left hook to the jaw. 'You didn't mess around with Alec Campbell in those days,' Alf said. 'Not that Alec was above criticism. When I came down from Canberra and pointed out the new techniques for preparing submissions for the minister, which he had been getting wrong for some time, Alec just said, "Oh God, what a bloody fool I've been".'

Despite the demands of his new job, he still had time for his children, as Mary remembers. 'When we were living up in Forrest Road and I was working at Kodak, which was very close to where Dad worked in town, we used to walk together down Forrest Road hill, which was very steep, to go to work. I was very fat when I was young, and I was terribly self-conscious about it. And when I said to Dad I was too fat he said, oh no, you're a pocket Venus. It was as if he knew how I felt, and wanted me to feel better about myself. He was empathetic: he knew how different people felt. He could talk to somebody with a totally different mindset and he just seemed to be able to switch, and to know exactly what people were thinking and how people were feeling. He was capable of using his ability to do that, not in a bad way, but for his own purposes. But he did seem to know what you thought and how you felt.'

Deirdre remembers him giving her Norman Lindsay's 'The Magic Pudding' on her eighth birthday. 'It was quite difficult to read, and I remember Dad read it aloud to me with all his usual enthusiasm for life. The book became an absolute favourite and I loved all the quirky characters. I think Dad liked that book rather a lot himself.' She recalls the house in west Hobart as 'always full of people coming and going. My four sisters and two brothers had friends coming to the house, and later two friends of my eldest sister boarded with us when they went to college in the city, and they all had callers.'

Politically, Alec was in his element. Labor dominated the federal landscape. The Chifley government, with large majorities in both houses, built on the 'cradle to grave' welfare system, and started the process of nationalising the banks and the national airline, Qantas. Although this met with Alec's approval, however, it turned out to be as far to the left as the electorate was prepared to go, and before the end of the decade there would be a strong conservative backlash. Meanwhile, with his new home, secure job and higher income, Alec had done all he wanted to professionally; he was entrenched in a secure government job and could look forward to superannuation and a pension on his retirement. The children were increasingly independent. For the first time in his life he had the time, resources and opportunity to look about him for some new, personal stimulus. He revived his earlier interest in sailing. Although older than most yachtsmen, and new to Hobart, he made up his mind to break into the exclusive world of yachting. Towards the end of 1947 he got a break when Gallipoli veteran Duncan Macrae, who had been badly wounded at Anzac Beach and who became an outspoken pro-conscription campaigner in Tasmania in 1916, offered him a position crewing on his Hobart-based yacht *Kintail*.

The move to Hobart would turn out to be a turning point in Alec's life. The windy city was much more cosmopolitan than Launceston, it was on the international shipping routes, and its relentless and unpredictable winds were about to sweep the well-grounded Alec off his feet. Wanting more than anything to sail with them, he could never have predicted how far these winds of change would take him from his past, from his home, from his family and, especially, from his wife of more than twenty years. When he sailed off on *Kintail* he would be leaving more than Hobart behind him.

CHAPTER 14

IN THE WAKE OF BASS AND FLINDERS

'At the end of the war I did not want to go back to the Launceston Railway Workshops. I had sold my house and bought a house on Forrest Road, Hobart. I was offered a transfer to the Commonwealth Department with superannuation and length-of-service rights, but without more qualifications than I had, I could see very little chance of promotion, so I enrolled at the university and completed a degree in Economics.'

In 1947 Alec broke into Hobart's well-established sailing community, then dominated by professional sailors half his age. By reviving his Anzac network he won a crew position with fellow Gallipoli veteran and Scotsman Duncan Macrae on his yacht *Kintail* in the third Sydney–Hobart race. Although Alec's previous experience was limited to sailing a Snipe dinghy out of Launceston, being thrown in the deep end could not have given the tireless adventurer a better start. Macrae first took Alec on a series of training runs in Hobart waters so he could get to know the vessel. As fellow crewmember Darrel Gates recalls, 'Macrae turned out to be a long-lost soul-mate.' Despite having lost the use of his legs after being shot in the back at Gallipoli, 'he had learned to sail magnificently. He could haul himself around the boat like a monkey on a rope. And he took to Alec and taught him everything he knew. We've still got charts at home that are marked with "Duncan says this is a safe anchorage". He was a master of the sea.'

For Alec it was another step along his lifelong path of self-development, but for the first time his motivation was not to improve his professional position but to pursue a recreation that had long attracted him personally. And like all his projects, he gave it everything he had. Unfortunately, this new venture would carry a heavy price, for in this world of men there would be no room for Kathleen or the children. It was another crossroads in his life. He had worked hard for his family, had committed himself to Kathleen and the children since 1924, providing for them through the hard times as best he could. Now some of the children were themselves in long-term relationships and in the workforce, and Kathleen wanted a more settled life. Alec the romantic, on the other hand, was a long-term fan of 'Sea Fever', the paean to the sea by English poet John Masefield, who had written so lyrically about the Anzacs at Gallipoli. Now, in this sailor's port, the poet's words were seducing Alec, as he too felt the lure of the sea as 'a wild call and clear call that may not be denied', and he could not resist. But in sailing away from Hobart, he was also sailing away from Kathleen.

They had been through so much together over the years but had grown apart since the move to Hobart, with all its distractions. As they developed different plans for the future, they began leading increasingly separate lives. No one was blamed, and there was no lasting hostility or resentment. According to the children, their parents simply drifted apart, developing different interests and values. Alec was immersed in his new obsession with sailing, Kathleen in her gardening. In Mary's view, 'The Depression killed off the romance for a lot of couples. It was such an awful experience, as for year after year they just had no money. Then, when they finally got money, they each felt they deserved a reward — but different kinds of rewards.'

Theirs had been a long and successful partnership. In 23 years they had together battled their way through the toughest of times to raise their large family, demonstrating extraordinary strength and resourcefulness. They had also evolved dramatically both as a team and as individuals. They had launched seven children into the world, all of whom would do well professionally, marry and have families of their own. They were not the same two people who had met in that Beaconsfield pub back in 1923. Kathleen had helped Alec develop from an itinerant carpenter to a respected leader of men. She had delivered, nursed and raised seven children while playing a key support role in Alec's professional life, and now she was exhausted and wanted to slow down. But Alec wanted to set off on new adventures, starting with ocean sailing. When the sailor took to the high seas he must have felt he was leaving his land-based cares behind — all that hard work, the struggle to pay the bills, wrestling over the children's future, political arguments. The Depression and the war were over, but the mundane pressures of family life persisted. Once out at sea there was nothing but the sky, the ocean and the yacht, all the banal burdens of life washed away by the sea. The appeal of Masefield's 'vagrant gypsy life' was irresistible.

Kathleen also took a well-earned holiday at this time, visiting Australia's most exciting postwar city, Sydney, where the family had been offered free accommodation. Alec had refused the offer but insisted Kathleen and the children go. It was a thrill for Kathleen and the children she took with her. 'It was one of the finest developing experiences we had as a family,' Cressey, now 22, remembers. 'We saw great art and top concert performances, attended fashion parades and enjoyed the life of the big city. I danced and dined and wined at Romano's and the Prince's and jitterbugged at the Troc. Mum knew it was important for us to have some insight into the big world outside our little island.'

Alone in Hobart between sailing trips, perhaps it was inevitable that 48-year-old Alec should meet someone else. At an interdepartmental meeting bringing together his unit and the Melbourne-based Commonwealth Social Services team, his eyes met those of Kate Corvan across the meeting room table. The two were involved in similar work, finding jobs and solving problems for people whose lives had been dislocated by the war. He worked with veterans with disabilities in Hobart and she worked on all sorts of social work cases in Melbourne. While searching for solutions to others' problems they discovered needs of their own, and they formed an attachment.

Later that year Kate attended a party, hosted by Alec in the empty Forrest Street house, for some visiting American social workers. Another guest was the now high-flying senator Bill Morrow, sporting a black homburg. Kate remembers being 'stimulated by Alec's fascinating political contacts — all left wing and all radical. They had ideas for Australia's future that were so exciting. I realised that Alec was a very interesting man and that we shared the same philosophy and radical, left-wing political point of view.' Thus began the second great partnership in Alec's life. For his part, he only hoped that the attacks of Bell's Palsy would not return too often, for the last thing he wanted was for this compassionate social worker to feel sorry for him.

Although very different from Kathleen, Kate Corvan, then 27, may have reminded Alec of a younger version of her namesake. She was a politically aware campaigner who still had the energy that Kathleen had spent. Perhaps, too, she was a companion whom Alec the opportunist needed to help him realise the adventures he still had planned. She certainly had a highly developed social conscience. After studying social work at the University of Sydney, Kate had been employed in Manpower-related organisations on the mainland, working as a social worker in munitions factories. Her brother had not returned from the war, having been captured in Timor, and this loss had deeply affected her. So she spent the war helping under-resourced people with transport, clothing and accommodation needs, and where she could soothing their anxieties about fathers, sons or brothers still away at the war. As she said later, 'I gave them as much practical help as possible.'

The tide of the budding relationship ebbed and flowed as Kate travelled back and forth from Melbourne for conferences. But Alec had his mind on other tides — notably his first Sydney–Hobart voyage in December 1947. This was pioneer sailing, for the inaugural event had been held only in 1945, when just nine yachts had taken part. Despite his inexperience, once they had sailed out of

Sydney Harbour through the heads and into rougher seas, Alec quickly shook off his seasickness, learned the ropes and pulled his weight, and *Kintail* made the trip to Hobart in her fastest ever time. John Bennetto, a shipmate and friend of the owner's son Malcolm, who had been sailing since childhood, recalls, 'Alec showed a remarkable adaptability to become a serious sailor in his late forties. It was a bloody good effort. He was very determined to learn how to become a good sailor and was always asking questions. And if he got something wrong he would always say, "That was silly, wasn't it." He was a great and humble learner.'

'Alec provided great comradeship too,' Bennetto says. 'He was always ready to give a hand, no matter what time of day or night, and he was always joking. His favourite expression on board was, "Are you looking at me, or are you asleep?" We became mates for life.' Since the first crew-member to be seasick was to shout the others a steak at the end of the voyage, when the moment came Alec rushed up forward to where he could throw up unseen behind the jib. 'The only trouble was,' Bennetto recalled with relish years later, 'Alec lost his false teeth in the process, so he had to survive till the end of the voyage without them — not that he ever complained. Nothing was ever wrong for Alec. He never whinged about anything. As he got sicker, Malcolm Macrae gave him senna tea to drink.' Alec got his own back by composing a rhyming verse, which Bennetto never forgot: 'It went, "Malcolm was a humourist / A really funny skunk. / He brewed up Alec a drink of senna tea / Which laid him on his bunk. / He writhed around in agony / And bolted for the dyke, / And all he wore was a sickly grin / And his little marlin spike." '

'We had done well,' Alec wrote later, 'as *Kintail* finished fourth across the line and fourth on handicap out of a fleet of 21 vessels.' More important, Alec had loved every minute of it. In ocean sailing he had found a new passion. Deirdre remembers his return: 'The back of the house looked out over the Derwent. When Dad sailed in the Sydney–Hobart we listened on the radio for the *Kintail* to be sighted coming in. We hung a sheet out the window so he could see us. I loved doing this and asked Dad as soon as he came though the door, "Did you see us?" He said he did.'

Alec was hooked on sailing. Determined to make himself more useful on future trips, he embarked on a course in celestial navigation, volunteered for several eight-metre class yacht delivery voyages from Hobart to Sydney or Melbourne to learn the ropes, and started to build his own H28 sailing craft with a new Hobart friend, Ken Dallas. *Trugannini* would be named after the famous nineteenth-century Aboriginal woman said to be the last surviving Tasmanian. The name reminded Alec of *Younah*, the book his grandmother had written about Aborigines in colonial Tasmania, and after which his parents' family home was subsequently named by Estelle.

Between voyages, Alec continued to help implement the Labor government's social policies, especially finding work for disabled veterans. In 1948, however, there was a huge shift in the national political mood. Conservative forces began to challenge and dismantle the structures Curtin and Chifley had erected during and immediately after the war to regulate the economy and protect the vulnerable and underprivileged. Now people wanted their individual freedoms back and began to complain of 'creeping socialism'. In the first major setback for the Left, the High Court blocked the Chifley government's nationalisation schemes for the banks and Qantas. Before long the conservatives had rolled back price controls and Labor's sweeping welfare provisions. With an election due the following year, it appeared that Menzies, now leading the Liberal Party (born out of the ashes of the UAP), would be returned to the Lodge.

Just as the old political order seemed to be changing at the national level as the certainties of the world built by the political Left crumbled, so too did the old order of Alec's personal life as the certainties of his marriage collapsed. Alec and Kathleen separated. They had simply developed in different directions. Back from Sydney, Kathleen began planning a new house and garden, which she would call 'Pax'. Alec decided to become a university student, taking up where he had left off in his WEA night courses during the Depression. He wanted to learn more about the new postwar economic thinking that was coming into vogue in the changed political climate — not only out of personal curiosity, but to acquire qualifications that would help him rise professionally. An office colleague, Bill Kalland, remembers the day Alec made this decision. 'We shared an office, and one day he looked up from his desk and said, "Bill, you've got a degree, haven't you?" "Yes, I got one when I was teaching at Burnie High School." "Well, tell me how you get a degree," Alec said.' Kalland told Alec all he could, and 'that was the last time we talked about it, but next thing I heard, Alec had rushed off to the University of Tasmania and started a degree then and there'.

At the end of 1948 the sailor ran away to sea again, signing on as crew in his second Sydney–Hobart yacht race, this time on *Nell Gwyn*, owned by Frank Hickman. The yacht acquitted herself well, as did Alec, who proved much handier than he had been during his first race. Back in Hobart, however, the old Labor activist could no longer ignore the dramatically changed political climate. In 1949 his old nemesis, 'Pig Iron Bob' Menzies, was elected as prime minister on a strongly anti-socialist platform. The conservative backlash had switched out that 'light on the hill' that Alec had shared with Curtin and Chifley. Menzies appeared unstoppable.

Alec had campaigned for Labor during the elections at his new campus, the University of Tasmania, described by fellow student Doug Padgham as 'a bit of a hothouse, where we were all fighting over ideas'. Padgham, a Menzies supporter, recalled that Alec could not be shifted from his socialist ideas: 'He believed these policies could right the wrongs of life in an unjust society.' The Right had targeted the universities. A Liberal Party official later summoned Padgham to a secret meeting in his car at the university car park. Would Padgham help compile a list of socialists and communists on campus? Padgham refused. The Liberals wanted to use this list both to discredit left-leaning individuals and to persuade voters to ban the CPA in the subsequent 1951 referendum. Padgham, who enjoyed his debates with Alec and other left-wingers, refused to cooperate. 'Anyway,' Padgham recalled, 'Alec was by no means a one-eyed left-winger. He was thoughtful and very intelligent, and was a complete gentleman, a courteous and pleasant man altogether.'

The Menzies government, later nicknamed the 'Ming Dynasty', ushered in 23 years of increasingly conservative rule that changed the character of Australian society. Menzies himself would win seven consecutive elections. The Right was in the ascendant again, and their victory pushed the old true-believer Alec Campbell out of politics. Now 51, and increasingly disillusioned by the dismantling of the structures and values he had worked so hard to establish, he began withdrawing from political activism. Without any proper public or parliamentary debate, Menzies committed troops to the anti-communist war in Korea, embroiling Australia in yet another international conflict just five years after the end of the war. Alec had had enough. He had done his bit for the community. Now he had embarked on a new series of adventures — the first, of the soul, would be ocean sailing; the second, of the mind, would be his university studies.

There could be no better way of getting away from the bleak turn of political events than by taking on a long, demanding sea voyage. This time he would follow in the wake of the great navigators Bass and Flinders, the first Europeans to sail around Tasmania (proving it was an island), in 1798. Now, 150 years later, Alec was signed on as navigator on Duncan Macrae's *Kintail* for a rerun of the expedition, and he embraced the opportunity with his usual enthusiasm. After only three years of serious sailing he was embarking on one of yachting's most challenging expeditions. 'Duncan Macrae had discussed with us, his crew, whether or not to take *Kintail* in the 1949 Sydney–Hobart,' the navigator and official voyage chronicler recorded. 'We had done well in the 1947 race, finishing fourth across the line and fourth place on handicap in a fleet of 21 yachts. Duncan had for some time thought of sailing round Tasmania and it was finally decided to miss the 1949 Sydney–Hobart and to take *Kintail* eastabout around Tasmania. The crew consisted of Duncan Macrae, Duncan's son Malcolm, Bill Vout, Alec Campbell, Les Chatterton, Hugh Wells, Tom Griffith and Keith Downey. John Bennetto joined us at Strahan.'

Since George Bass and Matthew Flinders had pioneered the route on the *Norfolk*, the circumnavigation had rarely been repeated. ('As far as we know,' Alec would write, 'only four yachts have circumnavigated Tasmania. They are *Tamima* (owned by D. O'May); *Saona* (Admiral Guy Wyatt); *Kilkie* (Victorian owned) and *Kintail* (Duncan Macrae).') It was a dangerous undertaking, as the rocky coastline was remote and seldom navigated, and the strong westerly winds had driven many ships to a watery grave on this lee shore. The logbook Alec kept during the 17-day journey revealed his growing knowledge of sailing and his cool, unflustered approach to danger. The trip around Tasmania would be his biggest adventure since sailing off to war in 1915.

The paralysis was recurring more frequently as Alec got older, and he and Macrae must at times have made a strange pair. Alec used to say, 'We may not be much use on our own, but together we make up one good man.' The unqualified success of this circumnavigation only whetted Alec's appetite. After another spell back at his government desk he competed in his third Sydney–Hobart yacht race, again on *Kintail*. Darrel Gates, who crewed with Alec on that race, would recall, 'Alec always had a joke. It did not matter whether it was day or night. A wave knocked us down off Cape Perpendicular at 3 a.m. and a lot of water rushed into the boat, so we had to get rid of it fast. When I dropped a bucket from the deck onto Alec who was bailing down below he quipped, bright as a button, "Darrel, it's three o'clock in the morning — this is no time for frivolities", which was typical of his memorable one-liners.'

Ocean racing was now his main preoccupation. Nothing was so exhilarating as to feel 'the wheel's kick and the wind's song and the white sail's shaking'. Having gained so much valuable experience, especially during the circumnavigation, in 1951 he was invited to crew on *Terra Nova* in his fourth Sydney–Hobart race. *Terra Nova* was owned by Ken Goulay, whose yacht *Malaran* he had glimpsed when departing Hobart on the circumnavigation. Darrel Gates was again a crewmate. 'By now Alec was one of the best crew-members on board, could do anything, and was always happy and always ready to go on deck anytime come rain, hail or shine.'

He still threw everything he had into his work too. Bill Kalland, 20 years his junior, reckons Alec had achieved a great deal. 'There was no stopping him. He used to get the newspapers every day and cut out the advertisements of companies wanting employees. Then he would call in an ex-serviceman or disabled person looking for a job, grab hold of them and march them down to the company advertising for employees, and waving the advertisement in front of the personnel officer at that company he would just say, "Here is the bloke I want you to hire for this job. You gotta take him on, you hear me!" Neither party seemed to have any choice, and it worked most of the time.' The work also realised Alec's long-held philosophy of mutual support and helping those in need. Whether they were founded on the spirit of mateship he had learned at Gallipoli or acquired during his political education at the Launceston Railway Workshops and in the unions, Alec believed deeply in the principles of compassionate socialism. Having faced his own physical challenges, he had developed a commitment to helping others overcome their disabilities. 'Because he had problems with his own facial disfigurement,' Kalland recalled, 'he knew how bad some of these crippled soldiers and citizens felt, and that helped him fight for them.'

Kalland, who for years sat on the other side of a large double desk, says Alec also 'had a wonderful network of people in high places, from the premier down, who all knew him and always did what he asked. He was very persuasive and took no nonsense. The fact that he had fought at Gallipoli helped too, because he knew what it was like for these World War 2 blokes to come back from the fighting. He worked hard, put in long hours, was very efficient and got amazing results. He also had a wide range of personal experience with different jobs. He had worked with people in the primary industries, building and carpentry, railways, railway workshops, unions, mining, ships — you name it. So he knew how to fit returned soldiers and the disabled into different jobs.' According to Kalland, who himself fought with a 9th Division gun regiment in the Second World War, 'Alec was also a charming person and very easy to get on with, and he had a great sense of humour that got everyone on side.'

In 1952 Alec decided to use a six-month long-service leave entitlement to travel overseas with Mac. He reckoned he had earned the break and had wanted to travel overseas for years. An old ambition had been to visit the ancestral home in Argyllshire, to see Inverlochy, where his grandfather Donald Campbell had lived, and to visit Inveraray Castle, the headquarters of the Campbell clan he had heard so much about. It was no coincidence that his new love, Kate Corvan, would be in England at the same time, on a working holiday to gain experience in the field of children's welfare. He hoped to catch up with her there.

Typically, the trip turned into an action-packed adventure. The brothers sailed to England on the Italian ship *Australia*, disembarking in Naples and working their way through Italy, Switzerland and France before reaching England. They visited Ireland, and Alec spent a few days in Sweden. Of course they travelled up to Argyllshire, where they visited Inveraray, toured the castle and met distant relatives among those branches of the family that had remained in Scotland after Donald's departure for the antipodes. Although the event would have been of limited interest to Scottish republicans like Alec and his brother, in February, while they were in England, the King died suddenly, prompting the recall of his heir and eldest daughter, Princess Elizabeth, from a holiday in Africa.

By a stroke of good luck Alec heard through the sailing grapevine in England about a yacht race across the treacherous North Sea from Dover to Marstrand, Sweden, and succeeded in securing a crew position at short notice as a foredeck hand on the British yacht *Nokoia*. Incidentally he demonstrated his sketchy grasp of European geography by phoning a friend on the day of departure, promising to call by the following day for a drink after the race. His friend

wasted no time in enlightening him! Despite Alec's ignorance of the
waters, the winds and the yacht, *Nokoia* was the third English yacht
across the line in the six-day race, and as a reward for his good
crewing Alec was made an honorary member of the Royal Ocean
Racing Club and the Royal Thames Yacht Club.

Having caught up with his Scottish family connections, seen
something of Europe, spent time with Kate in England and gained
valuable new sailing experience, it was time to go home. As soon as
he got back to Tasmania he enlisted for the next race — his fifth
Sydney–Hobart. In December he was appointed a senior crew-
member on Ken Goulay's *Terra Nova* again. The following year,
1953, he and partner Ken Dallas finally finished building their own
yacht, *Trugannini*, and began sea trials. He would take her out into
the harbour again to greet returning soldiers from the Korean War,
which ended in July. A few months later Alec sailed in his sixth
Sydney–Hobart on board *Fantasy*, owned by Dudley Burridge.
Darrel Gates, again a crewmate, recalls, 'By then Alec could have
skippered the yacht for the whole race. He was a great navigator, an
accurate chart reader and a reliable helmsman with a good nose for
the wind and should have been skipper of the yacht.'

In 1954 he completed his part-time university studies. At
around the same time the Queen visited Hobart on board the royal
yacht *Gothic*, bringing out thousands of sightseers on small boats to
greet her, including at least one unlikely republican. Alec and Ken
Dallas took *Trugannini* out for the occasion. Darrel Gates remembers, 'Alec was very afraid when he heard that co-skipper and
co-owner Ken Dallas was insisting on lowering the flag and saluting
when the Queen sailed by, because he knew Dallas was a very
clumsy man. He'd often leave the deck hatch open and fall down it,
and he left it open again this time. But when he stepped back to
salute the royal pennant, he fell backwards not down the hatch but
into the water! It amused people, because the Queen had not even
been watching.'

Alec's main sailing fixture for the year, however, was his
seventh Sydney–Hobart race, in which he crewed on *Southerly*

Buster, owned by *Terra Nova*'s Ken Goulay, again with Darrel Gates as a crewmate. 'Alec was as enthusiastic as ever, great company and still joking the whole time.' He never took part in the epic race again, but because he had sailed in the third race back in 1947 Alec claimed the honour of being the oldest Sydney–Hobart sailor, a status he held until his death in 2002. John Bennetto, who sailed with him in 1947, continued crewing the races without interruption until 2002, when he held the unmatchable record of having sailed in more than forty Sydney–Hobart yacht races.

In 1955, having graduated from the University of Tasmania with a degree in Economics, Alec was asked to produce his first scholarly work — an entry in the *Australian Dictionary of Biography* on his ancestor James Brumby, one of Tasmania's pioneer settlers. By now he had become more interested in history than politics. He was happy to be out of the union movement. The cold war anti-communist witch-hunt in Australia had spawned the Catholic-based Democratic Labor Party, which had fractured the ALP and divided the progressive vote, increasing the power of the Menzies-led Liberal/National Country Party coalition. It would be many years before Labor would recover from this reverse. Alec's political ideals were further shaken the following year when the Soviet Union invaded its socialist neighbour Hungary.

His main professional interests were now academic. He began delivering lectures on 'industrial methods', drawing on his long working experience. When Professor W. A. 'Mick' Townsley, whom he had befriended at university, published the history *Tasmania: From Colony to Statehood, 1803–1945*, he dedicated it 'To that evergreen veteran of Gallipoli Alec Campbell, through whom I came to know and love the Tasmanian community'. Armed with his new credentials, he also applied for, and received, promotion at the Department of Labour and National Service, becoming a Claiming and Research Officer. 'Getting a degree so late was unusual at that time,' Kate recalled later, 'but it opened up his intellectual life, and he made a lot of new academic friends, although he maintained his sailing friends as well.' Casting a pall over the year's successes, however, was the news of his mother's death at Beauty Point.

By the late 1950s the house Alec had been building on weekends and in the evenings was nearly finished. Since 1953, when he had bought the land in Lindisfarne, a picturesque suburb of Hobart, he had been working on this dream. Although the house was small, its charming interior was well designed and gave the appearance of a larger house, Estelle recalled. 'It had a spacious entrance hall with black and white tiles on the floor and big glass sliding doors opposite the main entrance. Off this were two bedrooms — one of these was the first room he built, and he lived in this room while finishing the house and entertained there (right royally) when he had visitors, including our mother and father who visited from Launceston to see the progress of the house. Also off the entrance hall was a large living/dining/sitting room, and separated from this was a breakfast bar and a modern kitchen with doors opening out to the back garden. The plumbing and wiring were about the only things Alec did not do himself.'

Perhaps the builder had always harboured dreams of starting a new family in this house. The children, of course, would be surprised, disappointed and sad, reluctant to let go of their father and all their precious childhood memories. But by then most of them had left home; even the youngest, Deirdre, was 18 years old. Alec now also decided to swallow the anchor and quit ocean sailing. He had lived out his 'Sea Fever'. Besides his seven Sydney–Hobart races, the Tasmania circumnavigation and the *Nokoia* race, he had participated in a number of interstate delivery voyages and other seagoing expeditions, and it was in his sixtieth year that he finally agreed to accept the concluding lines of Masefield's poem: 'And all I ask is a merry yarn from a laughing fellow-rover / And a quiet sleep and a sweet dream when the long trick's over.' That same year Alec decided to ask for the hand of the woman whom he had kept waiting for so long. What the 38-year-old Kate Corvan would make of the proposal from this middle-aged father of seven was an open question among their friends.

Alec's prized photograph of Estelle in Campbell clan — lost and found again

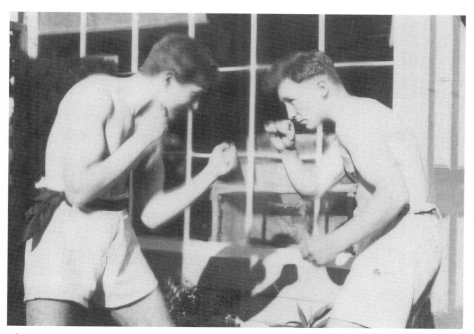

Alec (right), who became bantamweight champion of Tasmania, spars with a friend.

Alec and Kathleen exchanged these studio photographs shortly before their wedding in 1924.

The Campbells at Glen Roy, *c.* 1941 (*left to right,* back row: Deirdre, Kathleen, Greg, Cressey, Alec, Sam; *front row:* Geraldine, Jim, Mary)

State Council—Australian Railways Union.
Tasmanian Branch, 1939-40.

Left to Right. Back Row—A. Rubenach, W. J. R. Smith, J. Littlewood.
Middle Row—K. C. Phillips, F. W. Hall, A. C. White, F. Pinkard.
Front Row—J. Smith, E. R. Barnard, A. W. Campbell, W. Morrow, A. Ingles.

Alec (front row, centre) was re-elected president of the Australian Railways Union in 1939, with Bill Morrow (on his left) as secretary.

Alec (centre) sailed out of Hobart on the *Erica J* with members of the Royal Tasmanian Yacht Club, including Darrel Gates (in hat), 1950s.

The *Kintail* (w
Alec at the bo
returning to
Hobart after
the 1950
circumnavigat
of Tasmania

CHAPTER 15
THE HEART OF THE MATTER

'On return from Europe I built a house at Lindisfarne. In 1958 I married Kathleen Corvan. We have two children. I retired from the public service in 1964 but worked part time for the National Heart Foundation until 1980.'

Alec and Kate, daughter of Canon and Mrs C. Corvan of Hobart, married in June 1958 at St. John's Presbyterian Church in Hobart. Brought up as a Scottish Presbyterian, Alec had converted to Catholicism after returning from Gallipoli. Following his experiences during the Depression he broke with the church completely. Now he had married a Anglican. Not that religion seemed as important as it once had. The world was entering the space age: Sputnik III was photographed over Hobart that year, and the new entertainment medium of television was about to reach Tasmania. Alec witnessed these developments with irrepressible enthusiasm.

Kate's paternal family came from Ireland, while her mother's people were Scottish. Her clergyman father was the parish priest at St Johns, Newtown. Coincidentally, she too had been born in Launceston, but the family had subsequently moved down to Hobart. Later her work would take her to Melbourne. Like Alec, she came from a big family, in which she was the fourth child. Also like Alec, Kate had a minor disability: she had been born with dislocated hips, which led to a walking problem. As a child she had endured five operations by Melbourne specialists to correct the problem, all of which failed (she would learn later) because the appropriate operation should have been performed soon after birth. But the affliction never held her back and she enjoyed a normal childhood. After gaining an arts degree from the University of Tasmania, she took social studies at the University of Sydney before finding a government job as a social worker. Fellow students included Margaret Dovey (who married Gough Whitlam) and Peggy Kerr (whose husband, John Kerr, would be responsible for the dismissal of the Whitlam government in 1975).

Kate, by then a social worker with the Tasmanian Education Department, recognised that their values and ideas corresponded perfectly. 'Once I discovered he was trying to place handicapped returned soldiers in work, I knew he must be an exceptionally compassionate man. He was also so interesting and had so many fascinating friends, who were all interested in the politics of the Left. I quickly realised we shared the same philosophy and political point of view. And he was always taking up new challenges. He had an unquenchable thirst for education and meeting different groups of people from whom he could learn, like when he joined the Hobart History Society. He was exciting to be with — always taking up new hobbies, like art, and learning new skills, like musical appreciation and photography.' In photography, Alec was in fact picking up an interest he had first developed at age 14, long before he went to Gallipoli.

That Alec had served at Gallipoli was immaterial to Kate, apart from the mark it had left on his face, which interested her as a social worker. Alec had told her early in their acquaintance that he had served in the war. 'But there were a lot of people at that time that had been there, so it did not stand out in any particular way. They had these annual Anzac reunions, and he kept in touch with his group over the years. But although the war certainly had not scarred him deeply thanks to his strong character, I soon realised that the facial disfigurement from Gallipoli affected him deeply. He felt it counted against him in job interviews and at work. At the same time, it was the Bell's Palsy that had always driven him on to succeed in life. It put pressure on him to achieve things. He wanted to show that he could rise above the problem, that he would never be held back by it and could be better than the next man. And I really respected that.'

By then a widower, Sam Campbell had attended his son's second wedding but died the following year, severing a precious link with the past and an idyllic childhood. In 1962 Alec, now 63, demonstrated that he had lost none of his own vitality by fathering his eighth child, Neil. In the same year the Menzies government introduced an anti-inflationary credit squeeze that sent the price of goods and services into orbit. Now Kate had lost her income Alec was determined to put his economics degree to use, firing off a volley of job applications that stressed his new qualification. Eventually his persistence paid off, and he was promoted to the position of Economic Research Officer for the Department of Labour and National Service, a preferment hitherto unheard of for someone in his sixties. As Kate puts it, 'He had joined the department as a public servant but had now reached the level of academic.'

It was the pinnacle of his professional life. 'Alec thought, at last he really had achieved something in his life with that appointment, and he was very proud of himself.' In fact, he had probably won his position as much on his personal qualities as on the academic qualification he had worked so hard for. 'Alec had such high energy levels. For his age he had such a lot of go! And he was really good at that job, because he wouldn't hold back. He gave it everything he had. I loved the way he would just go and see employers and urge them to employ people. He was very successful because he would never take no for an answer. Of course, with his background in the Trades Hall and the ARU he knew who was who, what jobs were really available and what could be done.'

Public service rules, however, ensured that he would not have long to enjoy his new status, and two years later he was forced into retirement. Despite his reluctance, he would later acknowledge the prudence of the well-established rules preventing public servants from working beyond the statutory age. In any case, his old Labor mates had long gone — his longstanding ally Robert Cosgrove had lost office the year he married Kate — so there was no one he could appeal to. Alec did not care what employers thought of his advanced age, but he hated the thought of being unemployed. He had to find another occupation, and fast — especially with a new mouth to feed. And this could prove a challenge for a 65-year-old with an increasingly obvious facial deformity, in an economy still recovering from a crippling credit squeeze.

Within a few months he was contacted by Dr Robert Cutforth, director of the National Heart Foundation, who knew of Alec's formidable reputation for placing disabled people in the workforce. Cutforth, who had also heard that Alec 'knew absolutely everybody in Hobart', needed someone to help find jobs for patients who had suffered heart attacks — he got the job. For Alec, it was as good as working at Labour and National Service again, with the advantage of part-time hours. With the new Tasman Bridge, travelling to and from work became easier, and now he had more leisure time for his growing list of hobbies. Cutforth recalls, 'We were so lucky to get him. He was a well-connected and exceptionally experienced employment officer. Alec used to get a high percentage of patients back to work because he had so much knowledge of the workplace and was so forceful. He was a very good interviewer and was always very direct. He told patients that it was much better to go back to work than just sitting on their backside. He knew everyone, so could say, "Come on, don't you be lazy like your father was. Get back to work!" And as he had worked in so many jobs himself, he could find them work in a range of different fields. There was practically nothing he had not done. He set a good fitness example too, because he went walking with his son Neil up to his early eighties!'

One of Alec's first placements at the National Heart Foundation was for Kate, who was taken on as a social worker, a position she would hold for 15 years. Cutforth, who became friends with the Campbells, dining with them regularly, believes Alec and Kate made an unbeatable professional combination. 'They both had offices in the Royal Hobart Hospital. As a social worker with the NHF, Kate would interview the heart attack patients to find out their problems. If they wanted to stop work she would send them to Alec with special file notes. With his inside information he would persuade them to return to work, finding them jobs himself. They were a very successful team. Alec was especially committed. It was a labour of love for him.' By now the Menzies government had committed Australians to the Vietnam War, and Alec's experience proved invaluable when dealing with patients affected directly or indirectly by their involvement in the conflict.

With a steady job and regular income again, Alec embarked on a new mission. Despite his earlier resolution to put the sea behind him, he bought another yacht, the 23-foot *Arabella*, so he could teach his young son to sail in the sheltered waters around Hobart. He would sail her for the next ten years. Safe in Lindisfarne, they were spared the bushfires that killed 62 people in and around Hobart during 1967, destroying many homes and rural properties, and imprinting on Neil his first childhood memory. The following year Alec's socialist ideals were further strained when the Soviet Union invaded Czechoslovakia to crush the nascent democracy movement there, as it had in Hungary 12 years before. Kate recalls, 'Alec was very upset by these invasions. He was devastated by the brutality of the USSR, expressing his horror at their betrayal of socialist principles of international brotherhood. He recognised that it revealed big problems in the Soviet model, but he still maintained there was no real alternative to the socialist political philosophy best expressed by Labor.'

Alec supported the student-based anti–Vietnam War movement, which gathered momentum in the late sixties as more Australian conscripts were killed in the undeclared 'war against communism' so far from Australia's shores. After 1967, when Menzies' successor

Harold Holt drowned, the Liberal/National Country Party coalition seemed to lose their way. For decades they had been warning voters of the monolithic communist bloc's threat to Australia. Once the Soviets and China had fallen out, and US president Richard Nixon had made his historic visit to China (soon to be followed by the ALP's Gough Whitlam and other western leaders), the monolithic theory lost credibility, as did its more strident political promoters.

In 1969, in his seventieth year, Alec fathered his ninth child, Felicity. Angus had died a few years earlier, and Colin had only two more years to live, but their elder brother was still building a family. Kate recalls, 'I believed one child was a lonely child. We were old and we would not be around for very long, so it would be better to have two children to look after each other. I was very glad to have Felicity, but it was difficult because they were so far apart — there was seven years between them.' With so many birthdays, Alec began keeping a record in his diary so he could remember to telephone his children on their special day. Lindisfarne was big enough; anyway he had plenty of experience in adding or adapting rooms for new arrivals. As Neil recalls, 'Building that house in Lindisfarne during the 1950s — which was more or less the work of one man in his fifties with a full-time job — represented a pretty substantial achievement.'

Neil remembers Alec watching the first moon walk in 1969, and the deep impression it made on him. Born in the era of the horse and cart, he watched his television set in wonder as Neil Armstrong stepped onto the moon's surface, marvelling at this epic human adventure. But he had yet to finish his own. In the 1970s he started to build a series of boats for family and friends. Robert Cutforth recalls, 'He built a sailing dinghy for me on his verandah. He was such a skilled boat builder and taught me so much about traditional woodwork. I was the apprentice and he the master builder.' Neil remembers, 'He built various small boats for us on his workbench, which he had made years before from a wonderful tool chest — I remember how much he valued Huon pine. Dad and I spent a lot of time together when I was growing up. He built me a Sabot when I was about 11. I sailed the Sabot with the Derwent Sailing Squadron till I was 15, and he was always with me. He helped run the races for the squadron. Then I sailed a Laser with the Sandy Bay Sailing Club, and Felicity sailed an International Cadet with this club. We also cruised up the D'Entrecasteaux Channel on Arabella, and we joined the Vintage Boat Club.' Kate, too, remembers his love of boat building. 'He was always building something and made several sailing dinghies for the children. He also bought older fishing boats that were not so glamorous but were lovely boats, and they made wonderful holidays for the children.'

The true believer was delighted in 1972 when Whitlam's Labor Party, which had campaigned against Australia's involvement in the Vietnam War, finally defeated the Coalition, ending an epic quarter century of conservative government that had begun when 'Pig Iron' Bob had defeated Alec's old mentor Ben Chifley in 1949. Labor ran on a platform of change within Australia, withdrawal of troops from Vietnam and the abolition of conscription, all policies close to Alec's heart (he had opposed Australia's involvement in Vietnam from the start), and he watched the vigorous new Labor administration with interest. Whitlam also kick-started the Australian film industry, which enabled Peter Weir to make his highly successful film dramatisation *Gallipoli*. The film gave a new generation some appreciation of the Anzac experience; it also gave the legend another shot in the arm, and disposed people to regard with awe old soldiers like Alec, even if they did not resemble Mel Gibson.

Within three years the dream of a new Labor era was over. The year 1975 began badly in Hobart, when the *Lake Illawarra*, a bulk ore carrier, rammed a pylon of the new Tasman Bridge, bringing down the concrete roadway along with a number of motorists, and instantly sinking the ship. The bridge, on Alec's commuting route, would remain closed for more than two years. But worse was to come. In October the federal Opposition used its numbers in the Senate to block the Labor government's Appropriation Bills, denying them the funds they needed to govern. Three weeks later the governor-general, Sir John Kerr, acted to resolve the deadlock by dismissing the Whitlam government and inviting Liberal Party leader Malcolm Fraser to form a caretaker government that could guarantee supply. As the *Mercury* soon revealed to Hobart readers, Kerr had in fact planned the coup with Fraser, who was appalled both by the speed and radical nature of Whitlam's reforms and by the accumulation of political, financial and personal scandals that surrounded the Labor government. The dismissal would inevitably have reminded Alec of Sir Philip Game's removal of New South Wales Labor premier Jack Lang back in the turbulent days of the Depression, when he and fellow unionists at the Launceston Railway Workshops were themselves fighting for democratic reforms.

In 1980 Alec agreed to retire at last from his job as employment consultant with the Heart Foundation. Not that he had much choice, as Cutforth recalls. 'Unfortunately the NHF executives wanted to put more funds into research instead of patients, so rehabilitation was abandoned and we lost Alec's position — which was very bad for our patients as he was absolutely terrific and had revitalised so many of their lives. But as I said to Alec then, "I can't recommend to the board that they create a new career position for a man now in his eighties, can I?" And although he initially thought it might be worth a try, Alec finally agreed.'

Of course, retirement simply gave him more time to pursue his recreational activities. As soon as he got home Alec announced his intent to mount a series of family camping expeditions to explore the wilderness areas of Tasmania using a campervan and tents. He wanted to discover every part of the island that he had not yet seen. Between these treks he taught his second family the joys of sailing in their knockabout yacht *Arabella*, a Victorian couta boat, which they would sail during weekends. *Arabella* was a familiar sight along the Derwent River when the family was young, Kate recalls, recognised most easily by the nappies flying in the rigging. Not content with these outdoor activities, Alec constantly sought out new hobbies. He took a brewing course, producing his own beer 'with excellent results', according to Neil. After a picture-framing course, he began fashioning beautiful frames for his large collection of photographs — some taken with his new Nikon, others dating back more than eighty years. He won several prizes at the Hobart Photographic Society.

In 1983 Bob Hawke brought Labor back into government, having campaigned on the injustice of spiralling unemployment. A no-nonsense trade unionist, Hawke was in the pattern of Curtin and Chifley, on whom Alec had modelled himself, and far more to his liking than Whitlam had been. The two would later form a personal bond.

In 1986 Alec was distressed to hear of Kathleen's death in Launceston. His first wife had long since moved back to Beauty Point, where she had established the exotic country garden she had always dreamed of. She wrote a gardening book explaining all she had learned in her long and successful career growing vegetables and flowers. The large turnout at her funeral confirmed the strength of the family bonds she had created and how much she was loved. Sam moved into the house to maintain the garden according to her mother's gardening principles.

Always interested in big sailing events, in 1988 Alec went down to the harbour in Hobart to watch the arrival of the 11 tall ships of the London to Sydney Australian First Fleet Re-enactment Expedition (organised coincidentally by the author, who shared that yearning 'for a tall ship and a star to steer her by'). Kate recalls the old sailor's excitement when the colourful fleet of square riggers sailed in — the roaring forties abaft their beam, all canvas set. It was a happy moment in an otherwise sad year for Alec, who mourned the passing of his beloved brother and sidekick Mac. Of his siblings, only Estelle survived, and the two started spending more time together, making nostalgic visits to their childhood homes in Launceston and Cressy.

Out of the blue, Alec was offered the opportunity to make what would be his last great expedition — a pilgrimage to Gallipoli for the 75th anniversary of Anzac Day planned for the following April, 1990. He did not hesitate. He had spent much of his life regretting his decision to volunteer for the war, and became resolutely anti-British, anti-war and anti-monarchist after his experience, but a lot of water had flowed under the bridge. It was all so long ago — he had been a different person then. Anyway, the whole strange six-week adventure was almost lost to him now. He could hardly remember the place, and had always wondered what it was really like. Above all, Alec was an adventurer who seized the day. Of course, there were hundreds of other Gallipoli veterans, and there would not be funds for all of them to go. The ultimate decision would be made, as it had been in 1915, after a medical examination. So now, at 90 years old, Alec once more waited his turn in a growing queue of veterans, praying he would pass the medical examination as he had 75 years earlier. At least this time he did not have to adjust his age or get his parents' consent. Still, it was a nail-biting wait for the kid soldier.

ROLL CALL

Those heroes that shed their blood
and lost their lives . . .
You are now lying in the soil of a friendly country
Therefore rest in peace
There is no difference between the Johnnies
and the Mehmets to us where they lie side by side
here in this country of ours . . .
You the mothers
who sent their sons from faraway countries
Wipe away your tears
Your sons are now lying in our bosom
and are in peace
After having lost their lives on this land they have
become our sons as well

Kemal Atatürk

CHAPTER 16
A PILGRIMAGE

'The beach at Gallipoli seemed to have narrowed, but everything else looked the same. The old trenches are still there, filled with leaves and undergrowth. We could still find bits of barbed wire and other stuff — cans and the broken top of an old rum jar.'

Alec's medical examination in early 1990, no doubt administered a little more gently than the one he had undergone in 1915, went well. He certainly felt fit enough. He was the youngest of the group, of course, and was later heard to complain about having to travel 'with all those old codgers'. Nevertheless he was lucky to be selected as one of the 'landing force' of about 60 veterans short-listed from at least 350 applicants from all states of Australia for the all-expenses-paid tour. At 91, he was more than ten years younger than the oldest, John McLeery, who would turn 103 at Gallipoli on Anzac Day. Three other veterans in the party — Ted Matthews from Sydney, Len Hall from Perth and Walter Parker from Melbourne — would themselves attract media attention when they made the list of the last ten Australian Gallipoli survivors. Before the end of the decade Matthews, a signaller, and like Alec a carpenter in civilian life, would become the last Anzac survivor of the 25 April landings. This time the landing force would be led, not by British generals, 'who mucked the whole thing up by landing us on the wrong beach', as Matthews succinctly put it, but by Australia's own Labor prime minister, Bob Hawke, a rough-hewn former trade union leader like Alec.

Hawke promised to be a good travelling companion for the boys from 1915. The significance of the expedition was not lost on the Labor leader, who 'counted it a great personal privilege to be included in the pilgrimage'. He paid tribute to the courage of the veterans who had volunteered for Gallipoli once again. They had 'guts then and guts now', especially those among them who had put their ages up so they could serve their country. Some, he noted, had later adjusted their ages downward again so they could serve in the Second World War. 'With a track record like that, it is not surprising these veterans have volunteered to return to Gallipoli. But the most remarkable thing of all is that these veterans, all in their nineties or older, should be going to Gallipoli with exactly the same spirit which impelled them the first time, 75 years ago. When we read and hear what they themselves say — and they were great writers of letters, journals and diaries — two things stand out: their sense of adventure, and their determination to stick with their mates.'

Participating in this new 'invasion' were political leaders from Britain (Prime Minister Margaret Thatcher was there to honour the 21,255 British soldiers who died during the campaign), France (which lost some 10,000 men), New Zealand (2,701), India (1,350) and Canada (49 soldiers from Newfoundland). Like Australia, each participating nation sent parties of veterans too. Also attending were political representatives from Greece, which had provided the Allies with logistical support including use of the Aegean islands of Imbros and Lemnos (where Alec had first joined the 15th Battalion at Sarpi Camp). The event was hosted by Turgut Ozal, the president of Turkey (which had lost 86,692 during the campaign). Even high-ranking German representatives were present.

It would be the biggest and most lavish party Alec had been to since 1915. Underwriting the expedition by what was billed 'the world's oldest tour group' would cost the Australian government

$2.5 million. The ABC shelled out $1 million to cover the event and send live television images to audiences back home. Bob Hawke would be supported by the minister for Veterans' Affairs, Ben Humphreys. The new federal Opposition leader, John Hewson, also went along to confirm the bipartisan nature of the pilgrimage, as did the National Party's Tim Fischer. First World War Veterans' Association patron Bill Hall managed the veterans, and at least 150 military personnel accompanied the party, as did eight war widows, eight 'legatees' (who had lost fathers in the campaign), a team of administrators and a substantial media contingent. At least 1,300 defence personnel from Australia and New Zealand would also support the veterans at Gallipoli, and three ships would be anchored offshore. Many ordinary citizens had also been invited, and organisers expected a further 10,000 backpackers and tourists for the dawn service on the twenty-fifth. Ironically, given the shockingly inadequate medical resources in 1915, Alec and his fellow veterans were escorted by no less than seven doctors, 23 nurses, four RAAF aeromedicine specialists and unlimited medical supplies. Rumours that coffins or body bags were also carried on the plane were quickly scotched.

The return would bring back painful memories for some of the veterans, but not for Alec. Speaking before their departure to Radiowise journalist Peter Rubenstein, whose interviews with Alec and his family have been extracted throughout this book, Alec admitted that 'it might bring back some ghosts', but he was not at all worried. 'I was so young then, and yet I came through Gallipoli okay when a lot of more mature people didn't. But it was not a good place to serve at all, especially when the snow and the rain came. So I was one of the lucky ones. I can't think that any great trauma will occur, although I am remembering now more than I thought I would. I mean, you could go around looking for that sort of sadness if you wanted, but it is a long time ago. I think it is exciting, a marvellous thing. I am looking forward to it tremendously.

'It was a beautiful place, you know. The sea was beautiful and Anzac Cove was a pretty little beach and the steep hills and the background and the hilltop we called the Sphinx standing up high above the others. I'm looking forward to seeing Gallipoli again. Everyone that I've spoken to who is going is delighted to be seeing the place again. It was a lovely place. If conditions had been better . . . and the little bay, the cove, Anzac was a beautiful little cove, and the green Aegean Sea stretching way out to Imbros. The thing that was wrong was the conditions — you know, the lice and the fleas and the flies and all those things made it intolerable, and the poor food, and the sickness and the dysentery. But the place itself was beautiful.'

Kate had helped him pack for the trip, wishing she could go too. 'As he said, he was pretty young and he was able to recover. He had a varied life after he came back and his mind was more on the active things he was doing than worrying about the war. He certainly hasn't worried about the war. He is not like any of those people who have nightmares . . . He has never known that.'

Alec wrote his own account of the journey, and his unadorned narrative again reveals his continuing lively curiosity, range of interests and alert perceptiveness at this emotionally charged moment in his life.

Wednesday 18 April was a quiet day at the Lady Davidson Repatriation Centre. We had further medical checks and rest at this pleasant place. I had several visitors during the day — Neil, Jim, Andrew and Susan, and Peter, who was flying to Japan the next day for the launching of the Japanese yacht on their first attempt at the America's Cup. Chris and Jamie Jenkins and baby Eleanor also drove down and spent the afternoon with me. We all went to bed early in preparation for the Official Dinner. The Prime Minister and the Leader of the Opposition were there. Dinner was served in a huge tent. The day was cold and wet. It was raining the whole time we were in Sydney.

We left the Centre for the airport on Friday morning in two big buses. It was about an hour's drive, which I don't think I'll ever forget. We had a police escort, i.e. outriders on motor cycles clearing a way for us through the peak hour traffic in the centre of Sydney. I don't think

Alec and Mac in Argyllshire, 1952

Alec, still shy of his Bell's Palsy,
graduates from the University
of Hobart, 1955.

Alec married Kate Corvan,
20 years his junior, in 1958.

Returning to Gallipoli, 1990

Alec leads the Anzac Day parade in Hobart, 1995. *(The Mercury, Hobart)*

Alec and Kate with his nine children, Anzac Day, 2000 (*left to right*: Jim, Deirdre, Mary, Neil (partly hidden), Greg, Geraldine, Felicity, Cressey and Sam)

Kate and Alec steal a quiet moment between official functions, 2000.

(*The Mercury*, Hobart)

Proud Clan Campbell women farewell the old warrior outside St. David's Cathedral, Hobart.

(© Newspix/Tim Dub)

The old sea dog looks back across three centuries of an extraordinary life well lived.

(© Newspix/Craig Borrow)

we slowed down until we reached the airport and boarded the big jumbo jet 'The Spirit of Anzac' to Singapore.

We had a comfortable and interesting flight. It was surprising how long it took us to fly across Australia, it made me realize again what a big place Australia is. We flew over Ayers Rock. The pilot circled the Rock so we could see it. I had no problems during the long flight but my ears were ringing a little when we reached Singapore. We were taken on a very interesting bus tour of Singapore and in the afternoon and evening I went shopping. Singapore was a well organised, clean and tidy place. An amazing amount of swamp land has been reclaimed. I enjoyed the short time we had there.

The flight from Singapore was comfortable in the big plane but we were all tired on arrival in Istanbul. Istanbul is different from Singapore in all sorts of ways. I found it more interesting. Singapore is modern, very tidy streets and modern shops, while Istanbul is a sprawling mixture of shops, bazaars, mosques, old fortresses and apartment houses. It is a busy port with many big ships passing to and from the Black Sea ports. It reminded me of Cairo in 1915. We had a whole rest day there and I walked through the bazaars and narrow, interesting streets. I bought a leather jacket for myself and one for Kate and a few other small articles. I think the shop keepers expect you to bargain with them. I found I could usually get things for about 25 to 30 per cent less than the prices marked, especially if you had American dollars. The inflation rate in Turkey is 70 per cent, so it was not wise to leave with Turkish money. We stayed at the President Hotel, and when we arrived the whole hotel staff was in front to greet us. Service there was excellent. We did not particularly like Turkish food, it consisted mainly of soft cheese and bread and fruits. The meat was peculiar — some said it was goat.

We were taken for an interesting tour of the city by bus. We saw a lot, and it was well explained to us by our guide, a young Turk who had been educated in the USA. We were also taken for a tour of the

Bosporus on two Turkish ferry boats. It was here that we crossed from European Turkey into Asia.

We left Istanbul at 6.30 a.m. on Tuesday morning for Gelibolu, or rather the Boncuk Hotel about 5 miles from Gelibolu (this is the town that some of the AIF and the New Zealanders saw when they reached the top of Hill 60 from Lone Pine before being recalled during the August attack in 1915). Boncuk is a modern European-style hotel but the food was strange. A few of us hired a car to take us into Gelibolu, which is a fishing village on the Gelibolu Peninsula. I found this place interesting — lots of fishing boats in docks, not unlike but smaller than the Hobart fishermen's dock. The boats are about 25ft to 30ft long, half decked double unders. They have petrol engines and two long oars, which the fishermen use as our fishermen do, for the so-called 'Fisherman's Shove'. They also use 'Grab all' nets very like the ones used in Tasmania. I was glad we saw this place. We got back to the Boncuk Hotel in time for the evening meal.

The bus drive down the coast of the Sea of Marmara from Istanbul to Boncuk was interesting, mile after mile of prosperous looking farm land. Our guide told us this was owned by individual farmers, the property passing from father to first-born son. The farm houses were well built two-storied stone places painted white. The houses were mainly on the sea front, but not on each farm. There were very few fences and we could see no sign of irrigation. Crops appeared to be barley and other grains and some vineyards. I tasted a bottle of the local wine. Next day, ANZAC DAY, we were up at 2 a.m. Shower and shave, a cup of tea and off by bus to Anzac. It was still dark when we got there, but our bus had a slight delay on the road and this caused us to miss the opening of the international ceremony. There were crowds of people trying to get a place, some of them young 'back packers' who had camped here overnight. We had seats reserved and rugs provided to keep our legs warm. The ceremony was very impressive. I thought our uniformed troops compared very well with other troops.

After the ceremonies we were taken for a bus tour of the Gallipoli battle fields — Lone Pine, Quinn's Post and The Nek. There were beautifully kept pine trees planted around and the names of individual soldiers clearly marked on grave stones.

The levelling of the ground and the pine trees made these places look very different from what I remembered of them, but the rest of the place was just as I remembered it. The Beach at Gallipoli seemed to have narrowed but everything else looked the same. The old trenches are still there, filled with leaves and undergrowth. We could still find bits of barbed wire and other stuff — cans and the broken top of an old rum jar. It was a terrific experience to see this place again. I remembered all sorts of things I thought I had long ago forgotten. I walked along the beach to about where I thought the Fisherman's Hut and clump of olive trees was but I would have had to go too far into the scrub to have found it. About the place where I would have had to enter the scrub in search of the hut, a fishing boat was moored a few feet out from the shore. I was interested because Bean's diary of the Gallipoli campaign mentions a lone fishing boat being moored at this spot when the landing took place in 1915. I wondered if the owner of the boat I saw was connected in some way with the owners of the boat Bean talked about in 1915.

The drive back to the hotel along the shores of the narrows was comfortable but we were all tired out after a very long and very interesting day. After a rest we started the long drive along the shore of the Sea of Marmara to Istanbul. Next day we visited the War Museum, which consisted mainly of relics of the Gallipoli campaign. During this visit a Turkish military band entertained us at a concert that I thought wonderful. Bandsmen were dressed in period costumes, some dating back to the time of the European Crusades. The martial music the band played was splendid and inspiring. In the evening we left Istanbul for Singapore.

It had been an absolutely wonderful experience for me, and I think for all of us. The trip had been planned and organised to the last detail.

The 'carers' who looked after our well-being were a remarkable group of people. Most of them were skilled nurses devoted to their work. Gary Munting, our carer, is a nurse in charge of the Intensive Care Unit at the Tasmanian Repatriation Hospital. I could not imagine a more skilful and devoted person. The work he put into the task, by no means an easy one, went a long way to making the Gallipoli pilgrimage the great success it was.

As the media reports confirmed, contrary to the botched affair they were commemorating, the 1990 Gallipoli expedition was an unqualified success. The ABC coverage, too, went without a hitch, the event transmitted live all round Australia, where families such as Alec's were watching. When dawn broke on Anzac Day, 57 Australian veterans, including Alec (once again the kid soldier in the group), took their places for the commemorative service at peaceful Anzac Cove — at the very spot where, 75 years earlier to the hour, the first wave of Anzacs had landed amid a chaos of shellfire, bullets and death.

The prime minister, voice cracking and tears flowing unchecked, spoke for the nation when he said, 'For us, no place on earth more grimly symbolises the waste and futility of war than this scene of carnage where the campaign failed and 8,709 Australians were needlessly killed.' For this lesson to be understood, Hawke said, 'the story has to be taught to every new generation of Australians'. He paid tribute to Alec and his fellow veterans: 'They did not pretend to fathom the deep and immense tides of history which brought them so far from home, so far from all they knew and loved. Nor could they begin to imagine that the vast and terrible forces unleashed upon the world in 1914 would still be working their way through human history 75 years later. But they knew two things — they had a job to do, and in the end they could only rely on each other to see it through. At the heart of the Gallipoli tradition lay a commitment. It was a simple but deep commitment from one soldier to another, each to his fellow Australian. And that was where the great tradition of Australian mateship was enshrined and the essential nature of the nation's character was forged. Because it is that commitment to Australia that defined then and defines now what it is to be Australian.'

Buoyed up by the military band, the company then sang the national anthem followed by 'Soldiers of Australia' (to the tune of 'Waltzing Matilda'), before the baton was passed to other political leaders. The Turkish president graciously confirmed that all wrongs against his country were forgiven, and that it was Turkey's wish to remain a friend and ally of Australia. Then began the ceremony during which the political delegates laid wreaths at each of a series of sacred sites, starting with Anzac Cove, then Ari Burnu, Lone Pine, the Nek, Quinn's Post and Chunuk Bair. Finally, and most affecting for Alec and his fellow Anzacs, the last post was sounded.

The journey back to Australia took the veterans about the same time as it had taken Alec to sail from Anzac Cove to Lemnos in 1915. He was still excited when he got home. Interviewed by Peter Rubenstein, he seemed most elated about finding his old dugout below Hill 971. 'I wanted to look at Hay Valley, because it was a pleasant place, and we were there for a while, camping not far from the frontline trenches. There was a small sap that I had good reason to know, and I went looking for it and I couldn't see it, and then I fell into it! It had bush over the top of it, and I fell down into this wretched trench. Luckily it didn't hurt me, but the escorting soldiers had to haul me out. I also dropped my camera and they had to get that out too. But I was really thrilled to find my old trench again. And it is a pleasant enough place in peacetime.'

'Alec probably got more than most people would have out of the trip because he was the youngest,' Kate believes. 'He was keen to go out at night and have a look at Istanbul, whereas the others were just about ready for bed. So he had one of the Army servicemen take him out to have a look at the town, and the markets and things like that. One thing that struck him was looking behind the landing beach at Gallipoli, because in 1915 he had not seen much but the beachfront and all that part of it. But having looked at the land behind it, he said, "They were mad to think they could ever work their way through to Istanbul from there." With all the hilly areas and the forts along the way, he said, they could never have done it. They were wrong in their decision in the first place.'

The pilgrimage had been a great achievement. Speaking in Parliament the following month, the prime minister placed on record 'our thanks to all those involved in initiating, planning, organising and carrying through so successfully the memorable pilgrimage to Gallipoli on Anzac Day, 25 April 1990, the seventy-fifth anniversary of the Australians' landing at Anzac Cove'. He went on, 'The people of Australia are the inheritors and custodians of the Anzac tradition, because from the deeds and sacrifices of the Anzacs at Gallipoli there emerged a powerful sense of the Australian national identity. Despite the military failure of the Gallipoli campaign, the Anzacs forged an unsurpassed reputation for bravery, endurance, resourcefulness, irrepressible humour under pressure and above all loyalty to one another.' He argued for the ongoing relevance of the Anzac legend, because 'the commemoration of Anzac Day provides a continuing source of inspiration for all Australians, and the example of the Anzacs has been emulated many times, in war and in peace, by individuals and communities coping with natural disasters, tragedies of all kinds and, indeed, the challenges of everyday life'.

Finally, he paid 'a special tribute to those magnificent Anzacs who returned to honour their mates on Gallipoli. In 1915 these very men, and the thousands of their fellow Australians they represent, made a profound impact on the imagination of the Australian people and upon their sense of nationhood. Seventy-five years on they have made, I believe, no less an impact on a new generation of Australians. The most remarkable thing of all is that they have achieved that by showing exactly the same qualities which created the Anzac tradition so long ago. The way they bore themselves; the way they seemed to shrug off the weight of years; their sense of independence; their determination to see it through; the old sharp irreverent wit; their sense of mateship — in a word their sheer Australianness — was as evident in the pilgrimage as it had been 75 years ago, and I congratulate each and every one of these old diggers for teaching Australia the true meaning of the Anzac tradition.'

As an inexperienced 16-year-old in 1915, Alec had been disappointed not to get into 'the firing line' at Gallipoli. Now he was moving inexorably towards a firing line of a different kind, for by participating in this high-profile expedition he had placed himself on the media database. Frustrated by missing the 'action' then, he was about to get more than he wanted. Within a few years he would not be able to avoid the camera flashes and constant media attention. Unwittingly he had set himself up to become a prime target, the moment he became the last man standing.

CHAPTER 17
LAST MAN STANDING

'Dad often used to joke that if he went to war at 16 he would probably be the oldest Anzac left. Years ago, in the 1930s, that was his joke on Anzac Day. He realised even then that as the youngest Anzac there was a distinct possibility he would be the last one left alive.'

Back in Hobart, and finding himself something of a celebrity, Alec gave a series of local media interviews before putting Gallipoli behind him once more. That year they sold the house at Lindisfarne and moved in with Kate's mother in her humble little house in Bishop Street, Newtown. She needed the help, and the move would also be financially prudent, because the money they made from the sale of Lindisfarne would help fund their retirement. Alec settled back into a quieter life in Hobart. With the days of serious sailing and camping trips past, he now spent a lot of time at the Hobart Yacht Club talking to his old sailing friends, lending advice on boats and boat building. Estelle, who when they were children had done so much to enliven the lives of her brothers, especially her beloved Alec, died that year. Only Alec was left.

Resting comfortably in his favourite armchair at Bishop Street surrounded by memories, there was time for reflection. It was remarkable, looking back over his long life, how all the turns he had taken along his chosen path had led to this. Those first tentative steps towards self-improvement after the war — through the carpentry course and the car and wagon building — had set him on an inexorable course. The success of the first step inspired the next, resulting in a procession of hard-won professional and personal achievements. The disability he brought back from Gallipoli, far from holding him back, had spurred him on, consolidating his stubborn determination to succeed in all he did. Persistence, as his Scotch College headmaster once argued it would, had paid off.

His idealism had found many outlets — through his union work, through his career finding jobs for disabled war veterans, and later through his dedication to post-coronary placement at the National Heart Foundation, a commitment he pursued into his eighties. Alec's inclination towards being an all-rounder rather than a narrow specialist had led him in so many different and rewarding directions that he could claim with some justice to have truly experienced life to the full. He had tried his hand at everything, tasting as much as he could. So many times he had followed his heart rather than his head, letting his zest for life guide him. And he had done the Campbell clan proud, siring a big family, passing on the name, fighting for his country, serving his fellows in the social, industrial and political worlds. In his own way he had lived up to the ancient battle cry 'Cruachan!' He had had a good life.

He still marched on Anzac Day each year. Sometimes he featured in the state-wide media coverage, although few people outside Tasmania gave him a thought. He had kept a relatively low profile compared with some old soldiers on the mainland. When *Sydney Morning Herald* history writer Tony Stephens published a book on the last surviving Anzacs in the mid 1990s he knew nothing of Alec, so left him out of this otherwise definitive account. Stephens soon learned of his omission, however, and after tracking Alec down he kindly introduced the author to Alec and the other Gallipoli veterans he had contacted.

Things began to change in the second half of the 1990s, and it was no small irony that the catalyst should have been the election, in 1996, of the conservative John Howard's Liberal/National Party

Coalition. With Australia suffering the worst unemployment since the Depression, Howard campaigned successfully on a promise to create more jobs. Fortunately, all of Alec's children and grand-children were securely employed, but more than 12 per cent of Australian workers were without jobs. Just as the Scullin Labor government had been defeated by the Depression in 1931 in Alec's political heyday, the worsening economic situation now brought down the Labor government of Paul Keating, who had himself deposed Bob Hawke in a coup not long after Hawke's return from Gallipoli.

Not without qualms, the true believer was pleased when Howard promised more funds for Veterans' Affairs and announced plans for a $5 million ABC television series, 'Australians at War', to commemorate the service of soldiers like himself. Since both his father and grandfather had fought in the First World War, Howard had a personal interest in supporting the veterans. Nevertheless, his election victory must surely have reminded Alec of the triumph all those years ago of that other arch-conservative, when critics claimed Menzies had 'put the clocks back'. Politics aside, Alec would have been impressed by Howard's conduct following the Port Arthur massacre, when he swiftly clamped down on private firearms licensing. Tasmania in 1996 was a very different world from the one in which Alec had grown up, hunting rifle usually close to hand.

On Remembrance Day that year, public attention was drawn back to Gallipoli when the last veteran of the 25 April landings, Ted Matthews of Sydney (who had accompanied Alec on the great pilgrimage of 1990), appeared on national television. This was when the present author became involved with the story. Catching Matthews on television by chance, I set out to interview him on videotape for the Australian War Memorial historical records. Having established that Matthews was one of only ten Gallipoli survivors, I decided to interview all of these fascinating men who had such important stories to tell. One of them, it emerged, was Alec Campbell, the sole Tasmanian survivor. The other nine were

Ted Matthews, Fred Kelly and Les Leach (a New Zealander), from Sydney; Jack Buntine, Roy Longmore and Walter Parker, from Melbourne; Frank Isaacs and Len Hall, from Perth; and Doug Dibley, who lived in New Zealand. I would write of this group for the first time in an article in *The Australian* magazine published on Remembrance Day that year.

The die was cast, yet few journalists seemed interested in Alec's own long life. No one asked about his bush days or horse racing, his boxing career or carpentry work, his years as a union leader and peace campaigner, his experience as an ocean sailor and boat builder or his countless other interests. All these aspects of his rich life and inspiring character were distracting background. He had become simply a symbol. Despite having spent only six weeks at Anzac Cove, Alec Campbell had become the quintessential Gallipoli warrior, and he was expected to live up to the role. And since by a quirk of fate he was the youngest of the veterans, he would be increasingly relied upon by a nation reluctant to let go of the last living links with the legend. In November 1997 New Zealander Les Leach, like Alec a water carrier at Gallipoli, died in Sydney. He had been lucky to reach old age after a water can he was carrying stopped a Turkish bullet aimed at his heart.

When Ted Matthews died, aged 101, the following month, severing the last direct link with the first landings, John Howard authorised a state funeral — the first of its kind for an ordinary Gallipoli soldier, although Matthews did reach the rank of corporal. Doug Dibley, a stretcher bearer who had worked in the ambulance services alongside the legendary John Kirkpatrick Simpson, died next in New Zealand. In 1998, when the French government commemorated the eightieth anniversary of the end of the war by awarding Allied survivors of the battle of the Somme with the coveted Legion of Honour, the Department of Veterans' Affairs sent four of Australia's fittest veterans to France. The group comprised Ted Smout and Eric Abraham of Queensland, Charlie Mance of New South Wales and Howard Pope of South Australia.

Jack Buntine died in December that year. An original larrikin with a wry sense of humour, Buntine had been 'a crack shot who could knock a jam tin off a fence post at one hundred yards' and the last Australian winner of the Military Medal from Gallipoli. He was followed later that month by Fred Kelly, who had enlisted to 'keep an eye on' his younger brother but who ended up fighting at both Gallipoli and the Somme. With just five Gallipoli veterans surviving, media interest in Alec grew, notably when he celebrated his century at a large gathering of the clan in Hobart in February 1999. The big family occasion, attended by all his children, drew relatives from as far away as Perth and New Zealand. He received the traditional tele-gram from the Queen, but the old republican remained staunchly anti-monarchist, voted that way in the referendum later that year, and in his media interviews advised other voters to do likewise.

A few days after Alec's birthday gathering Len Hall died in Perth. Hall was the last survivor of the Light Horse to have served at Gallipoli, where he fought at the Nek in the bloody engagement Charles Bean would refer to as 'the tennis court of death'. He went on to serve under General Harry Chauvel in the charge of the Light Horse at Beersheba, which has been called the last great cavalry charge in history. He also rode into Damascus with T. E. Lawrence when the Turks were dislodged from that stronghold. Next to go was another Western Australian, Frank Isaacs, a seasoned fighter who had survived many dreadful battles both at Gallipoli and at the Somme, where he had once had to dig himself out from under a brick wall brought down by enemy fire. Isaacs died in April 1999.

By the turn of the millennium only two veterans besides Alec survived: Walter Parker, another water carrier at Gallipoli, now sadly depleted, having lost both his eyesight and power of speech; and Roy Longmore, who had been a tunneller at Gallipoli. At the Somme, wounded in both arms and legs, Longmore had been carried to a clearing station by captured German prisoners of war directed at gunpoint, a farmhouse door used as a makeshift stretcher. He had been wounded so badly he had thought he was 'a goner'. Both Parker and Longmore were from Melbourne, and both were now aged 104. With Walter Parker beyond interviewing, the spotlight swung between the affable giant Roy Longmore and Alec, with his increasingly troublesome and unsightly facial paralysis. To commemorate Australia Day, in early January 2000 Australia Post issued a special set of 'Last Anzacs' stamps, featuring early photographs of the three veterans. Walter Parker died later that month.

On turning 101 in February, Alec felt the call of the sea again. When his old *Kintail* shipmate John Bennetto heard of this, he 'could not resist the opportunity of taking that old sea dog out once more', so he prepared his vessel, *Mirrabooka II*, for the sail. 'Because he was so old I didn't want him walking down the gangplank, so I decided to lift him up from the wharf in a bosun's chair, swing him through the air and lower him down onto the deck. But Alec refused. "Johnny, I don't want to get in that dodgy little bosun's chair." So I just put my foot down. "Alec, you are now under captain's orders", and we swung him onto the deck.' And so they sailed through the Hobart waters Alec knew so well as he sipped his favourite whisky in the comfort of the cabin. Of course even this became a news event: Sydney-based Channel Nine presenter Ray Martin flew to Hobart to film the trip for a documentary he was producing on Alec. The network had helped fly Alec's children to Hobart for the biggest Campbell clan reunion outside Argyllshire, which Martin also filmed. Channel Nine also flew Alec and Kate to Canberra on a special RAAF jet to attend a function at the Australian War Memorial, where he met the prime minister and took tea with the Governor-General, Sir William Deane, at Yarralumba, again filmed by Martin's crew. Alec was becoming a TV star. On the steps of the Australian War Memorial he found himself the target of a scrum of enthusiastic young autograph seekers.

After these exertions Alec was happy to settle back in his comfortable armchair at New Town again. In September he followed the Sydney Olympic Games avidly on television, taking a special interest in the sailing events. Hearing that he was sitting still for a moment, Alec's granddaughter Katya Langenheim (Deirdre's daughter), who studied Fine Art at Monash University and worked at the Judith Pugh Gallery, paid a visit. Of the three portraits of her grandfather she painted on this occasion, two she promptly sold privately; the third she offered to the Tasmanian Art Gallery. Katya would inevitably remind Alec of his mother, another talented artist who trained in Melbourne.

On 1 January 2001 Australia celebrated the centenary of federation with a re-enactment of the proclamation of the Commonwealth in Sydney's Centennial Park. Watching the event on television, Alec would have been one of a tiny group who could claim to have participated in the original celebrations, when as a toddler he had accompanied his parents to the public picnic laid on by Launceston City Council to celebrate the birth of Australia. He turned 102 the following month, celebrating his birthday quietly with family at home. Later in the year he received a centenary medal, specially struck for the occasion, awarded to citizens who had contributed to the first 100 years of the Australian nation.

In June 2001 Roy Longmore died in his sleep in Melbourne at the grand age of 106. Alec Campbell was now alone.

On hearing the news, I phoned Kate to warn her of the next morning's front page news. Heaving a sigh, Kate said, 'I have been dreading this moment for years. Alec has had more attention than he ever wanted, and now it is going to get worse.' But she stoically agreed to do what needed to be done. An international search soon confirmed that Alec was not simply the last Australian but probably the last man standing from any country that had fought at Gallipoli in 1915. As the sole survivor of an estimated one million soldiers who participated in the campaign on all sides, including Turkey, Germany, Britain, France, New Zealand, Newfoundland (Canada), India and Australia, he had become the 'man in a million'. Little wonder the national spotlight now picked him out.

'Dad often used to joke,' Mary remembers, 'that if he went to war at 16 he would probably be the oldest Anzac left. Years ago, in the 1930s, that was his joke on Anzac Day. He realised even then that as the youngest Anzac there was a distinct possibility he would be the last one left alive.' On Remembrance Day, 11 November 2001, he dominated media reports covering Armistice Day.

Alec celebrated his 103rd birthday on 26 February 2002 with Kate, his children, grandchildren and great-grandchildren, friends, well-wishers and supporters from the RSL, who hosted a special function. On 25 April he came forward, as always, to lead the Anzac march through Hobart. On doctor's orders, this time he was driven, but he still insisted on laying a wreath at the Memorial. He was afterwards escorted for a lap of honour around the football ground where the recently inaugurated annual Anzac Day football match, the Alec Campbell Cup, was being played. Then he shared a beer at the RSL club with a group of Second World War veterans. It would be his last public appearance. Within a month, he was gone.

Alec died on 16 May 2002. He had been lucky. As a boy he had been thrown off horses and had spent an inordinate time with explosives and firearms; he had survived Gallipoli where so many others had not, there contracting a cocktail of illnesses that, while not finishing him, spared him the killing fields of the western front; he had survived sea voyages through the theatre of war where many ships were sunk; he had gone bush as a jackaroo and a drover, mustering scrub cattle in wild country; as a dare-devil jockey he had raced in many a country show; he had boxed men far bigger than himself who should have been able to 'eat him for breakfast'; he had stepped into a dozen union brawls; he had survived a hair-raising trip around the treacherous coast of Tasmania and no fewer than seven Sydney–Hobart yacht races, along with many other demanding ocean voyages. After all this and more, Alec died peacefully in his pyjamas in a neighbourhood nursing home managed by one of his granddaughters, Jo Hardy. His death was front page news in every major newspaper in Australia and was reported around the world.

Kate was heartbroken, as were his nine children, not to mention his 32 grandchildren, 35 great-grandchildren and two great-great-grandchildren. But their grief could not remain private for long, because he had become government property, and the machinery of the long-awaited state funeral was about to take over. Consequently, the last stage in his life story would have very little to do with the real Alec Campbell.

The public accolades might have been for Australia's top-ranking military commander rather than a humble Anzac water carrier. The governor-general, Peter Hollingworth, described Alec's passing as 'an occasion for Australians to pause and reflect on the passing of the generation that gave us our identity and character as a nation'. The prime minister pronounced, 'It is a big moment in this country's history, the severing of that link. On behalf of the nation, I honour his life. He was typical of a generation of Australians who through their sacrifice and bravery and decency created a legacy that has resonated through subsequent decades and generations. All Australians will forever be in debt to the Anzacs not only for what they did for us but for the legend, for the tradition, for the stoicism under fire, sense of mateship all those other great ideals that increasingly young Australians see as part of their inheritance. The wonderful thing is that the spirit and the tradition is growing stronger as the years go by. It must have been a source of enormous comfort and reassurance and pride for somebody like Alec Campbell in his later years to see the warm embrace of Anzac by the young people of today as they walk the cliffs of Gallipoli.'

'We thank him, we honour him, and our condolences go to his family,' recited the Opposition leader, Simon Crean. 'He was the last of the original Anzacs and our last living link with that Anzac tradition.' The minister for Veterans' Affairs, Danna Vale, declared, 'Mr Campbell and his fellow Anzacs fought with the kind of courage, integrity and honour that we will never forget.' Tasmanian premier Jim Bacon, less pompously, observed that 'it was important to remember him not just as a young man and a soldier. Alec glorified neither his own accomplishments in war nor his elevation as one of his country's heroes. He just enlisted, fought for his country then came back to Tasmania and got on with his life.' Tasmanian Senator Guy Barnett seized the moment for his state, pointing out, 'Mr Campbell has helped make Tasmania the great state it is for more than 100 years. He embodied the Tasmanian spirit as much as he embodied the spirit of Anzac.' The national president of the RSL, Major-General Peter Phillips, would remember Alec 'not as an old man but as that baby-faced 16-year-old in the 1915 photograph with that rather apprehensive look on his face. Alec Campbell may have been the last man standing from the Gallipoli campaign, but he was also a great Australian in his own right.' Les Carlyon, author of a highly regarded account of the campaign, commented simply, 'His death is actually the end of the story.'

John Howard cut short a state visit to China so as not to miss the opportunity to speak at the memorial service. The state funeral was, he declared, 'an occasion for all shades of Australian society to honour not only a person who deserves that by dint of his own bravery but also for what he represents and what his generation so preciously and heroically gave to us'. The governor-general, the pre-mier of Tasmania, state governors, political, military and religious leaders now cleared their diaries and set their sights on Hobart. There would be no half measures for Private Alec Campbell's send-off. Never mind that he had been on Anzac Beach for a mere six weeks; that he had subsequently renounced war, become a fervent trade unionist, union leader, Labor supporter and pacifist; or that he stood for political office on a socialist platform alongside a communist sympathiser and had become a committed republican. Had his old radical running mate Bill Morrow been alive, he would not have made the official guest list; he probably would not even have been allowed in!

The occasion was rich with ironies. Yet the funeral was not intended to commemorate Alec Campbell as an individual. It was a supremely national event — the last great opportunity to honour the 50,000 Australians who had served in that pitiless foreign field and the 8,709 who died there. His coffin draped in the Australian flag before the altar in St David's Cathedral, once again Alec was being called upon to serve a higher cause.

The main streets of Hobart were closed on the big day and crowds gathered early outside the little cathedral, rugged up against the chill of the windy city. The crowd watched as 'the top brass with their shrapnel', as Alec would have called them, began to file through the west door into the nave. Few commanders-in-chief or generals received the kind of attention accorded to Private Campbell, 2731 AIF, in Hobart on 24 May 2002. The officials included Prime Minister Howard, Governor-General Hollingworth, the state governors of Tasmania, Victoria and South Australia, the deputy prime minister; the leader of the Opposition; the British and New Zealand High Commissioners; the Archbishops of Australia and Hobart; the Chief of the Defence Force, Admiral Chris Barrie; the Chief of the Army, Major General Peter Cosgrove; the Chief of the Air Force and the Deputy Chief of the Navy. If Alec had been worried about meeting Lord Kitchener in life, we can only imagine his consternation in the face of this gathering at his death. His Sydney–Hobart shipmate Darrel Gates, shaking his head incredulously, commented after the funeral, 'Alec would have been so embarrassed with all the paraphernalia of that state funeral and would not have wanted any of it.'

Among the watching crowd would have been many representatives of the skilled trades. Noticeably absent from the official guest list, let alone from the speakers' list, however, were representatives of ACTU, the Trades Hall Council, the Australian Railways' Union, the Builders Workers' Industrial Union or any of the unions to which Alec had devoted so much energy. The upper echelons of the Catholic Church, from which he and Kathleen had broken irredeemably so many years ago, was well represented, however. He had always felt ambivalent about his own 'shrapnel' or 'ironmongery', as he called it. He might well have felt compromised by the ostentatious display of medals placed on purple cushions on the coffin of the six-week soldier, including the 1915 Gallipoli Star, the

British War Medal, the 1914–1918 Star, the 80th Anniversary Armistice Remembrance Medal and the Centenary Medal, complemented for the occasion by a bayonet and First World War cap once owned by Private Oscar Melrose. But Alec would have loved the bagpipes and the sight of so many family members wearing the Campbell tartan, and would have been gladdened to know that nearly one hundred members of his wider family had attended.

The prime minister began his tribute by extrapolating on Alec's life as embracing the rich history of Australia's first century following federation. The story of Alec's life, he said, was also the story of Australia from its first tentative steps to the great nation it had become. Even as the ranks of the veterans thinned, the spirit of Anzac was growing, as demonstrated by the bigger crowds at Anzac Day parades. By observing Alec's death, the nation was pledging itself to the ethos encapsulated by the Anzacs, who fought for the same sort of freedom, the prime minister claimed, that was being maintained by Australian troops at that moment in Afghanistan, East Timor and Bougainville. Fate had chosen wisely in selecting Alec Campbell as the last man standing, he said, because he was such a good family man — a friend, father, grandfather and great-great-grandfather of whom the nation should be proud. He was modest, unassuming, dedicated to hard work and self-improvement, with a great love of adventure, the sea and nature. The prime minister also conceded Alec's great commitment to serving his fellow man, which had included serving the disabled and the trade union movement. Alec's ability to love, his sense of endeavour, love of challenge and community service embodied the Anzac spirit, which would not die with him. It would not die because their sacrifice, spirit and values would always be with us.

This story has portrayed many different Alec Campbells. Perhaps the most representative image conjured up at the funeral service was evoked by his eldest daughter, Sam, a teacher. The man she recalled was the young railway worker in the 1930s, who every day, rain or shine, rode his bicycle three miles to and from work, who knew how to handle a horse and buggy, mend shoes on a boot-maker's last and milk Gertrude, the family cow. She remembered the avid reader who loved books — on politics, philosophy, economics and history, or sailing ships — though she could recollect no books on the war. He marched on Anzac Day, she said, only in memory of the young men claimed by the Gallipoli campaign. She remembered the excitement of their home at Glen Roy during the 1930s, when her parents' political meetings drew railwaymen, unionists, socialists, Labor politicians and teachers, all seeking ways in which to improve the conditions of workers during the dark days of the Depression. Sam remembered best the Australian Railways Union leader and the Trades Hall Council president who worked resolutely to help the unions, and the socialist who stood for election in Launceston in 1941. She was proud of his community service for the Manpower directorate in Queenstown, and recalled fondly how she and her siblings had hiked through the mountains and prospected for gold with their tireless father. She would always remember his energy, his unflagging readiness to explore new challenges, his devotion to study, his deep love of the sea, and the special grace with which he accepted his final role as the last man standing. He was, she told the congregation, an inspiring parent who passed on a respect for family, love, friendship, study and work. 'My father gave to me a sense that the world is out there, and it is for you. After all, I was descended from highland chieftains.'

For his second family, and for Kate, looking frail and diminutive tucked into her wool coat in the front pew, Neil spoke of his father's love of the sea, his tradesman's skills, his knowledge of politics and economics, his sense of history, and the way he helped others through his union leadership and his work for the disabled and for cardiac patients through the Heart Foundation.

After the service, his other children spoke of their own special legacies. Cressey, who became a nurse, always remembered her father saying, 'If a job is worth doing, do it properly and don't start anything if you can't finish it.' Greg, a teacher and administrator in adult education, remembered his parents' passion for self-sufficiency in the 1930s, a passion that had carried the family through the hard times. Mary recalled how her father made everyone he met feel pleased with themselves. He had the ability, not so much to make people like *him*, but to make them like themselves. And he believed in the joy and satisfaction to be derived from putting effort into 'working, talking, planning and loving — the whole disaster'. Jim, the academic of the family, spoke of how his father introduced him to the world of nature, inspiring in him a love of knowledge and a lifelong intellectual quest. Geraldine, a dietician's assistant, remembered her father's counsel to always do your utmost and give your best in everything you do in life. 'Dad had empathy and enormous energy,' said Deirdre, who worked in an art gallery. 'He lived his life with courage in many ways. I saw him not just as someone who set goals for himself and concentrated on attaining them, but as a man who loved to "seize the day", and that was his legacy for me.' Felicity, his last child, who trained in hospitality, recalled the strangeness of being picked up from school by a father who had served in the First World War when her classmates' fathers had been in the Second World War, yet despite his age he had put so much into fatherhood, offering a wonderful model for parenting.

Following Neil's eulogy, Alec's nephew Peter (Angus's son), a noted yachtsman, read Masefield's uplifting 'Sea Fever', whose imagery threaded through so much of Alec's life. After the traditional 'Ode of Remembrance', the haunting sound of the last post, played by army bugler Corporal Ashley Thompson, rang out in the hushed cathedral, sending the spirit of Alec Campbell on its way. Agonisingly slowly, the Triservice Federation Guard carried the coffin through the west door and out into the street between ranks of tartan-clad Campbell clan women. The coffin was gently placed on the gun carriage normally reserved for the heads of state, which was then escorted by the Guard, arms reversed, down the crowd-lined streets through the centre of Hobart. And so, to the measured drum beat from Chopin's poignant 'Funeral March', the body of

Alec Campbell made its exit from life's stage. Perhaps Alec himself was not the focus of this theatre, but once again he was serving a higher cause.

In the distance, ethereally, the firing party's three volleys rang out. Then, further off still, even more remote from the kid soldier we like to think we knew, the 21-gun salute echoed across the city. It was the sort of heavy artillery the diggers back on that desperate beach at Gallipoli might have wished they could draw on — to teach those bloody Turks with their 'Beachy Bill' a lesson.

Lest we forget.

ACKNOWLEDGEMENTS

From the start there seems to have been a guiding star over the writing of this book as countless people came forward to provide the most wonderful material for the story. In fact, there were so many contributors that I feel I worked with a team of co-authors.

Above all, members of the Campbell family were amazingly helpful, lending their support in so many ways. Indeed, the book could not have been written without the dedicated assistance of this wonderful family. They provided a wealth of original material, including Estelle's book on their shared childhood, *Donald Started It All*; the original of Alec's handwritten 'life story' (quoted at the start of most chapters), kindly donated by Colin Campbell; Alec's Gallipoli letter (found in an old trunk by Kate Campbell); his daughter Mary's memoir, *The Campbell Family*; Meg Hingston's *Forget Not: Campbells Down Under*; family photograph albums, letters and a range of supporting documents. Mary Burke, Jim Campbell, Kate Campbell, Neil Campbell and other members of this warm and generous family also patiently answered my endless questions and read early drafts of the manuscript. In many ways it is their book, since in a sense the story was written from within the family. At the same time, only the author can be held responsible for this interpretation of the material the family so generously provided. I hope they will accept my apology for any errors or omissions.

Special thanks are due to the children of Alec's first marriage to Kathleen — Sam, Cressey, Greg, Mary, Jim, Geraldine and Deirdre; to Kate, his second wife, for her generous support; and to the children of this marriage, Neil and Felicity. Peter Campbell provided background on Alec's circumnavigation of Tasmania, and David Campbell supplied material on the Campbell clan.

Historian Peter Rubenstein, of Radiowise Media Networks, who has recorded so many important audio interviews with war veterans, was an inspiration, generously providing comradeship and sharing transcripts of his far-sighted interviews with Alec, Kate Campbell and Mary. The Australian War Memorial, and in particular Dr Peter Stanley, generously supported this book from start to finish. Dr Stanley kindly invited the author to speak about Alec Campbell and the last ten Anzacs at the 2002 conference at Gallipoli, 'Australia in War and Peace', organised by the AWM in association with Curtin University. This occasion enabled the author to visit Gallipoli, locate Alec's dugout under Hill 971 and spend a memorable night on the beach at Anzac Cove, where Alec and his fellow Anzacs had landed.

Others who provided assistance include Alec's workmates Bill Kalland and Alf Hagger (Department of Labour and National Service) and Robert Cutforth (National Heart Foundation); his shipmates John Bennetto and Darrel Gates; Hadley's Hotel, Hobart; and Richard and Deirdre Vane-Tempest, who sustained me while I was researching in Tasmania. Glenda Lynch, of Researching Australia, found the diary and letter extracts used in the Gallipoli chapters. Launceston historians Marita Bardenhagen and Jill Koshin helped me track down information on Alec's early professional life. Scotch College Oakburn provided information and photographs. ABC Enterprises provided a video of the state funeral. Charlotte King gave late-night scholastic support. Camera World Hobart, Fletchers Photographics in Launceston and Konica Photo in Neutral Bay, Sydney, scanned the images most professionally. *The Australian* newspaper encouraged and helped consolidate my interest in Gallipoli over the years by publishing my stories on First World War veterans. Computerman, Seaforth, provided technical support. John Masefield's 'Sea Fever' is reproduced with permission of the Society of Authors UK, as the Literary Representative of the Estate of John Masefield.

At John Wiley & Sons Australia, Jane Ogilvie had the idea, inspiration and vision, and coached the author from start to finish; Peter Storer supported the project wholeheartedly; Jem Bates edited the manuscript with the care and attention to detail that General John Monash employed to win his battles.

Finally, I wish to thank those organisations that generously permitted use of the images reproduced in this book, including the Australian War Memorial; the Australian Army; the National Archives of Australia; Scotch College Oakburn, Launceston; *The Weekend Australian, The Mercury* (Hobart), *The Age* and the *Sydney Morning Herald*. Peter Nixon (www.peternixon.net/gallery) kindly provided the photograph of the Gallipoli war memorial used on page 187.

As always, I also thank my wife, Jane, for supporting me throughout the writing of this book. If I have overlooked any individual or organisation, please accept my apologies.

SOURCES

Chapter 1

Ted Matthews, video interview with author, 1997.

Neil Grant, *The Campbells of Argyll*, Franklin Watts, London, 1975.

David Campbell (Campbell Society of Australia), interview with author, 11 August 2002.

Cruachan: Campbell Clan Journal, Winter 2002, No. 86.

Meg Hingston, *Forget Not: The Campbells Down Under*, published privately, Launceston, 2002.

Estelle Campbell, *Donald Started it All*, published privately, Launceston, 1980.

Maitland and Krone, *The Cyclopedia of Tasmania*, Hobart, 1901.

Chapter 2

Estelle Campbell, *op. cit.*

Peter Rubenstein, Radiowise Media Networks.

Mary Burke, interview with author, September 2002.

Chapter 3

Scotch College Oakburn records, Launceston.

Peter Rubenstein, Radiowise Media Networks.

The Examiner, Launceston, 9 December 1912.

Chapter 4

Mary Burke, *The Campbell Family*, published privately, Hobart, 1993.

Lloyd Robson, *A History of Tasmania, Volume 2: Colony and State*, Oxford University Press, Melbourne, 1991.

Australian Imperial Force Attestation Paper, National Archives of Australia, Canberra.

John Meyers and Bryn Dolan, *Leaders of the Anzacs: Officers of the Australian and New Zealand Army Corps who died at Gallipoli* <www.anzacs.org>.
Video interview with Alec Campbell, 1997.
Peter Rubenstein, Radiowise Media Networks.

Chapter 5

Alec Campbell's letters to his mother, father and sister.
Diary entry, Lieutenant T. Miles, 12th Battalion, AIF, Australian War Memorial (AWM), Canberra.
Diary entry, Private E. King, 19th Battalion, AIF, AWM, Canberra.
Diary entry, Private John Dakin, 11th Battalion, AIF, AWM, Canberra.
Diary entry, Lieutenant L. W. Sutherland, 1st Squadron, AFC, AWM, Canberra.
Diary entry, Lieutenant T. E. Cozens, 21st Battalion, AIF, AWM, Canberra.
Letter to mother, Sergeant R. Adam, 11th Battalion, AIF, AWM, Canberra.
Peter Rubenstein, Radiowise Media Networks.
Lieutenant T. P. Chataway, *History of the 15th Battalion*, William Brooks and Co., Brisbane, 1948.

Chapter 6

Chataway, *op. cit.*
Kevin Fewster, *Gallipoli correspondent: The frontline diary of C. E. W. Bean*, Allen & Unwin, Sydney, 1983.
Reports from Gallipoli by Ellis Ashmead-Bartlett, published during 1915 in *The Times* (London).
Diary entry, Sergeant Cyril Lawrence, 2nd Field Company Engineers, AIF, AWM, Canberra.
Diary entry, Private N. McLeod, 23rd Battalion, AIF, AWM, Canberra.
Letter from Captain B. Duggan to his father, AWM, Canberra.
Peter Rubenstein, Radiowise Media Networks.

Chapter 7

Fewster, *op. cit.*
Alec Campbell video interview with author, 1997.
Peter Rubenstein, Radiowise Media Networks.
Diary entry, Private F. W. Muir, 1st Battalion, AIF, AWM, Canberra.
Diary entry, Captain Ivor Williams, 21st Battalion, AIF, AWM, Canberra.
Diary entry, CQMS A. Guppy, 14th Battalion, AIF, AWM, Canberra.
Diary entry, unknown soldier, 20th Battalion, AIF, AWM, Canberra.
Extract from letter, Major B. D. Jack, 54th Battalion, AIF, AWM, Canberra.

Diary entry, Sergeant H. Affleck, 1st AFA Brigade, AIF, AWM, Canberra.

The Anzac Book, Cassell, London, 1916 (written and illustrated by the soldiers at Gallipoli).

Diary entry, Private E. King, 19th Battalion, AIF, AWM, Canberra.

Diary entry, Private J. H. Turnbull, 8th Battalion, AIF, AWM, Canberra.

Chataway, *op. cit.*

Letter excerpt, Major P. J. Morgan, 17th Battery Field Artillery, AIF, AWM, Canberra.

Diary entry, unnamed soldier, 20th Battalion, AIF, AWM, Canberra.

Diary entry, Lieutenant-Colonel G. Murphy, 18th Battalion, AIF, AWM, Canberra.

W. Thomson (ed.), *Black's Medical Dictionary*, 28th edition, A. & C. Black, London, 1968.

Chapter 8

Fewster, *op. cit.*

Peter Rubenstein, Radiowise Media Networks.

Diary entry, Warrant Officer W. H. Garland, 2nd Battalion, AIF, AWM, Canberra.

Diary entry, Private J. Lennie, 4th Field Ambulance Brigade, AIF, AWM, Canberra.

Letter excerpt, Major E. Brind, 23rd Battalion, AIF, AWM, Canberra.

Diary entry, unnamed soldier, 20th Battalion, AIF, AWM, Canberra.

Diary entry, Lieutenant-Colonel G. Murphy, 18th Battalion, AIF, AWM, Canberra.

Diary entry, Captain Ivor Williams, 21st Battalion, AIF, AWM, Canberra.

Diary entry, CQMS A. Guppy, 14th Battalion, AIF, AWM, Canberra.

Letter excerpt, Lieutenant D. Caldwell, 27th Battalion, AIF, AWM, Canberra.

Diary entry, Lieutenant J. Bourke, 2nd Australian Field Gun Company, AIF, AWM, Canberra.

Letter excerpt, Colonel John Monash. AWM, Canberra.

Chataway, *op. cit.*

Margaret Lewis, research notes, AWM, September 2002.

Rosemary Derham, *The Silence Ruse: Escape from Gallipoli*, Cliff Books, Victoria, 1998.

Chapter 9

Chataway, *op. cit.*

Fewster, *op. cit.*

Peter Rubenstein, Radiowise Media Networks.

Chapter 10

Undated Sydney newspaper sports report believed to have been published in early 1920s. Held in Mary Burke's private collection.

Robson, *op cit.*, who states that in 1916 in Tasmania 48,493 people voted for conscription and 37,833 voted against. In 1917, 38,881 voted for conscription and 38,502 voted against.

The Examiner, Launceston, 1 March 1920.

Mary Burke, *op. cit.*

Launceston Municipal Transport, LCC Box 1. Unregistered papers and files.

John Reynolds, *Launceston: History of an Australian city*, Adult Education Board, Tasmania, and Macmillan, Melbourne, 1969.

Chapter 11

Greg Cooper and Grant Ross, *Tasmanian Railways 1871–1996: A Pictorial History*, Regal Press, Launceston, 1997.

W. A. Townsley, *Tasmania from Colony to Statehood 1803–1940*, St. David's Park Publishing, Hobart, 1991.

Reynolds, *op. cit.*

Chapter 12

Frank Taylor (former Australian Railways Union official), phone interview with author, 2 November 2002.

Geoffrey Serle, Inaugural ACTU Historical Lecture, Melbourne, 14 August 1997.

Chapter 13

David Horner, *Inside the War Cabinet*, Allen & Unwin, 1996.

Ralph Taylor, interview with author, 22 October 2002.

Material on the Manpower Minister, John Dedman, was supplied by AWM historian Chris Coulthard Clark, 22 October 2002.

Mary Burke, *op. cit.*

Peter Rubenstein, Radiowise Media Networks.

Alf Hagger, interview with author, 7 September 2002.

Chapter 14

Kate Campbell, interview with author, 9 September 2002.

John Bennetto, interview with author, 6 September 2002.

Alec Campbell's journal of *Kintail's* circumnavigation of Tasmania supplied by Peter Campbell.

Peter Rubenstein, Radiowise Media Networks.

Chapter 15

Bill Kalland, interview with author, 7 September 2002.
Dr Robert Cutforth, interview with author, 22 September 2002.
Jonathan King, *Battle for the Bicentenary*, Century Hutchinson, Sydney, 1989.
Peter Rubenstein, Radiowise Media Networks.

Chapter 16

Alec Campbell, 'Pilgrimage to Gallipoli', published in Tasmanian newsletter
    of Department of Veterans' Affairs, June 1990.
Bob Hawke, Hansard, May 1990.
Peter Rubenstein, Radiowise Media Networks.

Chapter 17

Mary Burke, interview with author, September 2002.
Sam Claridge, interview with the author, September 2002.
The Australian Magazine, 8 November 1997.
Peter Rubenstein, Radiowise Media Networks.
The Last Anzacs, documentary video produced by the author for Webster
    Publishing, 1998.
Heroes Return to the Somme, documentary video produced by the author for
    Webster Publishing and Department of Veterans Affairs, 1999.
Channel Nine Network, documentary on Alec Campbell presented by Ray
    Martin, Anzac Day 2002.
John Bennetto, interview with author, 6 September 2002.

Anzac Sector, Gallipoli 1915

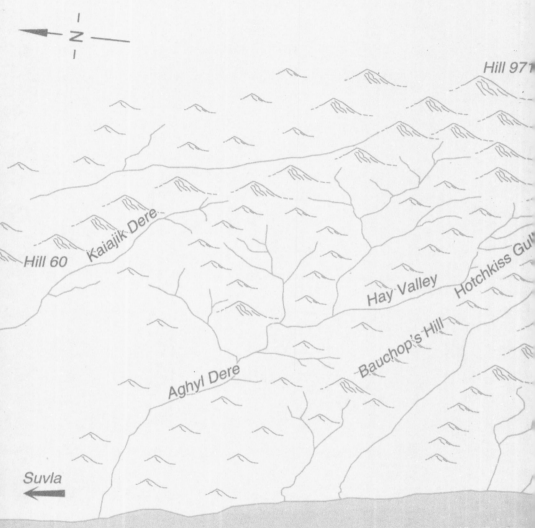

Hill 971

Kaiajik Dere

Hill 60

Hay Valley

Hotchkiss Gully

Bauchop's Hill

Aghyl Dere

Suvla

North Beach

AEGEAN SEA

1 kilometre